VANISHING WOMEN

V A N I S H I N G

Magic, Film, and Feminis

W O M E N KAREN BECKMAN

DUKE UNIVERSITY PRESS *Durham and London 2003*

© 2003 Duke University Press   All rights reserved
Printed in the United States of America on acid-free paper ∞
Typeset in Monotype Garamond by Tseng Information Systems
Library of Congress Cataloging-in-Publication Data appear
on the last printed page of this book.

For Michael, Siduri, and Lua

Contents

List of Illustrations

Acknowledgments

I want to begin by expressing my gratitude to Diana Fuss and Michael Wood, who have read far too many drafts of each of these chapters and have done so with meticulous care, great humor, and brilliance. They have both been models of intellectual generosity, and I offer them many, many thanks. Numerous other scholars have contributed to this work at various stages. Elisabeth Bronfen's early suggestions proved to be invaluable, as did my conversations with Jeff Nunokawa and Martin Harries. Eduardo Cadava, Craig Dworkin, John Fleming, Sander Gilman, Mark Hansen, Vicky Kahn, Tom Levin, Starry Schor, Elaine Showalter, and Susan Wolfson have all helped me in different ways in the course of my time at Princeton, and I thank them very much. Over the last few years I have learned a lot through my conversations with Sally Bachner, Anne Jamison, Gage McWeeney,

Julie Park, Eric Patton, Amada Sandoval, Lee Talley and Jiro Tanaka, and I am grateful to them for the contributions they have made to these pages. The responses I received to portions of chapter two from the Princeton Women's Studies Colloquium were extremely helpful. I thank Alexander Nehamas for inviting me to join the Princeton Society of Fellows, which has provided me with a vibrant and stimulating intellectual community in which to finish this book. I'm also grateful to the Cotsen fellows for their helpful comments on an earlier version of chapter five and to Mary Harper for her feedback on chapters two and five. I thank Allison Funk for sharing with me her wonderful thoughts and poems on vanishing women. Beth Harrison, Jennifer Houle, Marcia Rosh, Nancy Shillingford, and Marilyn Yates in the Department of English at Princeton are stars, and I'm grateful to them for all their help.

I wish to extend my thanks to the anonymous readers at Duke University Press for their incisive criticism and enthusiastic encouragement, which transformed this work, and to my editors, Fiona Morgan and Ken Wissoker, for their patience, advice, and support. I published versions of chapter four in *Critical Inquiry* and *Camera Obscura.* I thank the readers from *Critical Matrix,* the Body Parts Collective, and *Camera Obscura* for their comments. Summer fellowships from Princeton University enabled me to visit a number of key archives. I owe special thanks to the Mrs. Giles Whiting Foundation, which supported the final stages of the dissertation. A postdoctoral fellowship from the same foundation gave me time to turn the dissertation into a book. I also thank the Council of Graduate Schools and University Microfilms International for their support of this project. I thank the faculty members at the University of Rochester for their enthusiastic and helpful response to sections of this book and also for giving me the opportunity to keep doing what I like best.

I want to express warm gratitude to all the people who have looked after Siduri and Lua (and sometimes me) so well: Josh Engroff, Mrs. Chen, Shelley Davis, and the teachers of New World Montessori, Los Angeles; New Horizons Montessori, Princeton Junction; the Montessori School of New York at Brooklyn, and the Sunshine Daycare Center. I would also like to thank Joel Houkom, Ann-Marie Hardee, Sarah Levine, and Adam Schwartz for their sustaining friendship over the last few years. Two people I cared about died while I was writing this book: William Stanley Ireland and Daisy Johnson. These pages will always be intertwined with memories of them. I thank my family—Merrilee, Robert, and Mari Beckman, Jane and Lucy Johnson, Barbara and Claire Redrobe, Janek Redrobe-Steeg, and Ruth Wright—for their ongoing love and support. Michael, Siduri, and Lua are the magic of my life. This book is for them, with all my love.

VANISHING WOMEN

Figure 1. The vanishing lady. Reprinted from L. Frank Baum, *The Art of Decorating Dry Goods Windows and Interiors* (Chicago: Show Window Publishing Company, 1900). Courtesy of the Yale Collection of American Literature, Beinecke Rare Book and Manuscript Library.

In 1900 a Chicago department store advertised its new line of milli-
nery using L. Frank Baum's "vanishing lady," the latest technological
advance in the art of window dressing.[1] This display, featuring the
top half of a female mannequin, which would periodically disappear
and reappear dressed in endlessly new outfits, had a startling effect
on Chicago passersby. Hundreds flocked to see the female torso disappear and reappear. Indeed, so great was the public reaction to this
figure that "the second day the firm using it was compelled to put
up an iron railing in front of the plate glass for fear it would be broken by crowds."[2] Other contemporaneous show windows had used
mechanical figures to little effect. Yet Baum's vanishing lady, like the
late Victorian magic act that inspired it, produced a rare intensity of
excitement, suggesting that there might be something inherent to

the performance of female vanishing that unsettles, provokes, and arouses viewers in unexpected ways. But how do we account for the power of this vanishing lady to agitate and enthrall these ordinary Chicago shoppers? How can we explain this collective fascination with the woman who disappears?

Hovering on the border of two centuries, this strange moment in front of a department store window looks back nostalgically to a waning tradition of sideshows and stage magic, but it also looks forward impatiently to the newly emerging world of cinema, the vanishing lady's key twentieth-century venue.[3] Standing before Baum's show window in 1900, it would have been difficult for the casual shopper to lose herself in fantastical identifications with the female image on display, as she might have done in the darkened space of the cinema, not least because that image keeps evading her. As she watches the fashionable lady disappear and reappear, the crush of other bodies against her own threatens to ruin the integrity of her fantasy space and to destroy the screenlike window that marks the boundary between spectacle and spectator. Though the window should ideally function as a translucent mirror in which the face of the shopper dissolves and displaces the nondescript face of the mannequin, the spectators before Baum's window discover themselves not as fashionable individuals within the fantasy scene but as faces in a crowd that threatens to destroy the space of spectacle altogether.

Anne Friedberg has explicitly related Baum's windows to the cinema screen, and if we pursue her analogy between the window display and cinema we need to ask what this Chicago scene might tell us about the vanishing lady on film and her impact on viewing practices.[4] Critics of Hollywood cinema have made clear how narrative film, like the successful display window, encourages viewers to identify with the often ideologically problematic characters on-screen, effectively "disappearing" or assimilating potentially thoughtful and critical spectators into the diegetic space. But if the vanishing lady on-screen functions like her department store double, might she too not emerge as a compellingly disruptive force within the film, not because she discourages identification altogether but because she makes it more uncomfortable by rendering visible the kind of disappearances identification repeatedly effects? She makes spectators aware of the moments when they, like she, are no longer there, and this awareness might produce a critical presence within the spectator along-side those obediently identifying, and therefore vanishing, elements of the self. An agent provocateur across the spectacular realms of modernity, including magic, photography, and cinema, the vanishing lady produces desire and longing but also unrest. Given her disruptive potential, it may seem somewhat surprising to discover that she appears and disappears not only in experimental films that actively work against the narrative traditions of Hollywood but also in Hollywood films, fascist propaganda films, and the early short films that mark the beginnings of the medium. Why would this curious figure, who incites crowds to smash (albeit accidentally) the fantasy screen, the boundary between spectacle and spectator, appeal so broadly? What does the vanishing lady, inextricably and compulsively bound up with the invention and development of film, reveal about the medium as it defines itself through the visual representation of women?

Before we address these questions, we need first to consider exactly what kind of female image this protocinematic storefront spectacle constructs. [5] What model of femininity does the "illusion window" try to sell the consumer? While the idea of women as vanishing beings clearly descends from a long literary tradition of the fatally elusive woman, a tradition that includes Eve's disappearance in *Paradise Lost,* Spenser's *Faerie Queen,* Keats's "Belle Dame sans Merci," and the morbidly vanishing women of Hardy's *Poems of 1912–13,* the cultural texts I examine trace a divergent tradition of obstinately present females who are fantasized as going away, usually in spectacular ways. [6] Although by 1900 stage magic tricks had largely come and gone, only fourteen years earlier the Vanishing Lady Act had taken London by storm. This story begins in the late nineteenth century, when a divergent tradition of female vanishing developed in conjunction with a variety of new visual technologies—most notably photography and cinema—many of which were refined and developed by the early stage magicians. These technologies enabled the endless reproduction, circulation, and consumption of the female body. Within this modern proliferation and circulation of images of women, the threat of reproduction becomes both feminized and mechanized, and the vanishing women of the following chapters have to be understood in this context.

With the help of mirrors, trapdoors, elevators, photographs, and films, the visual image of "woman" emerges on the modern scene as utterly unstable and constantly prone to disappearance, in spite of, or perhaps because of, its endless reproducibility. The newly emerging department stores and mail order catalogues further emphasized this instability, as they encouraged women to shed outfits and self-images as quickly as does Baum's storefront mannequin. Harmless as it may seem, Baum's turn of the century American marketing campaign trades on a notion of woman as constantly changing and utterly disposable. It has its roots in Victorian Britain's magical disappearing acts, which emerged, not coincidentally, in conjunction with both British public discussions of a female population surplus and the British feminist movement. Like its Victorian predecessor, Baum's window appears, at first glance, to be nothing but a lighthearted, commercial form of entertainment. But if we push our way toward the railings to inspect the mannequin more closely it becomes clear that there is more to vanishing than meets the eye. The Chicago store window certainly entices us with its technical wizardry and its endless parade of colors and clothes. But are we not also compelled by the subtly gruesome spectacle of fashion fineries draped over a dismembered female body? Baum's illusion window may quite literally place femininity on a pedestal, yet his idealized woman possesses neither arms nor legs. Invisible from the waist down, this "woman" prefigures Freud's later claim that "for many years the vagina is virtually non-existent."[7] Surgically relieved of both sexuality and mobility, she moves only when she is moved by the mechanical force of the elevator. Creating the illusion that nothing ever *really* disappears, her returns distract our attention away from the mildly disturbing question of what happened to this lady's limbs.

The window stages a profound ambivalence about female presence. On the one hand, it tries to retain the female body by controlling its mobility, dismembering it and fixing it on a pole in order to reassure the window shoppers that this lady, elusive as she may seem, is going nowhere. Yet on the other hand, the spectacle simultaneously participates in a misogynist discourse that fantasizes the *complete* eradication of all women. The lower part of the body has already been taken care of, and each new disappearance implies that the remaining body parts will eventually follow in the footsteps of the legs.

In spite of this ambivalence, the vanishing lady's return does seem to be structurally necessary at the end of the well-known stage trick, and this fact encouraged me to think of her as a figure of feminist resilience, one who keeps coming back at a magician who endlessly enacts a collective fantasy of female eradication on the site of her body. Indeed, when I first began this project I hoped to mobilize this visibly vanishing woman as an alternative figure of female subjectivity in the visual realm, one who mediates between the worlds of presence and absence, both of which are, as feminist film theory has taught us, extremely problematic states of being or even nonbeing. Suspicious of my own triumphalism, however, I began to wonder whether I, too, was being tricked. Why did the vanishing lady so often appear as a smiling and willing accomplice to the magician? Was this really the new articulation of female subjectivity I was seeking?

My suspicions caused me to take another look at the sites of female vanishing and reappearance, and I discovered, on second glance, scenes littered with the traces of other, often unidentified bodies that had never been visible in the first place. While I had been preoccupied with the vanishing and return of a white female body that is always spectacularly visible — one that we miss when it is gone — I realized that these vanishing women all too frequently screen from view prior and more permanent disappearances. In these instances, though the vanishing woman first makes visible, then resists, a certain misogynist desire to make women go away, she may also serve as a prop for the very patriarchal violence she appears to withstand. This is not to say that she *never* resists patriarchal violence but merely to suggest that we need to be constantly aware of her ability to stand in for other bodies, to evoke the bodies of "others" through certain forms of "suggestion" such as the use of "oriental" costumes or names. Once the magician or his substitute — the window dresser, the doctor, the filmmaker — has set us at ease with the *comic* spectacle of the lady who disappears but always returns, the diverted spectator isn't likely to notice when the other bodies that disappear into and with the vanishing lady fail to return.

I explore these tactics of conflation and confusion in chapter one, which examines how from the 1860s on, the Victorian magician repeatedly collapses traces of the Indian male into the body of the white woman, making visible the close interconnections between British anxieties about male authority at home in the face of an increasingly empowered female population and imperial authority abroad. Encouraging astute and potentially troublesome spectators to fix their anxiety and care on the body of the female assistant, the magician—perhaps even in cahoots with the smiling lady—distracts our attention away from the more insidious ideological work that takes place before our eyes, leaving us feeling—wrongly—content and relieved at the apparent absence of violence about which we were momentarily so concerned. Lest this project become yet another example of ideological prestidigitation, I have sought in *Vanishing Women* to render visible not only the unacknowledged disappearances that occur in the very space of female vanishing that I suggest is useful to feminism but also how the vanishing lady—herself a subject under attack—might bear some of the responsibility for those other corporeal eradications. Magic transforms the emerging political voices of women and other "others" into bodies that move with apparent ease from the realm of the corporeal to the realm of fantasy. In short, magic tries to convince us that "surplus" bodies can be evaporated harmlessly and without trace. But the bodies in question do not always cooperate with the fantasy, and on many occasions at least some of them refuse to go away, making the spectacle of vanishing a particularly interesting site of ambivalence.

Vanishing Women grows out of stage magic's complicated relationship with the spectacular body of illusion, one that hovers somewhere between the real and the imaginal body, a body that the medium of film inherits from its magical forefathers. Spectacular vanishing relies upon a suspension of disbelief that allows us to suppose, if only momentarily, that when we "see" women disappearing from cabinets or being run through with swords we are witnessing an astonishing event *within* a physical realm that nevertheless confounds the laws of physical bodies. The audience, as a collective body, permits itself to take pleasure in the spectacle of violence because at some level it *knows* that the violence enacted is always illusory. However, although this knowledge might permit the audience's pleasure in moral terms, some of the pleasure of vanishing always derives from the possibility that the violence on stage *is* "real" and *is* being enacted on the physical bodies the audience sees before it. Without the possibility of death, stage magic would be nothing but a technical puzzle. Magic repeatedly presents the manipulation of fantasy or imaginal bodies *as if it were* the manipulation of real bodies. Within the realm of vanishing, the physical endlessly collapses into the fantastical with dizzying effects. Wherever there is vanishing, this confusion exists, making the question of how to move between real and symbolic violence in the context of a modern proliferation of mechanically reproduced insubstantial bodies one of the key problems with which this book wrestles.

Focusing on a series of vanishing women from different places, times, and media, I work to expose these elisions, rendering partially visible not only the moments when violent eradication takes place in the name of vanishing but the mechanisms by means of which these instances of violence try to render themselves invisible. In chapter four, for example, I juxtapose two films based on the same urban myth of an older woman who disappears: Alfred Hitchcock's *The Lady Vanishes* (1938) and Nazi filmmaker Veit Harlan's *Verwehte Spuren (Blown Away Traces,* 1938). In both films, after the older woman disappears those who associated with the woman prior to her disappearance deny her very existence, as though the act of witnessing were itself too dangerous to risk. In both films, a young woman proves the exception to this refusal to witness. She makes it her mission to uncover exactly how the lady vanished, where she went, and who was responsible. In terms of narrative content, the similarities between these films are astonishing, especially given their opposing positions on the ideological spectrum. This opposition becomes readable, I suggest, less at the narrative level than in the cinematographic techniques employed to create or disrupt the illusion of continuous narrative—the cut, the fade, the dissolve—causing us to think about how the politics of film editing intersects with the question of gender. Although the reader may at times wonder how a book that begins with Victorian stage magic and ends with Bette Davis finds itself considering Nazi editing practices, I hope my readings will show that important elements of the vanishing woman's story only come to light through particular, and sometimes peculiar, juxtapositions.

This book's oscillation between the magician-filmmaker's vanishing lady and the woman whom the state violently "disappears" for political reasons implies a relationship between these seemingly remote figures. How to articulate this relationship constitutes one of the most troublesome and persistent problems I encounter, and my methodological approach reflects the problem it addresses. Each chapter juxtaposes different types of discourse, all somehow related through the figure of the vanishing woman—conjuring and population studies, spiritualism and photography, psychoanalysis and classical mythology, comedy and propaganda, astrology and Hollywood films—while simultaneously interrogating the politics of such pairings. How, I ask, might these strange matches cause us to consider in more complex and subtle ways our movements between the space of the "real" and the "imaginal"?

Given that much of the violence of vanishing occurs as a result of the invisible conflation of these two spheres of being, one might think that an ethical imperative requires us persistently to separate the real from the imaginal or "psychic" body.[8] But what exactly does it mean to "hold onto" the material body? And how can we even distinguish between real and imaginal bodies within the context of magical disappearance, where magic might be described as the practice of collapsing the boundary between real and the imaginary through illusion? What can we do when the real body is not obvious or readily available? Must we then begin to imagine the real, and what does this act of imagination do to the idea of "necessary reality" we are trying to retain?

Spectacles of vanishing, frequently offered as harmless forms of entertainment, perform grotesque mutilations and violent physical eradications in ways that seem not only acceptable, because of their illusory status, but also delightful. Perhaps because of their status as "harmless entertainment," these magic tricks unselfconsciously make the potential violence of vanishing more readable, providing us with "eye-holds" in the smooth surface of the discourse of disappearance. Protesting our tendency to turn "real" violence into metaphors, however, Barbara Ehrenreich, in her forward to Klaus Theweleit's *Male Fantasies,* insists upon the supremacy of seeing over reading: "The reader's impulse is to engage in a kind of mental flight—that is to 'read' the murders as a story about something else, for example sex . . . or the Oedipal triangle . . . or anything to help the mind drift off. But Theweleit insists that we see and not 'read' the violence."[9] But before we condemn our habit of reading violence outright don't we need to consider where the temptation to 'read' violence comes from in the first place? Why does the mind 'fly' when it encounters violence? What compels us to turn acts of violence into stories about 'something else'? And why does the mind prefer one narrative over another when it is distracted away from seeing violence itself?[10]

In the case of murder, the movement of the mind away from the real body toward stories about something else suggests, perhaps, the impossibility of holding on to the material body in situations of extreme violence. Our repeated failure to focus on the real does not necessarily indicate the mind's unwillingness to deal with difficult material, although some minds are always more willing than others. The mental flights, acts of imagination, and translations of violence might rather reflect both the difficulty for the living of grasping the space of death and the struggle to do so anyway. Attempts to fix these dead bodies, to capture their "reality," tend to produce lists of physical mutilations that numb rather than engage the focused mind. Ehrenreich, for example, in Theweleit's *Male Fantasies,* writes of "heads with their faces blown off, bodies soaked red in their own blood, rivers clogged with bodies" (xi). Caught in a similar rhetorical dilemma, Diana Taylor, in *Disappearing Acts,* tries to articulate the responsibility of witnessing disappearance in Argentina by resorting to a hypnotic strategy of listing categories of real bodies, although she at least recognizes that such lists still emerge from the realm of the imagination rather than from the bodies themselves: "Somewhere behind those bodies, and simultaneously occluded and illuminated by them, one imagines the real bodies: male bodies, female bodies, some pregnant, almost all young. Thousands and thousands of tortured and mutilated bodies, dead bodies, bodies dumped into mass graves marked 'NN' (*Non Nombre,* or no name), or cut into pieces and burned in ovens, or thrown into the ocean from military planes. . . . How to think about these bodies that we know exist(ed) but that have vanished into thin air?" (140). Although lists of bodies and their tortures ostensibly commit themselves to seeing the real body, to resisting symbolization, in the case of vanished bodies we can only imagine such lists. We never see the bodies in question, not only because they are long dead but because the deaths of these bodies were disappeared along with the bodies themselves. Part of the violence of disappearance lies in the way it renders its victims fundamentally inaccessible. These bodies and their sufferings can be seen but only in the mind's eye, through acts of imagination, by reading the traces that violence carelessly, yet inevitably, leaves behind. "To see" in the context of disappearance might involve transcending the physical act of looking, seeing what is no longer, and perhaps was never, visible, and I have tried to suggest throughout the book that paying attention to, and reading, our distractions might well constitute the most effective resistance to certain modes of violence.

While the vanishing lady spectacle can shift our attention away from the violent eradication of material bodies, it would be misleading to suggest that I pursue this figure with the sole purpose of drawing back the curtain, of exposing the illusions that blind us to the sufferings and oppressions of real bodies. *Vanishing Women* deals primarily with neither the disappearance of material bodies nor the evanescence of the illusory body, although both types of body recur throughout the following chapters. The book aims rather to begin to theorize the space between these two categories, to think about the tensions that arise when the borders between real and imagined bodies become blurred, and film becomes my privileged example of this space. Through a series of close readings of particular instances of female vanishing at specific historical moments, I explore how and why these categories overlap as well as the ethical challenges and political possibilities that emerge out of this confusion.

I hope that the troubling juxtapositions contained both within and between chapters will illuminate connections between discourses that might hitherto have seemed unrelated, revealing particular aspects of a mode of representation or a sociohistorical anxiety that would otherwise go unnoticed. Both of the films I discuss in chapter four, for example, have been analyzed separately and have largely been considered to be apolitical, even trivial, in content. Critics have described *The Lady Vanishes* as "a top notch mystery melodrama" (*New York Post*), "the kind of hooey to which the popular picture-going public cottons" (*Variety*), and "one of the most comfortable and least substantial films" of Hitchcock's "English era" (Raymond Durgnat). Similarly, the Third Reich categorized Harlan's *Verwehte Spuren* as "künstlerisch wertvoll" (artistically worthwhile), in contrast to his explicit propaganda film, *Jud Süss* (1940), which was deemed "staatspolitisch und künstlerisch besonders wertvoll" (politically and artistically especially worthwhile).[11] After Harlan's trial in 1949, *Verwehte*

Spuren still maintained the reputation of an apolitical film. Indeed, in 1981 Siegfried Zielinski even went so far as to declare that this 1938 film "showed no sign of state politics."[12] By reading these two films together, however, the ideological function of the vanishing woman becomes quite clear. The family romance plot, which requires the mother to disappear for the heterosexual relationship to blossom in *Verwehte Spuren,* provides a perfect screen for other acts of violent eradication that wish to render themselves invisible. Harlan exploits the narrative of the necessarily disappearing mother (i.e., necessary within the heteronormative paradigm of the status quo) as a justification for the state's "necessary" eradication of all socially unwanted bodies, thereby configuring the subject's relationship to the state as a type of marriage. By contrast, Hitchcock's romantic couple only comes together through the act of *finding* the vanishing lady, and of exposing the hidden alliance between the film's surgeon and magician, who in this case, contrary to Walter Benjamin's claim that the two are polar opposites, have been in cahoots all along.[13]

Chapters one and four seem to privilege the disappearance of the material body, yet both also rely heavily on narratives of female eradication in the psychic realm. In Victorian Britain, for example, the perception of unmarried women as surplus bodies in need of deportation implies that marriage must function, among other things, as an institution of female disappearance. Although this mode of vanishing clearly seems to be of the psychic variety, when women fail to marry, the nation perceives their ongoing "presence" in physical not psychic terms. Veit Harlan's *Verwehte Spuren* takes the threat of heterosexual union one step further, when the disappearance of the daughter, Seraphim, into marriage can only happen once the mother has been literally erased. In contrast, chapter three focuses on narratives of psychic disappearance. While Freud's self-analysis fails in the face of his mother's psychic presence *and* absence, leading him to rely upon a maternal imago that oscillates endlessly between the two states of being, the hysterical patient struggles for physical survival in the face of her own psychic vanishing, experienced by patient and analyst alike as a physical phenomenon. Regardless of whether or not observers can reach out and touch a living body, can "know" at some level that a particular body has not really disappeared, is not "really" dead, nothing prevents us from experiencing psychic events in material or visual terms. In a discussion of a hysterical patient named "Mrs. Peters," for example, Juliet Mitchell writes: "She 'disappeared' in my company. This is hard to describe but I could see her physically vanishing. First her voice faded, then I found myself wanting to stretch out to stop her falling. She went down a psychic Black Hole."[14]

Mitchell tries to control the collapse of the psychic and physical by placing inverted commas around *disappeared* and by noting that the black hole is of the "psychic" variety, but she still "sees" the "physical" vanishing of Mrs. Peters and wants to respond physically to the downward motion of her patient's psychic body. This does not mean, however, that differentiation between the two realms is impossible or futile. Although Mrs. Peters's "disappearance" indicates that life for her seems currently unlivable, her participation—however tenuous—in the analytic scene does hold open the possibility of a future life or presence that is clearly denied to the physically eradicated body.

This confusion between the psychic and physical bodies becomes increasingly intertwined with the visual technologies that begin to emerge in the second half of the nineteenth century. In chapter two, I focus on Eva C., a French spiritualist medium who became renowned for her ability to render ghosts visible during her séances through the production of ectoplasm, a white, mucouslike substance that would pour out of her mouth, nostrils, nipples, and vagina. Eyewitnesses endlessly tried to capture her evanescent manifestations on photographs and film, yet, being themselves ghostly media of light and shadow, photography and film ultimately serve in these spiritualist testimonies as further sites of ontological anxiety. Indeed, by the end of chapter three, I come to suspect that the ghosts Eva C. reproduces are in fact the ghosts of visual technology itself, a suspicion that ultimately casts Eva as the camera's double, a machine capable of reproducing intangible moving images that hover somewhere between life and death for the entertainment of an audience.

If the vanishing woman does function as a substitute for the media that reproduce her, then those media may be more invested in her survival than we might initially have thought. Consequently, this figure potentially offers us interesting alternatives to the largely hostile relationships between female subject and camera that have been articulated in feminist discussions of photography and film to date.

Endlessly elusive, the vanishing woman persistently returns, simultaneously avoiding the perils of total presence and the powerlessness of utter absence or invisibility. Before we grasp too tightly the material body marked female, we need to ask ourselves whether this is really the body we want to retain.[15] And as we work to resist the violence enacted against real women might we not also imagine the disappearance of "women" as a potential goal of feminism, at least for those who find that label constraining? If women vanish, what other possibilities of being, physically, psychically, socially, and representationally, become thinkable for those of us now identifying, or identified, as women?

Hoping to understand the potential for pleasure and play within these implicitly threatening narratives of female disappearance, I end in chapter five by turning to one of Hollywood's camp icons: Bette Davis. She provides an apt focus for this inquiry first because she appeared in no less than four films about fading female stars, and, second, because in recent years her films have found themselves at the juncture of a number of important theoretical debates on the question of cinema and identity.[16] This chapter's discussion of falling film stars develops out of the arguments of chapter two, investigating further the relationship between media, presence, and gender through the ontological ambivalence of "the star," that repressed celestial body after which the luminous actors of Hollywood are named. Within the fallen star genre, we see Hollywood's most explicit meditation on the complicated relationship between film, being, and visibility. Actively drawing our attention to the fading star body, this genre stages the difficulty of spatial, visual, psychic, temporal, and oral presence in cinema in surprisingly critical ways. It challenges the paradigms of identificatory viewing and encourages us to think differently, at least for a moment, about how, where, and why we watch movies and when we become visible or invisible as we do so.

1

Surplus Bodies, Vanishing Women: Conjuring, Imperialism, and the Rhetoric of Disappearance, 1851–1901

When Prince Albert died in 1861, Queen Victoria vanished from public view. And although Victoria *was* in mourning for Albert, a certain stubbornness marks her refusal to appear. The nation resented her temporary disappearance to such an extent that a growing republican movement threatened to make her, and the monarchy in general, disappear for good. Politicians and newspapers pleaded with the queen to show herself, but a court memo published in the *Times* on April 6, 1864, illustrates the extent to which Victoria, well aware of the nation's dissatisfaction with her disappearance, resolutely refused to reemerge.

An erroneous idea seems generally to prevail, and has lately found expression in the newspapers, that the Queen is about to resume the place in society which she occupied before her great affliction; that is, that she is about again to hold levees and drawing rooms in person, and to appear as before at Court balls, concerts, etc. This idea cannot be too explicitly contradicted.

The Queen heartily appreciates the desire of her subjects to see her, and whatever she can do to gratify them in this loyal and affectionate wish she *will* do.

But there are other and higher duties than those of mere representation which are now thrown upon the Queen, alone and unassisted—duties which she cannot neglect without injury to the public service. . . . More the Queen *cannot* do; and more the kindness and good feeling of her people will surely not exact from her.

This memo reveals Victoria's determined refutation of the world of "mere representation," in spite of the increasingly obvious threat that her disappearance poses to the institution of the monarchy. She will *not* appear. She will *not* be seen. Gladstone states quite simply in an 1870 letter to Granville, "The Queen is invisible."[1] Even those who were permitted an audience with her had to contend with her visual instability. When Prime Minister Disraeli meets with Victoria in 1863, she appears then disappears in distinctly magical terms: "In less than five minutes from my entry, an opposite door opened and the Queen appeared. She was still in widow's mourning and seemed stouter than when I last saw her but this was perhaps only from her dress. . . . At last she asked after my wife, hoped she was well, and then with a graceful bow, vanished."[2] Here Disraeli constructs an elaborate scene of startling entrances and exits that he implicitly links to the queen's stoutness, and in the course of this chapter we will see that vanishing repeatedly occurs in response to various types of corporeal excess. As Adrienne Munich points out, British republicanism developed not in response to the Queen's absence alone but to the combination of this absence with both her excessive consumption and her excesses of mourning: "Above and well beyond her age's elaborate mourning customs, she engaged in rituals and trappings of loss, expanding upon them to the point where she exhausted her subjects' capacity to enjoy or sympathize with her performance. Histories and biographies stress the increasingly republican sentiments of her subjects, who resented their enormous financial investment in a monarch who barely showed her face."[3] The queen's withdrawal from public life has a private and personal explanation, but we can also read this withdrawal in the context of mid- to late Victorian Britain's fascination with the vanishing body and the vanishing female body in particular. Like the vanishing Victoria, the vanishing women of Britain can be read in various and even contradictory ways. Disappearance, masquerading as a certain kind of magical vanishing, can threaten to erase completely those bodies deemed superfluous or redundant. But it simultaneously offers a strategy of defiant resistance to the problematic paradigms of female visibility, a model of being that does not involve spectacular visibility. Although *disappearance* and *vanishing* may seem to signify the same thing, I want here to distinguish between these two words on the important grounds that while *disappearance* suggests a completed action *vanishing* is always in process. This inherent incompleteness becomes strategically useful at times when either an individual subject or the state itself tries to collapse magical vanishing into violent eradication, using the former as a screen for the latter. Because the action of vanishing offers terms of resistance from within itself, being never fully absent or fully present, it resists eradication even as it seems to support or mask it, and this ambivalent quality gives the term its political utility.

I begin this inquiry into the Victorian fascination with disappearing female bodies in 1851 because in this year the national census made the British public aware of a burgeoning female population, that left men in the minority. Extensive and elaborate debates about the "surplus woman problem" ensued, and these debates have received much critical attention within the field of Victorian studies. In this chapter, however, I want to suggest that a number of factors prevented the public discussions of the surplus woman from openly addressing the problem in its full dimensions. In order to access some of the material that is repressed from the public debate around this issue, but nevertheless is crucial to it, we need to turn to the spaces where collective fantasies make themselves visible. The British discussions of the surplus woman coincide with the world of stage magic's obsessive attempts to make women vanish. And only by reading the discourses of magical entertainment and population alongside each other can we render visible some of the repressed fantasies and fears that we need to understand in order to gain a fuller picture of what was actually at stake in these discussions of female surplus. This chapter aims to trace the metamorphoses of vanishing from 1851 through the end of the century, focusing in particular on the way a politicized discourse of human surplus and disappearance intersects with a specific moment in theater history. In 1886, magician Charles Bertram performed "The Vanishing Lady" for the first time on the British stage. The trick, which I suggest was from its inception highly politicized, captivated the imagination of the British public, appearing on the front page of the *Times* for an entire month. I will argue that this spectacle of vanishing both reflects and refutes Victorian anxieties about female surplus, offering us important insights about Britain's relationship not only with the early feminist movement but with the domestic political issues of unemployment and the care of the poor.

The questions of class and gender that emerge in the discourse of superfluous and vanishing women cannot be considered outside of Britain's relationship with its colonies. When *Punch* declares in 1850 that "the daughters of England are too numerous . . . and if the mother cannot otherwise get them off her hands, she must send them abroad into the world," it conflates the image of a daughter leaving home to make a living and become independent of her parents with enforced female emigration. This proximity of working women at home to the exportation of surplus women also points clearly to the relationship between domestic concerns about female emancipation and Britain's expansion beyond the boundary of its own island. Although Victorian Britain's surplus woman problem emerged explicitly as a question of gender, producing numerous debates and texts that form the foundation of British feminism, the surplus woman also needs to be considered within the history of imperialism. Population always emerges as a spatial issue, and we must consider it in relation to Britain's own geographical imagination. The rhetoric of surplus bodies reflects, among other things, a sense of spatial inadequacy and a subsequent desire for increased lebensraum. As we will see, many nineteenth-century narratives of female surplus fantasize the colonies, especially the "white colonies" of Australia, New Zealand, and the formerly British parts of the United States, as empty spaces into which unwanted British women might simply disappear.

As Britain tried, and failed, to rid itself of its unwanted bodies —

foreign and female—images of magical disappearance flooded the world of popular entertainment in striking and spectacular ways. Although the discourse of vanishing may seem to be confined to the realm of entertainment, these magical spectacles reveal something about the texture of the surplus woman problem that we would miss if we focused solely on the texts that deal explicitly with that issue. Having established a relationship between the surplus bodies of women and "natives" in the Victorian imagination, however, I want to make clear that I do not think the surplus woman question is in fact a purely, or even primarily, colonial issue, just as it would obviously not be useful to read Britain's relationship with India, for example, through the lens of gender or class alone. Rather, I want to argue that in the nineteenth century the discourses of gender and imperialism become increasingly intertwined with each other around the idea of vanishing in important and interesting ways. Here I want to align myself with the careful critical position articulated by Anne McClintock in *Imperial Leather:* "I write, then, in the conviction that history is not shaped around a single privileged social category. Race and class difference cannot, I believe, be understood as sequentially derivative of sexual difference, or vice versa. Rather, the formative categories of imperial modernity are articulated categories in the sense that they come into being in historical relation to each other and emerge only in dynamic, shifting and intimate interdependence. . . . I do not see race, class, gender and sexuality as structurally equivalent of each other. . . . Rather, these categories converge, merge and overdetermine each other in intricate and often contradictory ways."[4] Rather than leveling the discourse about surplus women and colonial subjects, I will try to think about how the spaces between these two categories of marked bodies work to complicate and refine our understanding of Victorian vanishings.

Only in magic do the hidden connections between surplus women, imperial expansion, and the fantasy of disappearance become clear. One might argue that popular culture works to stage things *as* harmless and, perhaps because of this assurance of harmlessness, that the interconnections between these spheres can become visible. But before we examine how the vanishing lady comes to embody the hopes and fears of a nation we first need to look more closely at nineteenth-century population discussions in order to establish how English women came to be confused with Indian men and how both ended up in the role of magician's assistant.

The Lottery of Life

Overpopulation dominated the thoughts of nineteenth-century Britons. As birth rates grew and people moved en masse from the country to the city, agricultural production fell, creating a panic about how the nation would sustain itself. At the end of the eighteenth century, an anonymous pamphlet declared that population growth would always outstrip available food resources, a simple fact of nature that would constantly threaten human happiness. The pamphlet, entitled *An Essay on the Principle of Population, as it Affects the Future Improvement of Society, with Remarks on the Speculations of Mr. Godwin, M. Condorcet, and Other Writers,* reappeared in 1803 in extended form as Robert Malthus's *Essay on Population.* Malthus, as though possessed by the problem of excess and redundancy, continued to revise and reprint four further editions of the same work over the next twenty-three years. In the face of what he deemed to be misguided benevolence, he argued that the nation should leave those incapable of providing for themselves to die. Public debate raged, and Malthus's essay solicited impassioned responses from prominent writers such as William Hazlitt (1807) and William Godwin (1820), whose work on human happiness had inspired Malthus's original pamphlet in 1798.[5]

"It has appeared that, from the inevitable laws of human nature, some human beings will be exposed to want," reasoned Malthus. "These are the unhappy persons who in the great lottery of life have drawn a blank."[6] Even if more people were to practice celibacy, he argued, a surplus would always exist. Like the human body, the social body seemed bound to produce waste, waste that Mother Nature would simply carry away in her natural sewage system: "The diminution in the number of marriages, however, was not sufficient to make up for the great decrease of mortality from the extinction of the plague, and the striking reduction of the deaths in the dysentery. While these and some other disorders became almost evanescent, consumption, palsy, apoplexy, gout, lunacy, and the smallpox, became more mortal. The widening of these drains was necessary to carry off the population which still remain redundant" (239–40). For

Malthus, human redundancy had less to do with any specific number of people and more to do with a particular section of society that he called the "abject poor," those who could do nothing for themselves, those whom the social body casts away, abjects. The abject poor were simply the feces of the social body, Malthus implied. And what could be more natural than that? In Malthus's contemplation of human waste, the process of social expulsion (the death of the abject poor) only served to confirm the health of the living social body and those who constituted it, just as the individual subject might assert itself in life through a contemplation of its own waste. As Julia Kristeva writes in her contemporary theorization of abjection, "These body fluids, this defilement, this shit are what life withstands, hardly and with difficulty, on the part of death. There, I am at the border of my condition as a living being. My body extricated itself, as being alive, from that border. Such wastes drop so that I might live."[7] In Malthus's formulation of identity, where the social body emerges only through the contemplation of its own waste, the nation or subject requires the visibility of the body's excess to mark the boundary between the "I" and the "not-I." Binding itself paradoxically to an unending visual fascination with the very thing it tries to eradicate, the subject or nation founds its sense of self on the spectacle of that self's surplus. Identity simultaneously yearns for and withstands the disappearance of its own excess. This paradoxical double bind provokes a crisis in mid-Victorian Britain, out of which emerges the idea of vanishing *as* spectacle.

The Body as Excess

According to Kristeva, those who continually define themselves in relation to the abject base their lives solely on a system of *exclusion:* "Put another way, it means that there are lives not sustained by *desire,* as desire is always for objects" (6). This statement cuts to the quick of Malthus's problem with human populations. Though he realizes that humans must reproduce in order to survive, he longs to eradicate the desiring body, and the desiring female body in particular, from his social vision. Acknowledging that the "passion between the sexes" is the strongest desire after the desire for food, Malthus knows he must find a place for it within his theory of society. But for Malthus, the sexual body, male or female, is constantly at war with the laboring male body on which society depends. As Catherine Gallagher argues, "Malthus turns the body into an absolute social problem. All individual bodily states, without exception, mean trouble for the state of society."[8] While on the one hand in his *Essay* Malthus advocates deferment of sexual gratification, on the other hand he dreads the moment when the laboring male body might lose its sexual desire altogether: "It is clearly the duty of each individual not to marry till he has a prospect of supporting his children; but it is at the same time to be wished that he should retain undiminished his desire of marriage, in order that he may exert himself to realize this prospect, and be stimulated to make provision for the support of greater numbers" (215).

Malthus encourages women to be virtuous and to abstain from sex until after marriage, but a by-product of this virtuous woman emerges: the image of woman as a cruel withholder of gratification, never more powerfully embodied than in his own construction of Mother Nature, a "kind though severe instructor" who is "ready to admonish us of our errors, by the infliction of some physical or moral evil" (238). Malthus's Mother Nature shows no pity. If a man comes to her feast and cannot get subsistence from his parents or his labor, he "has no claim of *right* to the smallest portion of food, and in fact has no business to be where he is" (249). And while some men might foolishly invite the man to dine in spite of his lack of credentials, Mother Nature never does: "She tells him to be gone, and will quickly execute her own orders" (249).

Although Malthus struggles to cast his discussion of overpopulation solely in class terms, women play a key role in his social vision. While matronly nature decides who deserves to feast and who to starve, the undisputed heroine of Malthusian society is the old maid, and the praise he affords her remains unparalleled in the *Essay*. The old maid provides a model for Malthus because in addition to living a vice-free life she "diminishes her own consumption" (272) by not having children. Here, as throughout the *Essay*, alimentary and sexual metaphors blur. The woman who reduces her oral (and vaginal) consumption at Mother Nature's feast diminishes the amount of "waste" she produces. But in this case waste is not anal but vaginal, not feces but families. This unmarried woman also works, thereby contributing to the nation's economy without either consuming or reproducing. While the matron with children "has subtracted from, rather than added to, the happiness of other parts of society" (271), the old maid contributes to the happiness of married couples by "depressing herself" (271) and redistributing her wealth among those who need it more: "She has really and truly contributed more to the happiness of the rest of the society arising from the pleasures of marriage, than if she had entered into this union herself, and had besides portioned twenty maidens with a hundred pounds each; whose particular happiness would have been balanced either by an increase in the general difficulties of rearing children and getting employment, or by the necessity of celibacy in twenty other maidens somewhere else" (272). Ironically, then, Malthus suggests that women can indeed find a place at Mother Nature's metaphorical dining table but only on the condition that they never eat. This benevolent image of the old maid contrasts strikingly with the matron with ten or twelve children. Although the matron's sons may have fought in wars for the nation and she may have served her country well, she appears for Malthus rather "in the character of a monopolist than that of a great benefactor to the state. If she had not married and had so many children, other members of the society might have enjoyed the satisfaction" (271). Malthus even goes so far as to insist on the rights of single women, stating that "with regard to rank, precedence, and the ceremonial attentions of society, they should be completely on a level with married women" (273). Although Malthus's support of the old maid clearly derives from his fear of the sexual woman, making him an unlikely advocate of women's rights, his respect for the single woman contrasts strikingly with later nineteenth-century attitudes toward this same figure. In the course of the century, enthusiasm for the old maid dwindles dramatically and, as population theorists apply the Malthusian rhetoric of abjection to female bodies in particular, unmarried women come under the sharpest attack.

"What Shall We Do with Our Old Maids?"

Popular opinion of unmarried women took a turn for the worse after the 1851 census revealed that there were "too many" of them in the country.[9] For every 1,000 men there were 1,042 women, and in the "marriageable" age group of twenty to twenty nine there were 1,090 women for every 1,000 men. This problem only intensified with time. Between 1851 and 1861, the ratio of women to men increased more dramatically than it ever had before, or ever would again, during the nineteenth century. By 1861, there were 1,053 women for every 1,000 men and 1,130 between the ages of twenty and twenty nine. The ratio of women to men increased almost as dramatically again between 1881 and 1891, growing from 1,055 to 1,063 women for every 1,000 men.[10] In addition, more women than ever were deciding not to marry, choosing instead to develop professional careers and female friendships. As Martha Vicinus argues in *Independent Women,* "By necessity and choice single women strengthened their friendships with each other and minimized their heterosexuality. It was convenient for them that some leading doctors claimed women had no sexual feelings until after experiencing intercourse."[11]

In addition to forming relationships that resisted the Victorian heterosexual imperative, the women of Britain also began to form political alliances during the 1850s and 1860s that would ultimately lead to universal suffrage. In the wake of the failure of the first Married Women's Property (MWP) Campaign of 1855, led by Barbara Leigh Smith and Bessie Rayner Parkes, the MWP Committee turned its attention to the question of employment and education, forming the basis of what came to be known as the Langham Place Circle.[12] During the second half of the century, the women of the Langham Place Circle made crucial feminist contributions to the surplus woman question through their journals, the *English Woman's Journal* (EWJ 1858–64) and the *Englishwoman's Review* (1866–1910). One of the most important voices in this debate was that of Jessie Boucherett, daughter of a Lincolnshire landowner who went to London in response to the EWJ's call to action. Once in London, Boucherett joined the staff of the EWJ, and helped to found the Society for the Promotion of the Employment of Women in 1859.

Boucherett's essays on the surplus woman question make at least three important interventions in the debate. First, Boucherett makes visible both the government's attempts to disappear these unwanted bodies into various institutions and the class structure embedded within these institutions. In 1864, she writes, "The national plan at present adopted in England for providing for superfluous women is that of shutting them up in workhouses."[13] In a later article in the *Englishwoman's Review,* she publishes a table comparing the numbers of governesses in various institutions responsible for "disappearing" surplus women, such as prisons, workhouses, and asylums, with the number of domestic servants. In 1866, only eleven governesses lived in workhouses, compared to 14,461 domestic servants. While there were seven governesses in prison in that same year, 904 domestic servants found themselves behind bars.[14] Boucherett works to expose how class functions within the surplus woman discourse. More importantly, she also rejects the idea that the surplus woman crisis is in any way a historical or statistical one, thereby bringing the very terms of the discussion under scrutiny. At the opening of her 1864 article "On the Cause of the Distress Prevalent among Single Women," she writes: "There is a general impression that the difficulty of providing for our large numbers of single women is occasioned solely by an inequality of the sexes; and that this inequality is something new, and the result of civilisation. I propose to show that it proceeds from some other cause, besides the inequality of numbers in the sexes, and also that both the difficulty and the inequality, far from being modern evils, are extremely ancient, and are felt in uncivilised as well as civilised communities" (268). Female surplus has nothing to do with a disparity between the number of men and women, she suggests, and everything to do with a misogynist tradition that views women as essentially superfluous, a line of argument she supports with statistics from Australia and the United States of America: "In countries where the men exceed the women in number, as in our own colony of Melbourne and in the United States, the women still find it difficult to live. Mr. Greg estimates the excess of men over women in the United States at 250,000 (a quarter of a million), yet it is stated by Dr. Channing, that in New York alone, in 1860, there were found 534 women who had to be their own bread-winners, and who could only earn a dollar (4 *s.*) a week, and a very large number besides who could earn nothing."[15] In this passage, Boucherett not only argues that the problem of the surplus woman is more conceptual than statistical; she also offers an important corrective to W. R. Greg, who, in his infamous 1862 essay "Why Are Women Redundant?" portrays the colonies as the ultimate empty fantasy space into which Britain might easily "disappear" thousands of unwanted female bodies.[16] According to Boucherett, the British colonies and the United States only threaten to produce *more* surplus.

Earlier in the century, in his *Essay,* Malthus had resisted turning to the colonies and North America as solutions to the population surplus at home, not only because of the difficulty of cultivating the land quickly enough to sustain the immigrants but because the "natives" of these lands presented such stumbling blocks (87). Given the unacceptability of "exterminating the inhabitants of the greatest part of Asia and Africa," bemoans Malthus, one would have to "civilize the various tribes of Tartars and Negroes," and this would "certainly be a work of considerable time, and of variable and uncertain success" (18). Unlike Malthus, however, Greg refuses to acknowledge the impossibility of universal happiness, and rather than happily contemplating the spectacle of his society's "waste products" he longs to make that waste disappear. Like the *Punch* article, which recommended sending England's "too numerous" daughters abroad, Greg tries to limit the threat of independent women going out to work through an elaborate fantasy of mass female emigration. Advocating the transportation of half a million women from overpopulated Britain to places where men lived alone, Greg believes that North American and colonial marriages could swallow up Britain's female excess so that the exported multitudes would never be seen again.

But the materiality of the body persistently disrupts Greg's fantasy of 500,000 disappearing women, largely because he fails to regard the women in question as real people with real bodies until his plan is well under way. When he eventually does work out the finer details of his master plan, Greg understands that in trying to escape the excesses of the female body he has in fact embarked on an overwhelmingly corporeal project. Greg suddenly realizes that these 500,000 female bodies will never simply evaporate. They have stomachs to feed and, he assumes, reputations to protect. At an average of 50 passengers per ship, he calculates that half a million women *with* chaperones would require ten thousand vessels or ten thousand voyages of the same vessel. Given that a round trip voyage to Australia took about seven months to complete, Greg's plan would have taken ten years to execute, without taking into account the new "surplus" bodies produced in the course of those years. These plans become even more ridiculous when read alongside the actual numbers of successful emigrations, which are very small. In 1874, for example, the Society for Female Middle Class Emigration, an organization designed to care for English women as they made the transition from one shore to another, reported that between 1861 and 1872 it had successfully settled 158 women abroad. An 1874 article entitled "Emigration" states that "In 1865, only five women were sent out; in 1868, five; in 1871, seven; and in 1872, five."[17]

It is not female bodies alone that trouble Greg's magical solution. Although he tries to imagine the colonies and the United States as empty spaces, containing only a handful of single British men, he feels compelled to stress that the exportation of British women would "redress the balance among the *free white population* of that country."[18] That Greg thought it necessary to mention the liberty and whiteness of the surplus women's future sexual partners reveals his anxiety about the exposure of single white women to the "otherness" of the colonies, about the lurking possibility that members of the not so free or white population might attempt to address the imbalance of the sexes themselves. Similarly, Greg worries about what single men abroad would do without British women "to satisfy their cravings and gratify their passions" (452). In this empty fantasy space, which promises to bring peace to the minds of overcrowded Britons, specters of masturbation, homosexuality, bestiality, and miscegenation abound.

Boucherett plays on Greg's anxiety about the status of white men in her 1869 reply to him, "How to Provide for Superfluous Women," where she suggests that one gets rid of surplus women not by exporting them but by educating and employing them, making them no longer superfluous. Well aware that this plan would set off fears about male unemployment, Boucherett, in a clever rhetorical move, reverses the causal chain of events, moving the responsibility for white male vulnerability away from women and onto the indigenous populations of the colonies. Instead of describing the displacement of men from British shores by working women, she creates a narrative that begins with "savages" displacing white men abroad and ends with the suffering of women: "In Queensland the demand for men is so great, that as the farmers cannot get Englishmen enough, they have imported South Sea Islanders to cultivate the land. What a strange spectacle does the great English Empire present to the world! Savages doing Englishmen's work abroad; men doing women's work at home;

and women starving, begging, and sinning, because they can get no honest employment" (41–42). The rhetorical force of Boucherett's argument here relies on her mockery of the *spectacle* of the British Empire, a spectacle determined by the visible interaction between Englishmen, Englishwomen, and savages. Greg fantasizes that Melbourne, New Zealand, and the United States would enable vast numbers of women simply to disappear, never to be seen again, bringing female surplus, "empty" space, and a rhetoric of disappearance together in a reassuring and invisible way. Boucherett does not fundamentally shift the paradigm of Greg's essay, which both posits colonized space as a dumping ground for Britain's material "waste" and thinks of that waste in terms of human life. Rather than challenging the notion that any human life can be excessive, Boucherett resists Greg's planned disappearing act by conjuring up a spectacle of colonial humiliation in which white women are spared by the presence of other surplus bodies onto which she can shift the blame. In her formulation of England, there is no "men's work" to be had at home. Englishmen's work, according to Boucherett, must be done abroad, and if the savages are doing it then *they* (rather than Englishwomen at home) must be the surplus bodies about which Greg should be concerned. Active, visible savages, feminized, impotent Englishmen, and suffering Englishwomen form the core of Boucherett's image of British imperialism.

Later in the same essay Boucherett tries to expose the violence of Greg's emigration model through her comparison of the Englishman's attempt to "disappear" the surplus female body into the imagined emptiness of the colonies with a New Zealand chief's cannibalistic consumption of his second wife. Again the feminist critique emerges at the expense of the indigenous people of New Zealand: "We have all laughed at the story of the New Zealand chief who, when asked how he had provided for his second wife, from whom he had parted at the recommendation of the Missionary, replied, "Me eat her." It was but his way of providing for superfluous women, and, if it had the disadvantage of being disagreeable to the woman herself, the same may be said of other plans proposed by much better instructed men than the chief" (47). Boucherett exposes and challenges Greg's fantasy of benevolent disappearance by eliding it with an image of the savage and foreign violence against women. As a strategy of feminist resistance, Boucherett presents a counterimage of "disappearance" as a markedly uncivilized, taboo form of murder. While this stance is important in illuminating and resisting a troubling aspect of the mid–nineteenth century's rhetorical treatment of women, we need to remain critical of the underlying assumption that "real violence"— like eating one's wife—always takes place elsewhere, that English *gentle*men, if violent, are actually only behaving like savages rather than the Englishmen they are. But in order to understand the role played by the interrelationship between these three subject positions in shaping Britain's discussions of women we need to look backward and read this "triangle" of Englishman, Englishwoman, and savage in the context of an earlier spectacle of empire. At the height of the surplus woman debate, the 1857 Indian Mutiny traumatized the nation with precisely this combination of spectacularly violent and visible savages, impotent and feminized Englishmen, and suffering Englishwomen.[19]

Indian Rebellion and the Cawnpore Massacre

The Indian "Mutiny" or "Rebellion" began in Meerut on May 10, 1857, when three regiments shot their officers and set off to recapture Delhi from the English.[20] The most frequently cited explanation for the revolt is the introduction of the Lee-Enfield cartridge, which was greased with cow and pig fat (offensive to Hindus and Muslims, respectively) and had to be bitten open to release the gunpowder. Although this new cartridge may well have served as a catalyst for unrest, the reasons for the rebellion were far more deeply rooted than any single problem could explain. As Edward Said argues in *Culture and Imperialism:* "The causes of the Mutiny were constitutive to British imperialism itself, to an army largely staffed by natives and officered by Sahibs, to the anomalies of rule by the East India Company. In addition, there was a great deal of underlying resentment about white Christian rule in a country of many other races and cultures, all of whom most probably regarded their subservience to the British as degrading" (146).

Between May and October 1857, discussions of the rebellion dominated the London *Times,* and many of these reports fixed on the sudden and violent eruption of English women and children onto the imperial scene. One telegraphic dispatch declared that "Delhi was in possession of the mutineers, who had massacred almost all the Europeans without regard to age or sex."[21] A Bombay *Times* article described how "half the station was in flames, and the terrified women and children of our soldiers were in the hands of the savage and infuriate crew, who murdered them under circumstances of unheard of barbarity."[22] In a letter from the Rev. T. C. Smith, M.A., Chaplain of Meerut, the most graphic of his descriptions focus on the deaths of women: "The inhabitants of the Suddur Bazaar and the city committed atrocities far greater than those of the Sepoys, as in the case of Captain McDonald's wife, whom they pursued some distance and frightfully mutilated . . . and Mrs. Chambers, wife of the Adjutant of the 11th Native Infantry, who was murdered in her garden during Mr. Chambers' absence on duty, her clothes having been set on fire before she was shot, and cut to pieces."[23]

Although women and children died at every stage of the revolt, this gendered violence came to a spectacular head on July 15, when the rebel leader Nana Sahib imprisoned two hundred European women and children and massacred them all with knives after sepoys refused to shoot them. Many of the bodies were thrown into a nearby well. Historian Ronald Hyam describes the scene immediately following the massacre: "When British soldiers arrived on the scene they found the house still littered with underwear and female hair and running in blood. . . . There was no evidence of rape. Women had torn their clothes in an attempt to barricade the doors. But the bodies were stripped, hair and limbs cut off. The soldiers divided the tresses of one girl and swore for every hair a sepoy should die."[24] Although Hyam states that there was no evidence of rape, the scene was from the beginning sexually overdetermined, for the rebels chose to imprison the European women and children in Cawnpore's *bibighar,* the house where, prior to 1840, European men had kept their Indian mistresses before English wives had been shipped out to India to join their spouses.[25] This fact, not mentioned in any of the numerous *Times* articles reporting on the event, would not only have placed the female body—both Indian and English—at the very heart of the rebellion's most gruesome moment, but would also have reminded the British of their early sexual relationships with Indian women, relationships that by 1858 were strictly taboo.

In the wake of these horrific murders on the site of European men's transgressive sexual intercourse with Indian women, the London *Times* became obsessed with voyeuristic fantasies of Indian men raping Englishwomen. In what appears to be a clear case of Englishmen projecting onto Indian men their own desires for the foreign body of the "other" woman, a series of "eyewitness" accounts of rape incidents appeared in the paper, in spite of the fact that there was, according to Hyam at least, no physical evidence to support these testimonies. These articles tease the reader, refusing to repeat the horror out of a sense of propriety even as they report the most graphic details: "There are some acts of atrocity so abominable that they will not even bear narration. . . . We cannot print these narratives—they are too foul for publication. We should have to speak of families murdered in cold blood—and murder was mercy!—of the violation of English ladies in the presence of their husbands, of their parents, of their children—and then, but not till then, of their assasination."[26] The same article even places Englishwomen at the very root of the revolt, suggesting that "to the great mass we doubt not that the plunder of English treasure, the violation of Englishwomen, the massacre of Englishmen, were the chief and immediate incentives to the bloody game."

In subsequent months, the descriptions of violence became increasingly graphic and sexualized. Although each account is marked by the author's awareness of crossing a line of discursive propriety, the events at Cawnpore somehow lifted a taboo on a certain type of public speech. One supposed eyewitness account from another clergyman in Bangalore appeared in the *Times* on August 25.

No words can express the feeling of horror which pervades society in India, we hear so many private accounts of the tragedy, which are too sickening to repeat. . . . They took 48 females, most of them girls of from 10–14, many delicately nurtured ladies—violated them, and kept them for the base purposes of the heads of the insurrection for a whole week. At the end of that time they made them strip themselves, and gave them up to the lowest of the people, to abuse in broad daylight in the streets of Delhi. They then commenced the work of torturing them to death, cutting off their breasts, fingers, and noses, and leaving them to die. One lady was three days dying. They flayed the face of another lady, and made her walk naked through the street. Poor Mrs. ——, the wife of an officer . . . was soon expecting her confinement. They violated her, then ripped her up, and, taking from her the unborn child, cast it and her into the flames.[27]

Karl Marx, responding to this report in the *New York Daily Tribune,* noted that the letter was obviously written by "a cowardly parson residing at Bangalore, Mysore, more than a thousand miles, as the bird flies, distant from the scene of the action."[28]

But what are we to make of the *Times'* compulsion to print blatantly false and ever more sensational accounts of the spectacle of female mutilation at Cawnpore? In *Allegories of Empire,* Jenny Sharpe writes: "In all those stories of 'Sepoy atrocities,' I would argue, the *English lady* circulates as a sign for the moral superiority of colonialism under threat of native insurrection. The slippage between the violation of English women as the object of rape and the violation of colonialism as the object of rebellion permits the moral value of the domestic woman—her self-sacrifice, duty, and devotion—to be extended to the social mission of colonialism. The signifier may be *woman,* but its signified is the value of colonialism she represents" (68). While I would agree with Sharpe that femininity intersects with colonialism in these accounts, we must be careful not to reduce the signification of *woman* to colonialism alone, effectively disappearing *women* altogether, excluding them entirely from the possibility of signification. For, while the narratives of colonial virtue that emerge in this period rely absolutely on the innocence of English female victims, as Sharpe suggests, it is important to remember that women "at home" are simply not what they used to be. Women are no longer necessarily self-sacrificing, dutiful, or devoted. In this year of the Mutiny *and* the founding of the Langham Place Circle, women are so numerous as to be deemed overabundant. They are often single, sometimes by choice; they work, they write, they want to be educated, they want to own property, and they want to vote. British men talk seriously about making these women (excessive in both their number and their demands) disappear into the (white) colonies, and it is within the context of these domestic debates that we need to consider the fictions of this traumatic event.

If the surplus woman did not disappear, British men might, or so they feared. Women had not only begun to provide for themselves, but they were threatening to take men's jobs, and we can read traces of this anxiety about white male redundancy throughout the reports of the Indian Rebellion. On one level, we might see these testimonies as an attempt on the part of the British public, through narrative repetition, to work through the trauma of this violence against its women. Britain did want its surplus women to disappear into the space of the colonies, but it longed for a disappearance that would not have to deal with either the materiality of the body or the violence inherent to disappearance. In short, it wanted magic, as Greg later quite explicitly states in "Why Are Women Redundant" in 1862 when he promises that if Britain follows his advice "the apparent redundance of women complained of now will vanish as if by magic, if, indeed, it be not replaced by a deficiency" (460). Like Boucherett's comparison of Greg's mass exportation plan with the New Zealand chief's cannibalism, the massacre at Cawnpore exposes the fact of the body within disappearance. Absolute disappearance is a violent act, the massacre reminds us, one that litters the space of eradication with material traces: breasts, fingers, noses, limbs, blood, hair.

In addition to making visible the violence of disappearance, the mutiny also exposed and exacerbated British men's fears that they were themselves superfluous by rendering them impotent in the face of the Indian aggression. Before the Mutiny, British male identity thrived on its image of itself as a defender of women, as a report in *Household Words* entitled "During My Stay In India" illustrates. Although the author writes after the Mutiny, on November 28, 1857, he looks back nostalgically to earlier days when the threat of white male retaliation actually seemed to mean something: "The fact is (or rather was) that, on any dangerous road, a lady, utterly unprotected, was safer than a gentleman . . . [the Indians] knew the perpetrators of an offence committed against a lady would be hunted down to the death."[29] But the narratives that proceed from the events at Cawnpore and elsewhere not only document the absence of the British man as the protector of women in their time of need but affirm the resilience and self-sufficiency of British women in India.

One of the most striking accounts of this sort is the tale of the unmarried Miss Wheeler, General Wheeler's daughter, shown in figure 2 defending herself against attacking sepoys. Although white men are

Figure 2. Miss Wheeler defending herself against the Sepoys at Cawnpore. Reprinted from Charles Ball, *The History of the Indian Mutiny*, vol. I (London: London Printing and Publishing Company, 1858).

utterly absent from this scene, Miss Wheeler copes quite well in the face of her four male attackers, and, according one Mr. Shepperd's report, she shot four Indians dead.[30] Another report suggests that she killed an Indian soldier, his mother, his two children, and his wife. But Charles Ball, in *A History of the Indian Mutiny,* works hard to dispute the veracity of this narrative, as though truth were actually a concern in British narratives of the rebellion. His defensiveness, I would suggest, stems less from a care about truth than from his desire to manage the emergence of a narrative of female potency.

It seems incredible that a young lady, reared amidst the refinements of high European society in India, could have had resolution, or physical energy, even in a state of absolute and uncontrollable frenzy, to commit a succession of acts amounting in the aggregate to one of such surpassing horror. Besides, a third version of the tale (and by far the most probable one), represents the heroic girl as defending herself from the brutal and licentious attack of four miscreant sepoys, with one of her murdered father's revolvers, which she had contrived to secrete, and

Figure 3. Death of Major Skene and his wife at Jhansi. Reprinted from Ball, *History of the Indian Mutiny.*

successfully used, to preserve her from dishonour. That in the excitement, terror, and desperation of the moment, the noble but ill-fated young lady should then have plunged into the well, to escape the atrocities that would in all probability have followed the discovery of her justifiable but desperate act of self-defence, may be reasonably assumed as a natural consequence of the frightful circumstances that surrounded her. (344–45)

Earlier in Ball's *History,* an engraving entitled "Death of Major Skene and His Wife at Jhansi" (fig. 3) depicts a bizarre scene in which Major Skene holds his dead wife in his arms, their dead child at their feet, while he shoots himself in the head, much to the surprise of the attacking sepoys. The picture seems to suggest that Mrs. Skene has been killed by the Indians and that to avoid the same fate, or perhaps to avoid life without Mrs. Skene, Major Skene turns his weapon on himself. A letter sent to a relative of Major Skene, however, tells a different story: "It is all true about poor Frank Gordon. He, Alice Skene, his wife, and a few peons managed to get into a small round tower when the disturbance began. . . . Gordon had a regular battery of guns, also revolvers; and he and Skene picked off the rebels as fast as they could fire, Mrs. Skene loading for them. . . . The rebels, after butchering all in the fort, brought ladders against the tower, and commenced swarming up. Frank Gordon was shot through the forehead, and was killed at once. Skene then saw it was no use going on any more, so he kissed his wife, shot her, and then himself" (274). The brutal rhetoric of the massacres not only mobilizes a language of extreme and fantastic violence against women, a violence marked as "un-British" in the extreme; it also allows British soldiers to execute their own wives and even be considered war heroes for doing so.

These accounts of the massacre had important consequences for Britain's treatment of the Indians. For even as the British denounced the "savage" nature of the events at Cawnpore the massacre simultaneously allowed British soldiers to drop any pretense of benevolence toward Indian soldiers, unleashing an unprecedented degree of brutality against them. Ronald Hyam, in *Britain's Imperial Century,* suggests that the massacre gave way to unbridled and premeditated violence on the part of the British: "Indian prisoners were blown from the mouths of cannon. The two sons of the emperor were murdered in cold blood. More serious was the indiscriminate slaughter in Delhi after its recapture — and even Palmerston wanted it razed to the ground" (225). Contemporary reports describe the British soldiers as "burning to inflict summary punishment on these brutal murderers." And the *Times,* ventriloquizing the voice of the nation, permits its soldiers to act with unlimited force: "Let it be known that England will support the officers who may be charged with the duty of suppressing this mutiny, and of inflicting condign punishment upon the bloodthirsty mutineers, however terrible may be the measures which they may see fit to adopt" (August 6, 1857:6). A letter from General Neill at Cawnpore, dated August 1, describes first how he tried and hanged all rebels who could not "prove a defence" then goes on: "But the chief rebels or ring leaders I make first clean up a certain portion of the pool of blood, still two inches deep. . . . To touch blood is most abhorrent to the high caste natives, they think by doing so they doom their souls to perdition. Let them think so."[31] Neill clearly feels justified in inflicting this type of religiously based humiliation on the rebels in the wake of their actions. It is important to note, however, that this extreme of punishment — making the rebels touch blood when this is abhorrent to them—seems remarkably similar to the problem of the fat-greased Lee-Enfield cartridge that the rebels were protesting in the first place. In other words, although the British used the rebellion to justify an increased level of violence toward the Indians, the main difference between British violence before and after the revolt is that the postrebellion violence both acknowledged itself *as* violence and then presented that violence as a *spectacle,* perhaps in response to the nature of the Cawnpore massacre, which left the British soldiers so visibly impotent.

British Conjurors, Indian Fakirs, and the Vanishing Lady Act

Throughout the nineteenth century, Indian jugglers and fakirs held a special place in the popular imagination. Travelers to India returned with incredible tales of the Indian rope trick, snake charming, walking on coals, and other magical feats. These performers also traveled around Britain performing conjuring tricks, and in many senses they defined the British understanding of "magic" as a public spectacle. As Albert A. Hopkins writes, "For British and American magicians, the 'Orient,' but India in particular, was the birthplace of magic, the standard unit with which to compare themselves. Many magicians traveled in India and returned with incredible stories of the Indian fakir, and throughout the nineteenth century, jugglers and fakirs were imported from India to entertain the British."[32] Given the familiarity of this magical figure, it is perhaps not surprising that the one benevolent Indian figure to emerge in the British coverage of the rebellion should be the fakir.[33] On August 5, 1857, a short London *Times* article entitled "A Bright Example" appeared amid reports of the slaughters at Cawnpore: "Among all the villanies and horrors of which we have been witnesses some pleasing traits of native character have been brought to light. . . . Yesterday a Faquir came in with a European child he had picked up on the Jumna. . . . He refused any present, but expressed a hope that a well might be made in his name to commemorate the act" (12). In direct contrast to the murdering sepoys at Cawnpore, the mystical figure of the Indian magician saves, rather than mutilates, European children and creates new wells in his name rather than polluting existing ones with the blood and body parts of English women and children.

By the time Wilkie Collins publishes *The Moonstone* in 1868, however, the figure of the Indian juggler has become infinitely more complicated. Although it was written eleven years after the Mutiny, the novel is set in 1848, a backward temporal move that complicates our ability to interpret the role of the Indian in this text.[34] Collins's three "jugglers," who are actually Brahmans in disguise, prove to be experts in the field of vanishing. After making the diamond disappear from Ablewhite's room, they disappear themselves, first through the roof then into the shores of India. In fact, the presence of the Indians contaminates "poor" Lady Verinder's entire household with a touch of magic. Unfortunately, however, by the end of the novel the British man fails to emerge in the role of conjuror. As the household tries to reconstruct the disappearance of the stone, Franklin Blake appears as the magician's assistant, first feminized, then orientalized as a result of his dose of laudanum, while the house servant Betteredge complains that he's nothing but the conjuror's boy: "And what does it all end in?" he complains. "It ends, Mr. Ezra Jennings, in a conjuring trick being performed on Mr. Franklin Blake, by a doctor's assistant with a bottle of laudanum—and by the living jingo, I'm appointed, in my old age, to be conjuror's boy!"[35] Importantly, the doctor's assistant, Ezra Jennings, who gets to play the magician in this bizarre conjuring spectacle, is marked as both female and "foreign." Jennings admits to Blake: "I was born, and partly brought up, in one of our colonies. My father was an Englishman; but my mother——" (420). These comments, and Jennings' own face, cause the not so astute Franklin to surmise two things: "He had suffered as few men suffer; and there was the mixture of some foreign race in his English blood" (420). Later, as Jennings relates to Blake the story of Mr. Candy's near death experience, he reveals that the racial instability of his identity mirrors the further impurity of his gender: "I laid the poor fellow's wasted hand back on the bed, and burst out crying. An hysterical relief, Mr. Blake—nothing more! Physiology says, and says truly, that some men are born with female constitutions—and I am one of them!" (422). When Betteredge complains about Blake and he becoming assistants to Jennings the magician, then, he voices anxieties not only about Englishmen making spectacles of themselves but also, and more specifically, about the way the spectacle of magic marks foreign blood and the female constitution as sites of power that threaten British men.

Mechanical Hindus, Indian Mutilation, and the
Professionalization of British Magic

In the second half of the nineteenth century, magic as spectacle undergoes some dramatic changes, most notable in the identity of the magician himself. Throughout the 1850s and 1860s, the figure of the British magician constantly defers, through adopted names and costumes, to the superior powers of the Indian fakirs and their inferior counterparts, the jugglers. But things began to change from around 1867, when John Nevil Maskelyne, who would later run Egyptian Hall, England's "home of mystery," was invited to perform his tricks at the Crystal Palace. Although conjuring was at this time regarded as nothing more than a type of sideshow at fairs and freak shows, Maskelyne began to shift the status of conjuring to a legitimate form of theatrical performance, one that would, by the 1880s, become an indisputable staple of the Victorian cultural diet. As Jasper Maskelyne, John Nevil's grandson, reports, "The new fashion in conjuring had captivated London's fancy. . . . The Davenports and their like faded into the background, making way for professional illusionists."[36] In 1873, Maskelyne began his tenancy at Egyptian Hall with the phenomenon of "Psycho," described by Jasper Maskelyne as "a dwarf figure to which the face of a mild Hindu was added. He had clockwork entrails, and was seated on a transparent glass cylinder" (47).

Anxious both to make the specter of the potent Indian magician disappear and to establish the British gentleman in his place, professional British conjuring began with the spectacle of the mechanized Hindu body. Although the British public received Psycho as a novel phenomenon, William Hazlitt had in fact already made the same rhetorical move fifty-two years earlier, transforming the Indian juggler from a figure whose skill made the British gentleman feel inadequate to a simple, mechanical curiosity. In his 1821 essay "The Indian Jugglers," Hazlitt begins by declaring both the awe and the sense of personal inadequacy that these performers inspire in him: "there is something in all this [Indian juggling] which he who does not admire may be quite sure he never really admired anything in the whole course of his life. . . . [Seeing Indian jugglers] makes me ashamed of myself. I ask what is there that I can do as well as this? Nothing. What have I been doing all my life?"[37] As the essay progresses, however, it becomes increasingly clear that Hazlitt invokes the perfection of Indian juggling only to set it up as a mechanical foil for the superior, though flawed, attempts of "true" artists to imitate nature: "The mechanical performer undertakes to emulate himself, not to equal another. But the artist undertakes to emulate another, or to do what nature has done, and this it appears is more difficult, *viz.* To copy what she has set before us in the face of nature or 'human divine face,' entire and without a blemish, than to keep up four brass balls at the same instant; for the one is done by the power of human skill and industry, and the other never was or will be" (81).

If British stage magic in the last quarter of the nineteenth century works to manage some of the anxieties that had dominated the 1850s and 1860s, as I suggest was the case, then Maskelyne's mechanization of Hindu potency simply did not go far enough. Although British audiences liked the novelty of the automaton, magic really only captivated the imagination of Britain when it began to manipulate the material body, making that body disappear and reappear at will. As if in direct response to Betteredge's fear of the orientalizing and feminizing effects of magic on the British male body, the Victorian conjuror begins to dress in evening suits rather than mystical magician's robes, and his assistants are almost invariably either Indian males or English females. Although conjuring postures as a lighthearted form of late Victorian entertainment, it takes on new resonances if we read it in the context of the nation's most controversial political debates. Stage magic, then, becomes an interesting and important site on which to read the ways in which the British public represented both its fears and its solutions to those fears.

One of the most popular tricks of the late nineteenth century, the Indian Basket Trick, brought back from India by the French magician Robert-Houdin, graphically enacts the mutilation of an Indian child. As Albert A. Hopkins describes it in *Magic,*

> Travelers in Hindostan have often told us that the Indians practice this wonderful trick upon public places. The Indian magician makes use of an oblong osier basket provided with a cover. He takes a child and incloses it in this basket, and around the latter buckles a belt. Grasping a sword, he thrusts it into the basket here and there, and pulls out the blade all dripping with blood.

The spectacle is shocking, and the feelings of the spectators become wrought up to a high pitch. The magician then opens the basket, which, to the surprise of all, is empty.

At a few yards distance cries are heard proceeding from the child who had been inclosed in the basket, and who is now running forward, sound and happy. (46)

Marking a dramatic shift away from the cup and ball tricks and card illusions of the eighteenth and early nineteenth centuries, this new magic draws on the political images of the day. The Indian Basket presents us with an extremely complex spectacle of Indian mutilation that has to be read in the context of the Indian Rebellion. But how exactly are we to interpret this violent spectacle? What kind of ideological work does it perform?

Any reading of the Indian Basket must focus on how the Indian body signifies in relation to the British body in the course of the performance. However, the fact that these tricks were live performances means that their signifiers were never fixed. Indeed, although the history of the trick is poorly documented, anecdotal reports in magicians' biographies, memoirs, and magazines make clear that the British body and the Indian body were at times interchangeable, fundamentally complicating any attempt to fix the way in which the trick operated at a sociopsychological level in late Victorian Britain. These tricks are never simple allegorical replays of the Indian Rebellion; indeed, if the allegorical references to British violence in India were not so disguised, the tricks would never have been so popular. Nevertheless, I would argue that the tricks, in their enactment of an extreme violence and mutilation between Indian and British bodies, do function as a type of subconscious remembering and working through of the events of 1857. Sometimes the British magician performed the trick in the guise of an Indian fakir, exactly as Hopkins describes it. In this instance, we might read the trick as an attempt on the part of the British gentleman to appropriate the power of the Indian male by adopting his dress and subject position. When the British magician penetrates the Indian boy with a sword, he enacts the same violence on Indian children that Indian men enacted on European women and children at Cawnpore, but the context remains one of "harmless entertainment," placing a distance between the British male and colonial violence. Similarly, the adoption of Indian dress serves to protect the reputation of the British man as *gentle*-man, tying brutality to the Indian body alone. On other occasions, however, the British magician performed this trick in an evening suit, shifting again the way the performance signifies. Rather than exposing the brutality of the Indian, the evening suit allows the Victorian gentleman, rendered impotent by the Indians at Cawnpore, to step into the role of active and potent avenger. But even here the magician protects his audience from having to acknowledge in any conscious way Britain's participation in this type of massacre because the scenario is repeatedly presented as a trick, and the mutilated body always ultimately reappears as whole.

Just as we can read the figure of the magician in multiple and sometimes contradictory ways, so the return of the Indian boy at the end of the trick opens itself to multiple readings. On one level, the boy's return authorizes any degree of violence on the part of the British conjuror. Whereas we "know" that Indian murderers are brutal because they dismember bodies and cannot put them back together again, the magician's spectacle of violence is harmless fun, the logic of the trick suggests, because the boy always returns alive at the end of the mutilation. In addition, the return of the living child at the end of the show might reflect British desires to imagine a way to restore the dismembered British bodies in India back to wholeness. More problematically, however, this return, which is indispensable to the magician's ability to perform atrocities onstage, further demonstrates the problem of British male impotence. Try as he might, the British gentleman seems incapable of thoroughly and successfully disappearing those bodies marked as surplus to the nation's requirements. At best, he magically "vanishes" these bodies, but, as I suggested earlier, vanishing is always incomplete, always undoes itself with the threat of reappearance. Like the return of the repressed, the vanishing Indian body keeps coming back at the British magician.

The Indian Basket is only one of many late-nineteenth- and early-twentieth-century tricks that centered on the mutilation of the young Indian body. In 1908, the *Magic Circular* reports another Victorian trick, the Dissected Messenger. The author notes: "Paget opens the basket, takes out and hands to Benson the dismembered body of an Indian youth (stuffed pieces). Benson thinks he has it all, but suddenly discovers he is a 'wing' short, becomes alarmed, and throws the lot on the floor. . . . The youth eventually emerges."[38] Again the integrity of the Indian body (which has in this description already become the body of a beast) lies in the hands of the nineteenth-century British gentleman, who may or may not be dressed as an adult Indian male. Likewise, the Indian Rope Trick involves the same key components of a violent Indian mutilator, a dismembered boy, the rhetoric of vanishing, and a magical restoration. As Maskelyne describes it in *White Magic,* "A boy must climb the rope to its top, and vanish. The fakir follows with a knife in his teeth, and slashes about in the air at the top, whereupon limbs, head and pieces of flesh cut from the boy's body fall to the ground. Finally, the fakir descends the rope, pulls it down and coils it up, throws the limbs and pieces of body into a bag, places the bag in a box which has previously been examined by the audience—and within a minute, the box opens and the boy jumps out alive and whole" (115–16). Like the Indian Basket, the Rope Trick simultaneously affirms and disavows the violence of disappearance, which constitutes a fundamental part of "benevolent" British imperialism. It also attempts to project the agency of brutality onto the body of the Indian "other" (who is also the violated body), and finally it portrays the impossibility of repressing the material fact of the body in pieces. Although the magician might work hard to get rid of the surplus Indian body, first by mutilating it, then by doubly burying it in a bag, then a box, this body keeps reconstituting itself, eternally returning. Like Malthus's abject poor, the Indian body, it seems, always exists as a site of excess within the spectacle of British imperialism.

Just as nineteenth-century population debates consistently blur the line between Britain's anxieties about surplus women at home and unruly "natives" abroad, so Victorian stage magic constantly substitutes a white female assistant for the body of the Indian boy. From the 1870s on, British magicians began to blow women out of canons, a trick that could not but recall the punishment of Indian soldiers at Cawnpore, whose bodies were decimated in precisely this way. Often dressing their female assistants in oriental robes, magicians pierced these women with swords, sawed them in half, and beheaded them, a series of tricks that drew their inspiration from earlier models of Indian mutilation. The Bodiless Lady, Stella, the Decapitated Princess, the Half Woman, and Vivisection are only a handful of the tricks that delighted British audiences.

Although these spectacles of mutilation and reconstitution, disappearance and return, enjoyed great popularity and did a lot to further the status of stage magic in Victorian society, *nothing* compares, either before or since, with the Vanishing Lady Trick as it appeared in 1886 on the stage of Britain's "Hall of Mystery," Egyptian Hall. Simultaneously arousing and managing the social and political concerns of the day, the Vanishing Lady captivated the public imagination in unprecedented ways. In addition to taking the London theater scene by storm, the trick caught the attention of the royal family (the Prince of Wales summoned his magician to give a command performance of the Vanishing Lady at Sandringham Palace on November 9, 1886), and provided the British press with a language of magical vanishing through which to examine the political problems of the day.

People, usually women, had been magically coming and going in more or less sophisticated forms from the late eighteenth century onward. On April 5, 1789, a poster for the Haymarket Theater, London, promised that Monsieur Comus, "lately arrived from Paris, will, by sleight of hand, convey his wife, who is 5 feet 8 inches high, under a cup, in the same manner as he would balls."[39] Late-eighteenth-century Paris was also home to the renowned "invisible lady," Frances, who baffled spectators. Hopkins, in *Magic,* describes the illusion in the following way.

> The spectator entered a well lighted hall in which, in part of a window, there was a box suspended by four brass chains attached by bows of ribbon. The box, which was surrounded by a grating, was provided with two panes of glass that permitted of seeing that it was absolutely empty. To one of the extremities was fixed a speaking trumpet. When a visitor spoke in the latter, he was answered by a hollow voice; and when he placed his face near the box, he even felt upon it the action of a mysterious breath. When he presented any object whatever in front of the mouthpiece and asked the voice to name it, an answer immediately came from the speaking tube. . . . People were lost in conjecture as to the secret of the experiment. (102–3)

As Jann Matlock has argued, Frances became an ideal of femininity, a genuine threat to those unfortunate women who led lives encumbered by a physical body.[40] Although Frances exists on a continuum with the nineteenth century's vanishing lady, an important difference distinguishes these two versions of decorporealized femininity. While Frances belongs to a misogynist discourse that fetishizes women without bodies, she nevertheless demonstrates a certain agency, power, and independence, even omniscience, through the continued and mysterious presence of her voice, an agency of which the vanishing lady appears, at least at first glance, to be completely devoid. Unlike Frances, the vanishing lady initially possesses a body. The male magician makes this body vanish, and, though it often returns at the end of the trick, the female body *seems* to lie completely in the hands of the magician, or so the trick would have us believe.

After Monsieur Comus, no further traces of vanishing women appear until 1838, when Mr. Sutton, an associate of the better known Professor Anderson, "Wizard of the North," advertised the Pie of Morocco (fig. 4). A broadsheet describes the pie trick as "a performance truly worthy of admiration, in which Mr. S. will cause one of the Ladies in the house to disappear, and afterwards to be found in the INSIDE OF A PIE." Taking Malthus's *Essay on Population* one step further, the pie trick not only limits the consumption of women in a time of surplus population but transforms the surplus female body into a nutritious meal for the worthy guests at Mother Nature's now cannibalistic feast. In this example, the disappearing act clearly marks the climax of the show. Not only does it close the performance; it also occupies the entire bottom half of the poster and is the only illustrated item on the program. As with most of the disappearing acts prior to 1886, Sutton's trick involved placing a lady under a basket, after which she escaped rather obviously through a trap door in the floor. In 1840, Professor Anderson himself advertised a performance of Magical Evaporation or Disappearance Extraordinary (the gender of the subject is unspecified, although most assistants were already female). And in 1857 Monsieur Robin presented Double Invisibilité at Egyptian Hall, in which he placed a man *and* a woman under a barrel and made them disappear.[41]

The 1880s, however, was *the* decade of the vanishing woman. She exploded onto the cultural scene with a forcefulness and panache un-

Fairy Tributes! - Enchanted Fruit! Magic Flight.
INCOMPATIBLES! OBERON'S REFECTORY! THE GAMBLER OUTWITTED! GOOD GENII

Petile's Pocket! Magic Power!

Pomona's Cornucopia.—This Illusion is dedicated to the Ladies.

Enchanted Watches! The Necromantic Money, &c. &c.

PART. II.

VENTRILOQUISM.

In this Part, Mr. SUTTON will introduce TWO JEW'S HARPS, and play a Medley Overture, and the Scotch Air of *"Roy's Wife"* with Variations. His performance on those insignificant instruments is truly wonderful, and always creates an extraordinary sensation. Mr. SUTTON will introduce the

SPEAKING AUTOMATON,

In imitation of the Roman Oracles. During the Conversation with this figure Mr. S. will

HOLD A LIGHTED CANDLE TO HIS LIPS,

And not a breath of air, or the least motion of the lips will be perceptible. This feat has never been attempted by any Ventriloquist on record, except by Mr. S.

HE WILL HOLD AMUSING COLLOQUIS,

With several supposed personages in various parts of the Theatre.

After which

Master VIOTTI COLLINS,

Son of the Celebrated English PAGANINI,

Will perform A SOLO ON THE VIOLIN introducing the DOUBLE HARMONICS in succession, which has never been attempted by any Performer, exc pt the great Master of the Art, SIGNOR PAGANINI. Accompanied by his Father and Infant Brother,

MASTER LINDLEY COLLINS,

Who will introduce A CONCERTO ON THE VIOLINCELLO, being positively the Youngest Performer on that Instrument in the World.

PART III.

EXPERIMENTS IN EGYPTIAN SORCERY,

Mr. S. will in the Centre of his Physical Cabinet, employ his science to excite the imagination of the audience on a variety of objects, which they will vainly endeavour to account for. These extraordinary feats, being different from each other will produce by turns wonder and amazement, and charm the eyes of the spectators intent upon penetrating the mysterious delusions presented to them. The

INFERNAL BOTTLE ; MIRACULOUS SHOT ;

And the RABBIT of the SANCTOSIA of the MAGII of ISPAHAN,

Will be Introduced.

Figure 4. The Pie of Morocco (1838). Courtesy of the Harry Price Library of Magical Literature, University of London.

rivaled by other stage tricks at any point in the century. Never had a magic trick been so prominent, so revered. And, although magicians never explicitly linked the popularity of this trick to the nation's political concerns, I want to suggest that the parallels between the worlds of magic and British politics are so striking that the two discourses beg to be introduced to each other.

Vanishing firmly establishes itself as female in 1886 with the introduction of French-born Hungarian magician Buatier de Kolta's new trick, known both in Paris and London as L'Escamotage d'une Dame en Personne Vivante or The Vanishing Lady. This vanishing verb, *escamoter,* has a number of interesting resonances in French beyond that of mere disappearance. Stemming from the word *escamote,* a conjuror's cork ball, this verb first suggests that any *escamotage* is always a kind of juggling act, but it also conjures up ideas of burking the question, filching someone's property, doing someone out of a job, and obtaining another's consent through trickery.[42] Similarly, the term marks the *escamoteur* not only as conjuror but as a "person who dodges the issue" and a "sneak thief," reminding us that there is something profoundly untrustworthy about the figure of the magician and about the concept of disappearance in general. Not only does he convince us with illusions, but he participates in some sort of theft. But the theft, the evidence of which he tries to render invisible, always inevitably leaves traces of itself. In the case of the Victorian vanishing lady, escamotage is haunted by the specter of colonial robbery and the illusions of imperialism, and the magician works hard to make the traces of these thefts disappear along with the body of his assistant.[43]

The lady first vanished on August 6, 1886, closing the second half of a longer variety performance that featured Zoë, the sketching automaton, A Spiritualist Sketch: Mrs. Daffodil Downy's Light and Dark Seance, plate dancing, telepathy, and a mechanical orchestra (figs. 5, 6, 7).[44] Buatier de Kolta had been engaged by Maskelyne and Cooke to perform the trick himself, but so successful was his run in Paris that he decided not to terminate his French performance prematurely. Instead, Maskelyne appointed a deputy: Charles Bertram, known as "royalty's magician" because of his frequent appearances at Sandringham Palace. A decade after the first performance, Bertram described the details of the momentous occasion.

Figures 5, 6, 7. L'Escamotage en Personne Vivante. Program from the Egyptian Hall, August 16, 1886. Courtesy of the Harry Houdini Collection, Library of Congress.

As this illusion is one which I think I can safely say is considered by every known professor of the magic art to be the most perfect and most startling stage trick which has ever been produced, I anticipate the desire of my reader, and enter into the details of the production of this trick at Egyptian Hall. . . . I was assisted in the illusion by Mlle. Patrice, a very beautiful young lady, tall and fair. And so that my reader may fully appreciate the value of the illusion, I may perhaps be allowed to mention that she weighed a little over nine stone—so that she was not by any means *petite*—a fact which greatly enhanced the effect of her disappearance. The illusion was arranged as follows:—The stage was clear of any furniture, though the scene used represented a drawing room interior. . . . On the center of the stage . . . an open copy of *The Times* newspaper was laid perfectly flat. Upon this was placed a chair made with a cane seat back. Mlle. Patrice was now introduced to the audience, and looked perfectly charming in a long white silk Grecian cos-

tume. . . . Upon seating herself upon the chair I informed her that I had the power to make her disappear, and that I could send her unseen to any place which it pleased her to name. She desired to go to "Arcadia," which was constructed into meaning the (Burlington) "Arcade" here opposite, from which she could quickly return. Giving her a little bottle to smell "containing a potent liquid," she fell into an apparent deep sleep, with her head drooping gracefully on one side. I then produced a large red silk shawl, seven feet square, which was given for examination to the audience. This was lightly placed over her head and tied at the back, and then was lightly drawn downwards, so as to completely envelope her. I walked round the chair, and after again showing that she was still underneath the veil, I stood for a moment at the side of the chair. I touched the veil lightly with both hands, whereupon it disappeared, as had the lady also, nothing being left except her dainty lace handkerchief upon the seat of the chair. Looking round the theatre I inquired, "Where

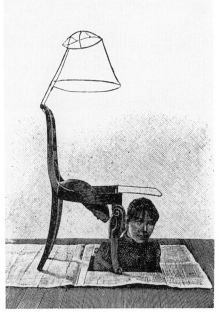

Figure 8. Bautier de Kolta's Disappearing Lady. Reprinted from Albert A. Hopkins, *Magic: Stage Illusions, Special Effects, and Trick Photography* (New York: Munn, 1898). Courtesy of the Theater Collection, Rare Books and Special Collections, Princeton University Library.

are you?" "Here!" she exclaimed, and there she was, seated in the gallery beside some astonished person, absolutely ignorant of her presence, and oftentimes greatly frightened at her being there.[45] (fig. 8)

A number of features distinguish this trick as different from earlier disappearing acts. First, it takes place not in an orientalized setting — a standard feature of many nineteenth-century conjuring acts — but in the heart of Victorian domesticity, the drawing room, already a place of disappearance or "withdrawal" from public view. Britain's ongoing concern with female surplus (the trick appears only four years after the passing of the second Married Women's Property Act) reflects itself here first in the excessive corporeality of the unmarried *Mademoiselle* Patrice, who is not "in any way *petite*," and then again in the interpretation of her desire to go to Arcadia, a place of rustic simplicity, as actually being a desire to go shopping in the Burlington Arcade.[46] Bertram's emphasis on Patrice's size contrasts strikingly with descriptions of Maskelyne's own assistant (and wife). Jasper Maskelyne writes, "Demure little Early Victorian as she was, the roses from the audience almost hid her when the performance ended."[47] This perceived corporeal expansion in magicians' assistants tells us less about female bodies, I would suggest, than about a late Victorian sense that female bodies were taking up more space than ever before as a result of their growing independence. Mademoiselle Patrice perfectly represents this shift, for she was in fact an accomplished magician in her own right, quite an anomaly for the period. So skilled was she that the royal family summoned her, like Bertram, to perform at Sandringham on numerous occasions. Indeed, in *Isn't It Wonderful?* Bertram, obviously threatened by his assistant's accomplishments, can only acknowledge her prowess via a backhanded compliment, praising her at the expense of the rest of her sex: "This lady had the honour of performing on several occasions at Sandringham before T.R.H. the Prince and Princess of Wales. Her success is phenomenal, as good conjuring requires qualities found very seldom indeed in a woman, and she may perhaps be taken as the exception which proves the rule that ladies do not make good *prestidigitateuses*" (119–20). Clearly, the trick served to reinforce Bertram's anxiety about female power. As in the Indian tricks, the vanishing lady keeps returning at the end of her supposed disappearance, signaling the magician's innocence and playfulness but also his impotence. The return represents the impossibility of vanishing's completion, emphasizing further the radical and disruptive potential of this woman's resilience.

Unlike earlier vanishing lady tricks, de Kolta's Escamotage d'une Dame not only made the lady disappear but made the apparatus of disappearance — in this case the silk cloth — disappear along with her, causing one reviewer in the *Times* to refer to the act as a "double illusion."[48] The disappearance of the cloth, which, unlike the lady, never returns, matters for two reasons. First, it renders invisible the mechanism of vanishing along with the body in question, something that, as I argue later in the book, becomes key for the political appropriation of the vanishing woman. This piece of silk is also remarkable as the only remaining visible trace of the exotic Orient that this very British, very domestic conjuring scene works hard to repress. However, although the red silk shawl — which Bertram, in another appropriation of "oriental" labor, claims to have "produced" himself —

may be this scenario's only *visible* remnant of the British magician's debt to the now vanished Indian and Chinese magicians, the success of this new version of the trick depends absolutely on another invisible trace of the colonies and of India in particular. What marked de Kolta's illusion as original and unfathomable was the placement of the *Times* newspaper beneath the chair of the vanishing lady, apparently making it impossible for her to escape through a trap door in the stage, as previous vanishing ladies had so obviously done. Spectators simply could not imagine how Patrice might work her way through the newspaper without (1) making a noise, and (2) tearing the paper. In his explanation of the trick's mechanics in *Magic*, Hopkins reveals the secret and invisible agent of disappearance, explaining that "if the newspaper is carefully examined, it will be found to be made of India rubber and to contain a large rent at about the center" (43). For the British, India rubber, or *caoutchouc,* had been an agent of disappearance since 1770, when Priestly first discovered that it could remove pencil marks from paper. And the metaphorical potential of this colonial export was exploited as early as 1837 when Dickens wrote in *Pickwick Papers* that "The unwonted lines . . . in Mr. Pickwick's clear and open brow gradually melted away . . . like the marks of a black-lead pencil beneath the softening influence of India rubber."[49] During the second half of the nineteenth century, demand for rubber increased dramatically for various reasons, resulting in the transplantation of rubber seeds from the Amazon Valley to numerous British colonies, primarily Malaya, Ceylon, and India.[50]

Although W. R. Greg had once fantasized that the excesses of Britain might one day simply vanish into the empty space of the colonies, by 1886 it was becoming clear that this dream had doubly failed. In addition to there being a growing imbalance between the male and female populations in Britain, women were becoming more demanding than ever, while colonial subjects were proving increasingly difficult to ignore. The annexation of Burma in February 1886, for example, provoked strong resistance from the Burmese population for both religious and political reasons.[51] Apparently killing two birds with one stone, Bertram first does away with the body not just of any woman but of the woman who is unmarried, overly corporeal, overly consuming, and overly accomplished in the professional realm. Next he disappears the remaining visible trace of the potent oriental magician and colonial laborers, the silk shawl. Finally, he mobilizes India (through the India rubber mat) as an *invisible* site of disappearance into which both the surplus woman *and* the colonial other can vanish without even making a dent in the news of the day.

But what was the news of the day? What would the vanishing lady have seen had she picked up the paper and read it instead of disappearing through it in August 1886? Ironically, she would first have encountered news of herself. Between August 2 and August 30, the front page of the *Times* ran an advertisement for L'Escamotage d'une Dame en Personne Vivante every day, advertisements that ran alongside descriptions of the Ceylon Show at the Royal Agricultural Hall, the Colonial and India Exhibition (which promised to provide an "Illustration of the Products and Resources of the British Empire"), and the Miniature Japanese Village at Hyde Park. On August 2, the front page declared that, "Buatier de Kolta, the marvellous HUNGARIAN CONJUROR, who is creating such a profound sensation in Paris, has been ENGAGED at very great expense to perform in conjunction with Maskelyne and Cooke." Two days later, the advertisement had to acknowledge that de Kolta himself would not appear at Egyptian Hall: "Buatier de Kolta's marvellous illusion L'ESCAMITAGE EN PERSONNE VIVANTI, will be introduced on Saturday next, August 7 — Mr. Maskelyne begs to announce that Mr. Chas. Bertram and Mademoiselle Patrice have been deputed to produce this startling illusion until the arrival of the originator, which has been delayed for a short time in consequence of his enormous success in Paris." The same notice announced that Bertram would perform a private showing of the trick on Friday, August 6. Reviews of the performance soon began to appear. The front page of August 10 declared, "Immense success of Buatier de Kolta's marvellous illusion received with breathless astonishment, culminating in unbounded enthusiasm. A morning paper of August 9 in a long descriptive article, says, 'M de Kolta's invention is certainly one of the most ingenious effects of its kind yet produced, even on the stage of the Egyptian Hall.'" In the course of the month, advertisements for imitations also hit the front page of the *Times*. On August 26, in addition to the daily advertisement of de Kolta's trick, it announced "The Marvellous Disappearance of a Lady" at the London Pavillion and the "Mysterious Disappearance of a Young Lady" at the Royal Aquarium. Variations sprang up around the country, but, as the *Morning Post* declared on August 7, 1887, "The clumsy attempts at imitation have given luster to the original feat, which stands preeminent like a rich Brazilian gem in the midst of a French paste" (quoted in Bertram, *Isn't It Wonderful?* 128).

Although the front page of the *Times* preoccupied itself with magic in August 1886, the "Latest Intelligence" section of the paper primarily addressed the ongoing problem of the Bulgarian Revolution, one of the major European political crises of 1885–86. Bulgaria, once a part of the Ottoman Empire, revolted in 1876 and gained independence with the help of Russia's intervention in the Russo-Turkish wars (1877–78). Prince Alexander of Battenberg became ruler of Bulgaria, but he grew increasingly unpopular with Russia for a number of reasons. Major A. von Huhn writes in 1886: "I have already hinted shortly what the principle charges are that were brought against Prince Alexander in Russia: his German origin, his disinclination to allow himself to be treated like a subordinate by Russian consuls and generals, his endeavours to raise national feeling amongst the Bulgarians, and to make something more of Bulgaria than a mere Russian province."[52] Amid rumors of a Russian assassination of the prince, the *Times,* drawing on the trick that had become the talk of the town, dramatically announced on August 26 that, "Prince Alexander has disappeared": "General anxiety about Prince Alexander's fate has been manifested today. As he had been kidnapped by desperados it was natural that rumours of his assassination should be circulated. In Russian circles, however, it is affirmed, as if from positive knowledge, that he is alive" (3). Victoria, who had herself become increasingly more visible since being crowned empress of India in 1876, emerges in this context as an agent determined to get the bottom of this Russian escamotage, and the *Times* reassured its readers that, "the Queen of England has telegraphed to Bucharest asking where the Prince is" (3).[53]

Although the prince soon reappeared, Britain continued to think about this political crisis in magical terms, as the cartoon and poem that appeared in *Punch; or the London Charivari,* on October 9, 1886, entitled "The Latest Trick. Will It Succeed?" effectively illustrates (fig. 9). The cartoon depicts Russia as a magician holding the cloak of diplomacy, under which he attempts to vanish a dejected female embodiment of Bulgaria, whose chair sits squarely in the middle not of the *Times* but of the Treaty of Berlin. The accompanying poem elaborates on the image.

Figure 9. "The Latest Trick. Will It Succeed?" Reprinted from *Punch; or, the London Charivari*, October 9, 1886.

The Latest Trick (n.a.)

An amateur Wizard, of character shady,
A conjuror doubtful, though wearing a crown,
Is trying the trick of the Vanishing Lady,
Which lately so greatly has taken the Town.

A very old trick in a somewhat new setting,
But possibly little the worse for its age.
After going the rounds, it appears to be getting
A place on the foreign political stage.
. . .
The juggler is frankly a juggler, he tells us:
His object hard cash, and his mode sleight of hand;
But 'tis for our good that diplomacy sells us,
Its motives are lofty, its objects are grand.
. . .

But even Imperial Jugglers must juggle
With deftness of passing and swiftness of stroke,
And he will need smartness and skill if he'd smuggle
That form unsuspected from under that cloak.

Finesse with effrontery, palming with patter,
Must go to the making a Royal VERBECK.
He who thinks that brute force will settle the matter,
May make a mistake, and meet with a check.

Hey Presto! Bulgarians' freedom to banish
Were quite *à la Russe,* a true Romanoff deed.
But what if the Vanishing Lady won't vanish?
The trick is a taking one. Will it succeed?[54]

In choosing the British spectacle of escamotage as a metaphor for Russia's forceful, and ultimately unsuccessful, possession of Bulgaria, this *Punch* cartoon exposes the implicit violence and misogyny of the Vanishing Lady Act, the success of which turns on the thrill of imagining momentarily that the female body can be disappeared without trace or consequence, but it also makes the connection between magic and international politics more explicit than it had ever been on the Victorian stage.

The cartoon attempts to lampoon Russian imperialism, revealing it, through the analogy with the vanishing lady, to be nothing more than an insidious act of trickery, one that presents smuggling and theft as lofty and grand political acts. However, the poem inadvertently implies a parallel with Britain's own acts of political escamotage through its repeated invocation of that repressed figure of Victorian magic, the Indian juggler.[55] Haunted by the inevitable ending of the magician's trick, the poem concludes by asking, "But what if the Vanishing Lady won't vanish? / The trick is a taking one. Will it succeed?" Any Victorian reader of the poem would have known that, though the lady would of course vanish, she would always reappear unless the magician chooses either to make a spectacle of his own impotence or to make his violence visible. For the failure to return the woman's body at the end of the trick suggests either that the magician is unable to do so or that the body in question has *not* magically vanished but has been completely eradicated, at which point the trick moves out of the realm of light entertainment and into the sphere of something more grim. Although these questions about the success of vanishing speak first of Bulgaria, they also reflect Britain's fears about the increasing demands of women at home and colonial subjects abroad.

But how do we read the failure of Russia's attempt to vanish Bulgaria implied by this cartoon back onto the scene of British politics? At first glance, it would seem that the imperialist British escamoteur has to emerge as a failed figure, one unable to eradicate successfully either his overly corporeal surplus women or his rebellious colonial subjects. Indeed, at one level true success—getting rid of this and most other women—eludes everyone, except as a kind of fantasy, for the success of the stage trick is to make the lady vanish but not really. If the lady doesn't come back, the trick is not a trick anymore, merely an act of exportation or eradication. However, this cartoon does distinguish British vanishing from the tricks of Russian imperialists by collapsing the geographical space of Bulgaria and its inhabitants into the visible body of the vanishing woman who always returns, thereby rendering the Russian attempts at escamotage doomed to a double failure—at both the real and fantastical levels—because the imperialist vanishing act remains visible. In contrast, the "superior" British magician carefully separates the spectacular female body, about whose well-being we actually care, from the less visible traces of British colonized space, traces of which disappear along with the lady but never come back. This failure to return usually goes unnoticed, and it is only when we as spectators refuse the reassurance offered by the lady's return that the magician is really in trouble. So, although the return of the vanishing lady in Britain may seem, from a feminist perspective, to represent a moment of triumph over the patriarchal magician, we need to be careful that our focus on issues of gender, and our enjoyment of the spectacle of white female resilience that asserts itself in the single word *here,* do not make us unconsciously indifferent to the permanent disappearance of the veil and what it comes to represent. In the context of the recent mobilization of feminist discourse in the service of America's "liberation" of Afghan women, this task of looking beyond the success of the newly visible woman and of asking what disappears along with the veil has never been more urgent.

2

Insubstantial Media: Ectoplasm, Exposure, and the Stillbirth of Film

By the end of the nineteenth century, European and American audiences had temporarily lost interest in stage magic and the vanishing lady no longer held any particular theatrical appeal. Charles Bertram, the magician who had introduced the Vanishing Lady Act on the British stage, writes in 1896: "No place of entertainment was complete without its vanishing lady, but . . . the illusions which were attempted elsewhere lost all their significance, and eventually 'wore out' what was a most startling and marvellous feat."[1] Not coincidentally, 1896 is also the year in which John Maskelyne, director of London's primary magic theater, Egyptian Hall, introduced moving pictures into his magic shows.[2] Magicians included film in their repertoire in the hope of revitalizing the public's interest in magic, but ultimately the new medium only worked to consolidate magic's demise.

As Jasper Maskelyne writes, "It was Mr. Devant who was responsible for obtaining for the Egyptian Hall some of the first moving picture shows ever seen in England. Little did anyone guess then that the novelty to which a few minutes of the Maskelyne programme was devoted each evening was subsequently to oust conjuring to a very great degree from public interest, and to contribute largely toward the condition of things which eventually caused Maskelyne's Theatre to be taken over by the b.b.c." (91).[3]

Unaware of the ousting that was soon to take place, however, turn of the century magicians enthusiastically performed their best tricks before the camera. The Maskelynes and Mr. Devant shot illusions on the roof of Egyptian Hall with a machine purchased from R. W. Paul, while in France another magician found himself entranced by the new medium. When the Lumière brothers first presented the Cinématographe in Paris in 1895, Georges Méliès, renowned magician and owner of the Théâtre de Robert-Houdin, Paris's equivalent of Egyptian Hall, was one of the guests.[4] Describing the display as "un truc extraordinaire" (an extraordinary trick), Méliès became determined to buy a machine for his magic theater, but the Lumières refused to sell the Cinématographe until late 1897.[5] Undeterred, Méliès traveled to London in February 1896, where he, too, purchased a projector from R. W. Paul. Then, either through his own invention or through acquiring the rights to the Isolatograph, designed by his friends the Isola brothers, Méliès found himself in possession of the power of filmmaking.[6]

As the vanishing lady disappeared from the stage, she rose like a phoenix from the ashes, making an immediate and ghostly comeback in this newly emerging world of film. Many trick films from the early years of cinema feature vanishing and reappearing bodies, both male and female.[7] It is striking, however, that between 1896 and 1898, three filmmakers from different countries all chose to reproduce the particular version of the Vanishing Lady Act first performed by Charles Bertram in Britain in 1886. In 1896, Méliès made *The Vanishing Lady* (*L'Escamotage d'une Dame Chez Robert-Houdin,* October-November), performing the original stage trick with one crucial alteration. In Charles Bertram's stage version of L'Escamotage d'une Dame, his assistant, Mademoiselle Patrice, reappeared not as a body but as a voice in the audience, asserting her presence with a single word: "Here!" In the silent medium of film, however, in which the voice temporarily disappears as a mode of presence, the vanishing lady's screen come-back becomes something of a challenge. Denying the vanished lady a full visual reappearance, Méliès removes the cloth to reveal a grue-some and charred skeleton in the chair where his assistant once sat.[8] Apparently unaffected by Méliès's attempt to give some closure to the repetitive comings and goings of the magician's assistant, how-ever, the vanishing lady rises again from the ashes (literally, this time), making two further early cinematic appearances. In 1897, R. W. Paul made *The Vanishing Lady*, with Charles Bertram as the star magician, and in 1898 Thomas Edison produced another version of the same trick, with the slight variation that instead of turning into a skeleton the lady never returns at all (figs. 10, 11, 12). Each of these conjur-ing films strives, albeit unsuccessfully, to stage the eradication of the spectacular woman once and for all. Ghostlike, the charred female skeleton repeatedly dons its flesh and returns to haunt the screen. But why did these filmmakers from England and the United States choose to imitate Méliès's film at a historical moment when, accord-ing to Bertram at least, the vanishing lady had worn herself out as a figure of public interest?

Female Exposure

Film historians have worked hard to establish the *pre* of this "pre-historic" period of cinema, arguing for the importance of separat-ing it from later narrative film as well as for the relative transpar-ency of these early works. Tom Gunning, for example, distinguishes pre-1906 cinema—"the cinema of attractions"—from later narrative film, though he does carefully refuse any absolute separation between the two: "Although different from the fascination in storytelling ex-ploited by the cinema from the time of Griffith, it is not necessarily opposed to it. In fact *the cinema of attractions does not disappear with the dominance of narrative, but rather goes underground,* both into certain avant-garde practices and as a component of narrative films, more evident in some genres (e.g. the musical) than in others."[9] The porous nature of Gunning's historical boundaries here makes his view one of the most useful, but from the perspective of the vanishing woman even his historical paradigm is too rigid. The vanishing lady, for example,

Figures 10, 11, 12.
The Vanishing Lady
(Thomas Edison,
1898). Courtesy of
the Paper Print
Collection of the
Library of Congress
Motion Picture,
Broadcasting, and
Recorded Sound
Division.

does go underground, reemerging as a showpiece trick in particular narrative genres like the musical.[10] But, in addition to occasionally reviving an earlier "cinema of attractions," she also emerges as a narrative feature in post-1906 film and comes to play a central role in the development of these later film plots.

In contrast to Gunning, Barry Salt resists the continuity between trick films and later narrative film with surprising passion. In "Film Form, 1900–1906," he declares with more than a hint of aggravation: "It is my view that excessive attention has been devoted to early trick films, and in particular those of Méliès, in view of the fact that they proved a dead end as far as the development of the cinema is concerned. . . . This is not to say that they have no other interesting qualities, just that enough is enough. . . . There is no necessity to describe these techniques . . . or to comment on the films in which they appear. Their occurrence and manner of execution are always quite obvious."[11] But what causes Salt to rail so against the "excessive attention" paid to these "dead ends," a term that emphasizes the separation of pre- and post-1906 cinema and reinforces the idea that the road to Hollywood began neither at Egyptian Hall nor at the Théâtre de Robert-Houdin? Why does Salt feel compelled to monitor the interest other viewers obviously *do* have in these short films?

One reason to revisit these short early films is that they have traditionally received far less attention from feminist film critics than the later films of the Hollywood studios, leaving the relationship between these two periods vastly undertheorized from a feminist perspective.[12] As Linda Williams writes in "Film Body," "To a certain extent we know what the status of this body becomes as a relay to the body of the spectator within the already formulated institution of classical narrative films and their system of suture. To a certain extent we also know how these films constitute the male viewer within the film as a surrogate for the look of the male spectator and the female body as site of the spectacle. But we know much less about the position of these male and female bodies in the 'prehistoric' and 'primitive' stages of the evolution of the cinema, before codes of narrative, editing, and mise-en-scène were fully established" (509). Williams draws our attention to the gap that exists between feminist thought on Hollywood film and early film scholarship and raises questions that encourage us to begin moving back and forth across the divide. Provoked, then, by Salt's prohibition on looking back, I return to these early films in order to think further about what their repeated resuscitation of the vanishing female body reveals about the development of cinema and the anxieties it produced.

Although feminist film theory has in many ways moved beyond the debate initiated by Laura Mulvey about women in film as either objects to be looked at or sites of absence, Constance Balides usefully draws our attention to the fact that many of the questions that have been so fully explored in the context of classical narrative film have remained quite unthought in relation to early film. Beginning to address this gap, then, Balides argues in "Scenarios of Exposure in the Practice of Everyday Life" that the "exposure" of women, the practice of "turning women characters into spectacles," does not confine itself to the Hollywood films on which feminists have primarily focused but also constitutes a central feature of early or "primitive" cinema.[13] But how successful were these attempts at exposure? What exactly does early film render visible? Although Balides rightly identifies a pattern of trying to expose the female body, these attempts are intimately bound up with the attempt to understand the medium of film itself. The vanishing lady provides such a compelling figure to filmmakers because, as a result of her ability to make a spectacle out of the vanishing body, she emerges as a perfect emblem for the cinematic image, which constantly wrestles with the difficulty of fixing bodily presence on the screen. Through a return to the vanishing lady, the medium of film finds a narrative that allows it to explore the possibility of its own existence.

The triple appearance of the vanishing lady in just three years suggests that she plays an essential role in the birth of film and that she embodies something about the medium itself that captured the imaginations of filmmakers in France, Britain, and the United States. In spite of the general lack of feminist attention given to this period, the vanishing lady did briefly enter feminist film discussions at the end of the 1970s. In her important article "The Lady Vanishes: Women, Magic, and the Movies" (1979), for example, Lucy Fischer states, "Though we are all accustomed to crediting Méliès with the birth of film magic, the implications of the genre for the *image of women* have not been examined. In addition to being the 'father' of film fantasy, Méliès may also have to stand as the inadvertent patriarch of a particular cinematic vision of women."[14] Fischer qualifies her judgment of Méliès by acknowledging that his vision of women is in fact "simply a convention borrowed from theatrical magic" (40). But in spite of this allowance, Fischer insists that by making women disappear and appear the magician/filmmaker still demonstrates his power over the female body, rendering her nothing more than "a *function* of the male will*" (32). These early films, she claims, do more than demonstrate feats of prestidigitation; they also "articulate a discourse toward women" (31). In decorporealizing the female body, she maintains that these films betray an anxiety about the physicality of that body, most strikingly in relation to that body's reproductive capacity, and she views Méliès's cinematic magic as a form of "womb-envy," a jealous desire for the ability to give birth. Fischer supports her argument by suggesting that the magician's acts, "producing rabbits out of hats or flowers from cones," function as "symbolic imitations of birth, and their occurrence at the hand of the male magician seems to speak an *envy* of what is, essentially, the *female procreative function*" (47). In these films, the "woman as mother" emerges as an emblem for the medium of film itself, the ultimate reproduction machine.

Responding in 1981 to Fischer's reading of Méliès, Linda Williams resists the idea of cinematic vanishing as an exclusively female affair and even suggests that we cannot privilege vanishing per se as a defining feature of these early films: "Fischer is quite right to stress the significance of magic which exerts power over women's bodies, decorporealizing and reducing them to the status of a decorative object. But it is simply not accurate to privilege the disappearance of women in Méliès films, any more than it would be accurate to privilege her magical appearance. In fact, there are probably an equal number of magical appearances and disappearances of men in these films, or of any object for that matter, since the staging of appearance and disappearance is the primary way Méliès exercises the illusory power of his simulation machine."[15] Williams then usefully develops Fischer's argument beyond the paradigm of male envy of the reproductive capacity of women, drawing our attention to the important relationship between the film bodies on screen, which both vanish and appear, and the simulation machines that (re)produce them: "While Lucy Fischer emphasizes the envious male's appropriation of female procreative powers in the construction of this machine that gives 'birth' to women, I would stress instead that this spewing forth of identical female bodies only calls attention even more to the status of these bodies as totally mastered, infinitely reproducible *images* whose potential threat of castration has been disavowed by the fetish object of the machine with which they are associated" (531). But even as we recognize the simulation machine's disavowal of the threat of castration posed by the woman's body, the fact that the machine "totally masters" these threatening bodies through infinite reproduction re-invokes the specter of the mother's body that the image-making process tries to control. As an icon for the medium of film itself, the vanishing woman can never be properly mastered by the simulation machine of cinema, for the threat she poses reemerges with every cinematic image.

Although in "The Lady Vanishes" Fischer focuses mainly on the women who disappear at the hands of male magicians, she does briefly discuss the rare occurrence of female magicians in early films as evidence to support her claim that, although these films act out the male magician's control over the female body, they actually "bespeak his perception of relative weakness" (42). Fischer astutely reads a variety of examples of female magic as sites of female power that are inseparable from the female body's capacity to reproduce itself. But in noting how the ability to reproduce and manifest bodies functions in these films as a mode of power we should not forget that vanishing has a power of its own. Fischer's oppositional stance toward female vanishing seems like a logical feminist response to the scenarios that stage the repeated eradication of women. Yet the recent work of numerous theorists, including Terry Castle, Avery F. Gordon, Peggy Phelan, and Patricia White, suggests that there might well be politically strategic reasons for taking the vanishing lady as a paradoxical model of resistance to violent eradication.[16] Hovering in the space between absence and presence, she challenges us to think not only about the "presence" of particular women but also about the very possibility of presence per se. And though this lady's unstable existence may trouble us her lack of complete presence ultimately equips her to resist both exposure and eradication. In this sense, the vanishing lady has a deep affinity with the *a* of *différance*. Derrida asks: "What am I to do in order to speak of the *a* of *différance*? It goes without saying that it cannot be *exposed*. One can expose only that which at a certain moment can become *present,* manifest, that which can be shown, presented as something present, a being-present in its truth, in the truth of a presence or the presence of a presence. . . . Reserving itself, not exposing itself, in regular fashion it exceeds the order of truth at a certain precise point, but without dissimulating itself as something, as a mysterious being, in the occult of nonknowledge or in a hole with interminable borders (for example, in a topology of castration). In every exposition it would be exposed to disappearing as disappearance."[17] Like the *a,* the vanishing lady cannot be exposed because she is never fully present. So, although Balides rightly claims that the "exposure" of women is not limited to Hollywood film but "constitutes a central feature of early cinema" (20), we need to remember the extent to which these attempts at exposure fail, and fail without allowing that body simply to fall into "a hole."

As mentioned earlier, Ellis Hanson suggests in his introduction to *Outtakes: Essays on Queer Theory and Film* that we have to deal with vanishing every time we sit back to watch a movie: "The outtake raises the possibility that to be taken out—to be taken out to the movies, to be taken out of the movies—is often to be taken in (perhaps knowingly), to be seduced for better or worse by the spectacle of one's own disappearance—which is to say, one's own constitution—as a subject."[18] Hanson and the movies remind us that subjectivity itself always begins in vanishing, a vanishing most fully explored in Lacan's discussion of the term *aphanisis.*[19] He writes: "Now, *aphanisis* is to be situated in a more radical way at the level at which the subject manifests himself in this movement of disappearance that I have described as lethal" (207–8). Later, elaborating upon this statement, he continues, "hence the division of the subject—when the subject appears somewhere as meaning, he is manifested elsewhere as 'fading,' as disappearance. There is, then, one might say, a matter of life and death between the unary signifier and the subject, *qua* binary signifier, cause of his disappearance" (218). All subjects—male or female—must necessarily undergo the experience of aphanisis, which would seem to suggest that vanishing is not necessarily a gendered phenomenon.[20] Furthermore, as Elisabeth Bronfen has pointed out, Lacan's discussion of aphanisis retells Freud's story of the fort-da game, which I will discuss in more detail in the next chapter, replacing the fading maternal body of Freud's narrative with the fading of the subject.[21]

But, although this act of displacement may reformulate vanishing as a universal phenomenon, less explicitly tied to femininity than in Freud's earlier text, might we not also read Lacan's "reiteration" of Freud as yet another repetition of maternal vanishing? As with all vanishing woman narratives, the woman ultimately reappears, if only as a trace. In the case of Lacan, she reemerges as an exemplary figure in this story of the subject's fading: "It is in the interval between these two signifiers that resides the desire offered to the mapping of the subject in the experience of the discourse of the Other, of the first Other he has to deal with, let us say, by way of illustration, the mother" (*Four Fundamental Concepts*, 218). Like film, psychoanalysis finds itself wrestling with the impossibility of presence through a discourse of vanishing that seems inextricably linked to the figure of the mother. In this sense, even the "universal" vanishing of the subject that Hanson links to the act of watching movies emerges within the discourse of psychoanalysis as an implicitly gendered experience.

Although vanishing threatens the existence of the subject, Hanson's phrase, "for better or worse," implies that vanishing also has its advantages. But what are the better forms of vanishing and how can they help us think about cinema's potentially radical role in identity formation and transformation? On one level, we might simply understand the "payoff" of vanishing as the ability to "appear somewhere as meaning" (Lacan, *Four Fundamental Concepts*, 218). But we might also read the vanishing of the self as a particularly interesting form of agency, explored in an early film entitled *Hooligan Assists the Magician* (Edison, November 16, 1900). Like the vanishing lady films I have discussed, *Hooligan* reveals disappearance as the site for a battle between the sexes, but in this exceptional case the lady comes out on top precisely as a result of her ability to vanish. A magician appears onstage and materializes two barrels. Hooligan, a male assistant, enters the frame and makes the magician disappear. A woman dressed in white then pops up in one of the barrels waving what appears to be a large, rubber sausage, with which she hits Hooligan over the head. When Hooligan turns to face his phallic female tormentor, she vanishes. Another woman appears in the second barrel, armed with the same flexible weapon, and the two take turns beating Hooligan. Unlike his female counterpart, Hooligan the *male* assistant does possess the rare power to make the magician vanish, but he remains incapable of exerting any control over the female bodies onstage. These women torture Hooligan with a combination of their phallic sexual excess (the sausages) and their capacity for self-vanishing. In the absence of a sufficiently passive female assistant, the male assistant turns his powers on the body of the magician, transforming the magic stage from a reassuring site of patriarchal authority into a disruptive space where men treat men as they used to treat women and women appropriate and transcend the powers that were once male prerogatives.

These vanishing ladies provide no comfort for those who dread the excesses of female presence, for this film attributes the power to make oneself disappear at will to women alone. The passive vanishing of the magician's assistant becomes an active form of power in the hands of these cinematic women. Much to his frustration, Hooligan can never lay his hands on either woman. Each time he turns to grab one of them, she vanishes. Furious, Hooligan smashes the barrels. But with impressive resilience, one of the women appears yet again in a reconstituted barrel, and this time she tauntingly waves her sausage before Hooligan's eyes. He reaches for the first woman's hat but succeeds only in pulling yards of cloth out of the barrel. The same scenario repeats with the second woman. The films in this genre anxiously attempt to grab the "truth" of a materiality marked female in the midst of an uncertainty of the body made newly visible by the invention of film. *Hooligan Assists the Magician* resists this attempt, however, through its stubborn literalization of the object in question, offering yards of white cotton to Hooligan in response to his search for female "material." This defiant substitution of one type of material for another does not confine itself to the world of film. In fact, in the early decades of the twentieth century sexologists, psychologists, spiritualists, and photographers repeatedly gather together in the hope of documenting and fixing the elusive truth of presence through the unstable spectacle of the medium's body and the vanishing images it produces. Like Hooligan, however, they find themselves faced with a series of women who vanish before their eyes, leaving behind them only a selection of cotton wool, cheesecloth, and linen. But just as the early magic films of Edison, Méliès, and Paul reflect on the medium itself through the materialization and dematerialization of the female body, so the spiritualistic medium struggles to materialize the absent bodies of the "departed." Trying to ascertain the authenticity of these visible spirits, scientists and skeptics turn to the "honest" media of film and photography. But these truth machines fail to function as passive recorders of the spiritualist scene and gradually play an increasingly active role in shaping the form and content of the séances themselves. Ultimately, rather than film and photography documenting the manifestation of spirits, the séance becomes a space for staging the birth of film itself. Although the relationship between spiritualism, spirit photography, and cinema has received remarkably little attention, a closer look at the visual technology of this period reveals the complicated ways in which, through the figure of the vanishing woman, one medium defines and shapes itself in relation to another.

Magic and the Media

Late-nineteenth-century stage magicians and filmmakers had a complex and largely antagonistic relationship with the spirit world. They were at once fascinated by the manifestations of the spiritualistic medium and determined to "expose" them. Magicians like John Maskelyne devoted substantial portions of their time to uncovering the fraudulent nature of spirit manifestations by duplicating them on the magic stage without the aid of the "other world." The most famous of these exposures occurred in 1906, in response to a challenge from the spiritualist Archdeacon Colley, who, claiming that his manifestations could never be reproduced without the aid of the spirit world, called on John Maskelyne to produce a woman from his side. John, who repeatedly insisted upon that he had never had any help from spirits, successfully reproduced Colley's illusion. In his description, Jasper Maskelyne reports that: "a white mist began to issue from his left side. This mist thickened till it formed a hand, growing from his side. The hand was followed by an arm; gradually, there materialized a golden-haired spirit form. She floated from his side horizontally, while J. N. himself stood with shut eyes and white face, apparently in a trance . . . and then . . . vanished from before the audience's eyes."[22] But in choosing to expose spiritualists through imitation magicians were all too frequently mistaken for spiritualists themselves in spite of their protestations. Writing in 1924 of his relationship with Sir Arthur Conan Doyle, for example, American magician and skeptic Harry Houdini complains: "Sir Arthur thinks that I have great mediumistic powers and that some of my feats are done with the aid of spirits. Everything I do is accomplished by material means, humanly possible, no matter how baffling it is to the layman."[23]

The magicians' complicated fascination with spiritualism seeped into the films they made at the end of the nineteenth century. In his extensive study of the relationship between magic and the cinema, Erik Barnouw writes, "The spectacular, century-long successes of ghosts, phantoms, skeletons and other apparitions made it inevitable that they should come to haunt the motion picture."[24] He goes on to cite four examples of the spirit films listed in *The British Film Catalogue, 1895–1970:*

> *The Corsican Brothers* (1898). Ghost of a man's twin shows him visions of how he was killed in a duel.
> *Faust and Mephistopheles* (1898). Satan conjures vision of girl, for whom old man signs pact and is made young.
> *Photographing a Ghost* (1898). Photographer tries to take picture of a ghost, but it won't keep still and then vanishes.
> *The Gambler's Wife* (1899). Gambler is stopped from shooting himself by wife's spirit. (89)

Photographing a Ghost represents a particularly interesting example of the intrusion of the ghostly body and the practice of spirit photography into the world of film. Like the magician, this film mocks the practice of spiritualism even as it exploits the general public's interest in ghosts. But, in addition to representing the ghostly body, this film simultaneously stages a quiet exposure of the inadequacies of the medium of photography in order to assert the supremacy of film in relation to insubstantial matters. As the photographer fails to capture the ghost because of its refusal to stay still, the moving picture delights in the spirit's mobility, implicitly declaring itself the new master of the insubstantial, ectoplasmic body. In some ways, then, this is less a ghost film than a film about the ghost of photography and its haunting of cinema. The persistence of vision that film offers here also seems to promise a simultaneous persistence of visibility, knowability, and truth. Because of its ability to represent temporality and sequence, film promises to capture the elusive in a way that photography cannot. In practice, however, the medium of film proved to be as impotent in the face of disembodied spirits as its ancestor. Spirit photography and film share a desire to capture and master a "truth" that comes to be represented by the insubstantial body. These desires are constantly frustrated, however, not only because the objects they seek, such as ghosts and vanishing women, can never be fixed but because both media generate the very ectoplasmic bodies that cause them such anguish. These ghost hunts become self-reflexive projects in that they mobilize the media of photography and cinema in order to capture and expose the "truth" and "presence" of photographs and films.

Ghosts and Photographs

From its inception in 1839, photography always had an implicit relationship with the realm of the intangible. But after 1861, when William Mumler produced the first spirit photograph, this relationship became ever more explicit, and the new medium found itself increasingly entwined with the mysterious world of spiritualism. A precursor to the discourse of psychoanalysis, spiritualism worked to conjure up, capture, and control the images and voices of the past. And while magicians like Maskelyne busied themselves with exposing the fraudulent nature of spiritualist practices, spiritualism worked literally to expose on film the insubstantial bodies of ghostly presences.

Photography seemed to promise a new method of seizing what was "really" there, of capturing the "truth" of matter as one experienced it, of fixing the visual certainty of any situation. It offered a form of vision that promised to transcend the eye and allow us to see what we might otherwise miss. But because of its appeal as a medium of truth photography's supposed ability to catch what the eye missed placed it in close proximity to the magical and the mystical. Nadar, in his 1900 memoir *My Life as a Photographer,* contrasting photography with other nineteenth-century inventions, including the telephone, the electric light bulb, the phonograph, and the radio, extends the medium's capacities one step further when he asks, "But do not all these miracles pale when compared to the most astonishing and disturbing one of all, that one which seems finally to endow man himself with the divine power of creation: the power to give physical form to the insubstantial image that vanishes as soon as it is perceived, leaving no shadow in the mirror, no ripple on the surface of the water?"[25] For Nadar here, the camera catches and makes physical an image that is in the physical realm quite insubstantial, that leaves no trace of itself *except* in the photograph. Photography here enables "man himself" to resist the inevitable disappearance of experience, to materialize the elusive and evanescent elements of life, and to have "divine power" over the troubling realm of the insubstantial. For James Coates in 1911, the ability of photography to fix with equal success "the visible, the material invisible, and the immaterial invisible or the psychic" is nothing less than a scientific fact.[26] Defending against those who dismiss spirit photography with contempt, Coates turns to X-ray photography, astronomical photography, and sound recording ("photophonographic records") as proof that the photography of "material, though invisible objects" is an everyday occurrence (viii).

This somewhat mystical notion of the camera as a machine capable of capturing and literally exposing an elusive truth persists today in contemporary theorizations of the medium. The catalog of a recent photography exhibition at the Los Angeles County Museum of Art, for example, entitled *Ghosts in the Shell: Photography and the Human Soul, 1850–2000,* declares, "Whatever it may be called — personality, individual, self, soul, character, 'invariant of consciousness,' or software — what persists of being human continues to be found embedded within, lurking behind, projected upon, or subsiding beneath the human face, and the photographic representation of the face remains the principal tool of our time for delineating the ghost in the shell."[27] Here the photograph appears again as a vehicle for fixing, "delineating," rendering visible a truth that constantly threatens either to elude us completely or to vanish on appearance, for controlling the world that exists "within, behind, upon, or beneath." However, these scientific, material, indexical qualities of photography are repeatedly haunted not only by the ghostliness of the traces that the photograph tries to control but by the ghostly nature of the photograph itself, which always testifies to the absence of bodies in the very act of representing them. As Eduardo Cadava writes, "In photographing someone, we know that the photograph will survive him — it begins, even during his life, to circulate without him, figuring and anticipating his death each time it is looked at. The photograph is a farewell. It belongs to the afterlife of the photographed. It is permanently inflamed by the instantaneous flash of death."[28] To be present in an image is also to become, of necessity, a "presence," in the ghostly sense of the word. These lurking presences continually alert, then evade the gaze, making the photograph a site of endless vanishing. As Régis Durand writes in "How To See (Photographically)," "Photographic images, then, whatever their apparent subject, are images *in crisis*. Something in them is always trying to run off, to vanish."[29] In light of this statement, it is interesting to note that the French phrase for changing a photographic plate is *escamoter une plaque,* suggesting that the plate itself must vanish in order for the image to be exposed. And as I will demonstrate in the course of this chapter, the technologies of visual reproduction always disappear at the moment of image manifestation. The crisis of the image is temporal as well as physical. Just as the photograph's subject tries to "run off, to vanish," so, too, does the moment in which the photograph occurs. Thierry De Duve suggests, "It is the sudden vanishing of the present tense, splitting into the contradiction of being simultaneously too late and too early, that is properly unbearable."[30] Photography literally makes the present *tense.* Presence becomes a physical and grammatical impossibility at the very moment when this temporal and physical state is inscribed in the image.

Just as film explores its anxieties about materiality through the repeated representation of vanishing women, so photography turns to the female body as a crucial site for exploration and exposition. Also like film, spirit photography conducts its investigations not through the bodies of women in general but through the particularly shining examples of women we have come to know as stars. Prior to the invention of cinema, the late nineteenth century had already produced early photographic versions of this female phenomenon, the best known of these being the spirit Katie King, who emerged in the 1870s as a paragon of female beauty. Robert Dale Owen declared in 1874, "I cannot conceive of a disembodied spirit more gentle, graceful, exhibiting a more beautiful character, material or spiritual, than she does."[31] Given the centrality of these shining female spectacles to spirit photography, it is somewhat surprising that film did not displace photography as the primary mode of documenting séances in the same way that it had previously ousted those stage magicians who had contributed so much to its development. Although, as I have suggested, filmmakers were interested in ghosts, the relationship did not seem to be reciprocal, and the spiritualist movement seemed, at least at first glance, to exclude the medium of film from the scene of the séance completely. But in spite of this attempt the ghost of cinema persistently haunted the séances. While some attention has been paid to early film's interest in and development of the nineteenth-century tradition of spiritualist photography, particularly in the work of Tom Gunning and Erik Barnouw, interestingly, the other side of this relationship has been largely ignored.[32] How did spirit photography respond to the invention of film? What impact, if any, did film have on spiritualist practices? In the next section, I will turn my attention to the question of how spiritualism dealt with the one ghost it tried to repress and what this repression reveals about the medium of film itself.

All about Eva

The early decades of the twentieth century produced a new kind of medium, of which the Frenchwoman Eva C. was, as her name suggests, the first and most spectacular example. Arthur Conan Doyle, a central figure in the British Society for Psychical Research, writes: "The first materializing medium who can be said to have been investigated with scientific care was this girl Eva, or Eva C., as she is usually described, her second name being Carriere."[33] Theodore Besterman confirms Conan Doyle's opinion of Eva's primacy in his 1930 retrospective case study of her: "It was the phenomena produced by Eva C. that first decisively drew the attention of scientific men on the Continent of Europe to the so-called 'ectoplasm' (better called teleplasm) and materializations alleged to be extruded from the bodies of certain specially endowed individuals known as mediums."[34] Distinguishing this new medium from her predecessors was both the scientific apparatus that came to play a central role in the spiritualistic séance and her production of a mysterious white substance known as ectoplasm, for which the *American Heritage Dictionary* provides four intriguing definitions: "1. *Biology*. The outer portion of the continuous phase of cytoplasm of a cell, sometimes distinguishable as a somewhat rigid, gelled layer beneath the cell membrane. 2a. The visible substance believed to emanate from the body of a spiritualistic medium during communication with the dead. b. An immaterial substance, especially the transparent corporeal presence of a spirit or ghost. 3. *Informal.* An image projected onto a movie screen." To speak of ectoplasm, it seems, is to speak of film, at least according to the dictionary. But this cinematic definition also seems to suggest that ectoplasm throws the "movies" into crisis, for what we find in this definition is not film itself but a reach for film, an incomplete manifestation of cinema. Ectoplasm hovers in the space between photography and film, becoming an image on-screen but only that—a single image that cannot move. And this dictionary definition, which distracts our attention away from the final entry with its signal of informality, encapsulates the relationship between film and spirit photography that played itself out around the body of elusive matter that spewed forth from the body of Eva C.

Given that film is in one sense, then, inseparable from ectoplasm, it is interesting to note that this new form of spiritual manifestation almost never came into direct contact with cinema, although the vast tomes of spiritualist literature written on the phenomenon of ectoplasm did rely on exhaustive photographic evidence. But, in this world where absent figures so frequently reappear as presences, film becomes the unnamed ghost haunting twentieth-century spirit photography. Although the bizarre manifestations produced by a variety of media clearly reveal an ongoing exploration of female materiality, photography, and the world of ghosts, the spiritualist séance also becomes a stage for the birth of film itself, in spite of the fact that film had already been born elsewhere. But this birth, which, in the context of the séance, ultimately proves to be a stillbirth, provides us with an important and neglected site for thinking further about visual technology's relationship with materiality as well as about early film's compulsive return to the vanishing female body.

Eva, a young woman in her twenties, began her mediumship in 1902. After undergoing a series of traumatic investigations in Algiers with Professor Charles Richet, who first coined the term *ectoplasm,* Eva was taken into the home of another central figure in the French spiritualist scene, Madame Bisson, whose contributions to spiritualism were so great that Conan Doyle believed that "it is probable that Madame Bisson will take a place beside her compatriot Madame Curie in the annals of science" (107).[35] Under the "care" of Madame Bisson, Eva produced impressive quantities of ectoplasm, which were, like Eva herself, exhaustively examined by the German psychologist and sexologist Dr. Baron von Schrenck-Notzing. While late-nineteenth-century spirit Katie King became an object of male desire, (dis)embodying the most appealing aspects of femininity, the spiritual material that emerged from Eva's orifices evoked fascination but also disgust. After witnessing one of Eva's manifestations, magician and skeptic Harry Houdini wrote, "Up to the present day nothing has crossed my path to make me think that the Great Almighty will allow emanations from a human body of such horrible, revolting, viscous substances as Baron von Schrenck-Notzing claims."[36] Tom Gunning has noted that the appearance of ectoplasm on the spiritualist scene gave séances "an oddly physiological turn," but surprisingly little has been said about the gendered nature of this mucouslike substance. How, one wonders, could the descriptions of a white viscous substance pouring from the mouth, vagina, and nipples of Eva C. not conjure up the female bodily fluids of breast milk and vaginal discharge? Although the scientific investigations of these manifestations ostensibly take ectoplasm, "this horrible, revolting, viscous substance," as their object, there can be no doubt when one reads the case studies of Eva C. that it is also the female body that science and visual technology work so tirelessly to expose both physically and photographically.

At the opening of his 629-page case study of Eva C., Schrenck-Notzing lists a seemingly endless number of "facts" about Eva's body, mind, character, and personal history: "Hair color blonde. Body well nourished. In her second year of life she is to have suffered from nerve-induced convulsions, endured no serious illnesses. Menses began in twelfth year and are generally regular. Occasional tendency to bladder complaints after a bout of cystitis about six years ago. . . . Inner organs healthy. Pulse small and weak. . . . No signs of degeneration."[37] This list continues for several pages, drawing every aspect of Eva's body and mind to the reader's attention. As though this initial exposure of the "truth" of Eva were not enough, Schrenck-Notzing proceeds to document the almost daily physical examinations of Eva's body, which took place prior to every séance.

Eva undressed completely before Mme Bisson (if requested, also before other ladies who were present). She then put on the black tricot tights, without any opening, which reached to the hips, and which were repeatedly examined by me; over this she put on the black dress, which had an opening only at the breast, and which had been similarly painstakingly examined by me. The medium gave us several times the opportunity of examining her body while she was still in a half-dressed state and before the dress was sewn up. . . . But after this had been done she also allowed us to touch the entire surface of her body and to establish again that there were not concealed on it any kind of materials or utensils. The tricot and dress are so thin that the whole superficial anatomy of the body showed through the light fabric. It was impossible for the subject to touch her body, particularly its lower parts, without tearing or ripping the material.[38]

Clearly, this elaborate preparation ritual is rife with anxiety about the manifestation not of spirits but of the threatening shadow of an active female sexuality. Women congregate in respectable parlors first to witness Eva undressing, then to touch "the entire surface" of her body. Gentlemen scientists painstakingly and repeatedly examine the woman's tights and dresses in search of openings. Eva wears transparent clothing that not only reveals her "whole superficial anatomy" to the audience but also renders visible any attempt on her part to touch "the lower parts" of her body. The séance is haunted not by deceased loved ones but by the specters of lesbianism and masturbation as well as by the desire of the doctors obsessively to "manhandle" the trappings of femininity.[39]

Although Eva appears to exist as pure spectacle, a closer look at the preparation rites for each séance suggests that, even as she seems to embody the ultimate female image, her examiners construct her as nothing but a series of gaping holes. After thoroughly searching for any openings in Eva's clothes, Schrenk-Notzing turns his attention to the openings of Eva's body itself: "In order to exclude the possibility of her having concealed rolled-up bits of material in a hollow tooth, in her cheeks, in the external part of the ear or in the nose, before each sitting I made her breathe heavily, closing in turn each nostril, open her mouth widely (to examine her cheeks), examined her ears and their external passages, her armpits, the black felt slippers she was to put on her feet, and finally her hair and scalp" (quoted in Besterman, *Some Modern Mediums,* 85). Here the spectacular surface of the medium's body collapses into the endless possibilities of that body's orifices. In the course of the attempt at exposure, Eva C. disappears as a material presence in her own right, emerging primarily as a potential container for "real matter," an empty vessel, a lack, a multiplicitous hole. In spite of Schrenck-Notzing's vigilance, however, this search for the guilty orifice is haunted by the absence of the female orifice that *does* actually produce a white, mucouslike substance—the vagina—even though Schrenck-Notzing earlier signals an awareness of this place of secretion when he expresses concern that the medium might try to touch her "lower parts."[40] The vagina undergoes a double disappearance. It first vanishes in its representation as nothing but a hole, a site of lack, and then in its exclusion from Schrenck-Notzing's inventory of female orifices, where it becomes the absent hole, the missing site of lack.

Although the scientific apparatus of spiritualism worked rigorously to expose visually the outpourings of this female body, Eva's materializations were paradoxically predicated upon her own vanishability and general lack of self. Schrenck-Notzing comments on the medium's "große Willenschwäche" (major weaknesses of will), her "Mangel an Selbstständigkeit" (lack of independence), and her "Passivität" (passivity), which makes her particularly easy to hypnotize. Tom Gunning comments further on this quality of the media: "All mediums, men or women, had to be, in Spiritualist parlance, feminine, or negative (borrowing again from electricity and magnetism, a technical term which also has implications for photography), in order to let the spirit world manifest itself" ("Phantom Images," 52). Like Freud's hysterical patient Anna O., whose spells of *absence* made hypnosis possible, Eva's production of matter relied on her own disappearance.[41] Indeed, at the moment of manifestation she frequently cried out "Je suis prise" (I am taken), asserting her absence even at the peak of her visibility.[42]

All about Ectoplasm

The production of ectoplasm from Eva's orifices resembled nothing so much as a spectacular birthing scene. Figure 13 shows Eva C. in the "capable" hands of two men in white, each holding a hand and a

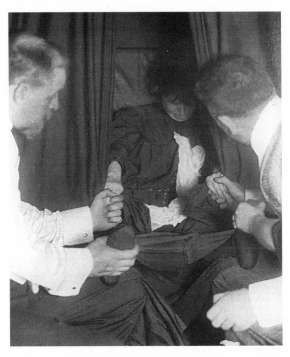

Figure 13. Eva C. and the birth of ectoplasm. Photograph taken June 7, 1911. Reprinted from Freiherrn von Schrenck-Notzing, *Materialisationsphaenomene* (Munich: Ernst Reinhardt, 1923).

foot, while she sits and strains, legs apart, until the ectoplasm finally appears from the inner recesses of her body. Some combination of birth moans, sighs, and shrieks of sexual ecstasy usually accompanied these scenes. In *Some Modern Mediums,* Besterman, for example, writes of "convulsive groans and long-drawn expirations" (91). In addition to discovering how Eva actually bore this substance, scientists were keen to determine what kind of "baby" she was delivering into this world. What exactly was "ectoplasm"? Eva generally declared herself incapable of providing samples of the white viscous substance for scientific experimentation, claiming that it would disintegrate when touched. Just as she vanished whenever ectoplasm appeared, so ectoplasm, mimicking its "mother," disappeared in the restored presence of the medium. On repeated occasions, Schrenck-Notzing tried to grasp the ectoplasm, only to find that "die Masse verschwindet" (the mass vanishes) (*Materialisationsphaenomene,* 72). In the face of this evanescence, photography played a crucial role. As a medium of the moment, photography bore the responsibility of capturing the truth, the essence of the ephemeral. Both Schrenck-Notzing and Madame Bisson photographed Eva continuously, but rather than substantiating the claims of the truth seekers these published photographs repeatedly contradict the written testimonies of eyewitnesses. Instead of offering images of a substance that was once present but has since vanished, the photographs depict material that was, at least according to the reports of Schrenck-Notzing, never there in the first place. Witnesses of Eva's materializations repeatedly stress the moist, mucouslike nature of the ectoplasm. During a séance in Biarritz in June 1910, when Schrenck-Notzing manages to touch the ectoplasm for a few brief moments before it disappears, he portrays it in the following way: "It is hard to describe this mass; it gave the impression of a flat, striped, stringy, sticky, cool, living substance; the same showed no form of scent, light-grey whitish color. My fingers remained moist from the contact" (76). If we turn to any of the many photographs published by Schrenck-Notzing in support of his claims, however, there exists a noticeable disjunction between what the eyewitness claims he saw and felt and what we see in the photograph. We look for signs of a mysterious, moist, living substance. What we find are pieces of cheesecloth, some of which seem to have been stuffed into the medium's mouth, offering us a spectacle not of the free-flowing "truth" of feminine interiority but of a silent and gagged woman (figs. 14, 15).

While Schrenck-Notzing represses all trace of this disparity between text and image, Fred Gettings, who published *Ghosts in Photographs: The Extraordinary Story of Spirit Photographs* in 1978, explains it away with an argument whose circularity is nothing less than disarming.

> Now, the point is that ectoplasm—especially when isolated on a single negative—often resembles cotton wool or clouds, and at other times a fine linen, or cheesecloth. This in itself has encouraged much fraud, with pseudo-ectoplasmic manifestations, simply because when photographs are taken of genuine manifestations—such as a humanoid form resting within a bed of ectoplasm, it all too frequently gives the appearance of a simple photographic montage resting in cotton wool. Again, ecto-

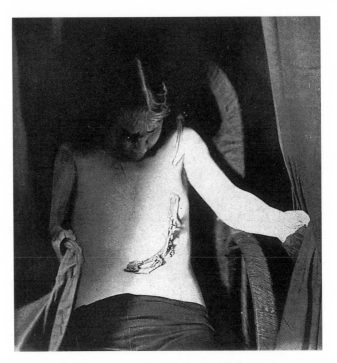

Figure 14. Eva C., January 9, 1913. Reprinted from Schrenck-Notzing, *Materialisationsphaenomene*.

plasmic faces are often rather like newspaper cuttings or doll's heads, and while it is easy to dismiss photographs of such manifestations as amateurish frauds, there is irrefutable evidence in a vast psychic literature that such materializations are genuine products of mediumship.[43]

Ectoplasm looks like cheesecloth in the photographs, Gettings suggests, because ectoplasm, when photographed, looks like cheesecloth. But according to Schrenck-Notzing's study of Eva ectoplasm does not really look or feel like cheesecloth at all.

One séance with Eva C. finally provided Schrenck-Notzing with three small samples of ectoplasm of the nonvanishing variety. When tested, these fragments turned out to be bits of skin. In response to Schrenck-Notzing's report on his findings, Theodore Besterman became quite irate, largely due to Schrenck-Notzing's failure to address the inconsistencies inherent to his own definitions of ectoplasm.

After emphatically and repeatedly stating that the materialisations are composed of "plastic substance," the so-called tele-

Figure 15. Eva C., August 21, 1911. Reprinted from Schrenck-Notzing, *Materialisationsphaenomene.*

plasm, which emanates from the medium's body, he suggests that bits of human skin may be "produced during the sitting," that is consist of teleplasm! After alleging that the slightest touch of this teleplasm is painful to the medium, that violent interference with it would make her ill, and that its removal might even cause her death, he himself asks for bits of teleplasm to be so removed and has his wish granted! After pointing more than once to the teleplasm's alleged speedy disintegration and disappearance on being interfered with as a proof of its super-normal nature, he secures, examines, analyses, and permanently preserves a portion of that same teleplasm! (*Some Modern Mediums,* 87)

The discovery that ectoplasm is made of human skin throws our understanding of the limits of the medium's body into crisis. Is ecto-plasm the "outer" layer of a foreign body from another world, as its name suggests? Or is it rather the living matter of a creature from afar, as *teleplasm,* Besterman's preferred term, implies? How do we reconcile these definitions with the claim that the substance comes from *inside* the medium's body? The outer layer comes from inside; the living matter from far away turns out to be the all too familiar matter of dead skin. This skin, however, does not define the outer limit of the human form; rather, like the skin of a baby, it issues from the deep interiors of the female body. And, just as *ectoplasm* leads us to "a moving image projected on a screen," so this French skin, born out of the body of a woman (the first woman, Eva), leads us back to the material of film. Jean-Luc Nancy writes: "*Film* and its French equivalent *pellicule*—from *pellis,* the skin—at first have the same meaning, stemming from the same origin. It is a small skin, a thin skin. The English word *film* first meant "membrane."[44]

Besterman expresses frustration with the "scientific" findings of Schrenck-Notzing primarily because the "truth" of ectoplasm cannot be fully exposed and any attempt to fix its meaning dissolves into paradoxes. The medium literally turns our thinking on bodily limits inside out. Refusing either to reveal or conceal herself properly, Eva C. embodies the vanishing woman's ambivalence as she seeps through visual and epistemological boundaries with the fluidity of ectoplasm itself. Her ambivalence challenges and invites the camera to document and expose this space of the in-between. Ultimately, however, the camera captures the truth of neither ectoplasm nor femininity but of an image of itself, of photographic reproduction. Tom Gunning suggests that, "The medium herself became a sort of camera, her spiritual negativity bodying forth a positive image, as the human body behaves like an uncanny photomat, dispensing images from its orifices" ("Phantomimages" 58). Although the images of human faces, bodies, and body parts that appear on the surface of the ectoplasm clearly exist in a close relationship with photography, Gunning's comparison of the medium with the photomat does not account for the fact that these are *moving* images. Although the spirit manifestations look exactly like two-dimensional photographs, Schrenck-Notzing's descriptions stress the mobility of these images. And, although film is largely repressed from the spiritualistic scene, the cinema returns to haunt the séances through the ectoplasm's meanderings.

Furthermore, film also reproduces itself in narrative form. On February 23, 1913, Schrenck-Notzing describes a séance that exactly reenacts the plot of the 1898 film *Photographing a Ghost,* which we might usefully recall here: "Photographer tries to take picture of a ghost, but it won't keep still and then it vanishes."[45] In *Materialisationsphaenomene,* Schrenck-Notzing writes: "Suddenly, after about 30 minutes, a life-size phantom with masculine facial features appeared by the opening of the curtains behind Eva's chair in the corner of the cabinet. He was already fully developed on the first exposition (fig. 16). Eva rose, stepped to the side and opened the curtain with her right hand, in order not to hide the picture with her body. Flashlight photograph taken. . . . Mme. Bisson extinguished the red lamp in the back of the cabinet. A second attempt at a photograph failed, because the phantom had moved off sideways to the left out of the field of vision of the camera. The same then vanished without trace in the direction of the back wall" (27). In this 1913 reproduction of an earlier film, photography fails to expose either the ghost or the female medium. Instead, Eva doubly reproduces the birth of the moving image. First she manifests an ectoplasmic moving image; then this ghostly matter proceeds to reenact the star role of an 1898 film, whose plot exposes the inability of photography fully to capture the insubstantial moving body.

A frustration with photography's failure to capture properly the ectoplasm or moving image recurs throughout the literature of this period. Besterman complains: "We shall see later that the method of *recording* what occurred at the sittings remains in doubt; and even six or eight cameras, of however varied kinds, cannot do more than register what is before them at the moment of the flashlight exposure. They cannot record the *development* of the phenomena, or, what is often vital, the sequence of various, often seemingly insignificant, events" (*Some Modern Mediums,* 82). At the very moment when the camera should fix and capture the phantom's vanishing body, the image fails because of its inability to deal with temporality, with the sequence of events. Besterman's comments betray a certain longing, a desire for a different kind of recording machine, one that would capture the moment before and after the "flashlight exposure," one able to reproduce "development" and "sequence." He yearns for a machine that could document movement, the quivering to and fro of this elusive woman's essence. In short, he wants the movies.

But what are we to make of this anachronistic desire for a medium

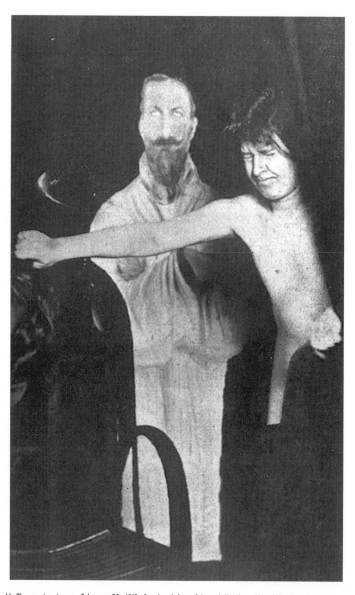

Figure 16. The moving image, February 23, 1913. Reprinted from Schrenck-Notzing, *Materialisationsphaenomene.*

that already exists? In *Burning with Desire,* Geoffrey Batchen describes the desire to photograph that logically should precede the official invention of photography in 1839 as a similar, albeit paradoxical, type of anachronism: "My own shift of analysis from 1839 to the earlier desire to photograph at one level obeys this traditional logic of priority, merely revising the usual historical account to place the desire to photograph before the invention of photography and 1800 before 1839. However, this shift from invention to desire also opens up the whole question of temporality. For example, we must ask whether the desire to photograph simply preceded photography or whether photography was in fact always already there."[46] Drawing on the work of Eduardo Cadava, Batchen suggests that the desire for photography can in some senses never precede photography if photography was always already there.[47] Like Besterman's longing for a cinema that already exists, the desire for photography is always anachronistic. But how can we explain this persistence of desire and longing? Even if we accept the idea that photography as a form of light writing has always existed, we might read the continued longing for photography and film as a desire for ever more sophisticated technological developments, for the "perfect" reproduction machine. However, we can better understand the interminable desire for photography and film after their inventions by focusing not on the technologies themselves but on what they come to represent—namely, the possibility of exposing and capturing an elusive form of "truth," the possibility of fixing both knowledge and presence. Each time these media betray the promises they offer, which they necessarily must, they vanish as we have imagined them and we must desire and reinvent them all over again.

This frustrating appearance and subsequent disappearance of cinema features quite literally in Schrenck-Notzing's report of two séances he attended on June 25 and July 13, 1913, with the polish medium Fräulein Stanislawa P. These séances differ from the other recorded séances of the period because they were not photographed but filmed.[48] Schrenck-Notzing writes: "On both evenings we succeeded for the first time in operating the cinématograph for several minutes at a time. The film from the first evening contained about 360 pictures, that from the second evening more than 400. Each shoot shows the material going back into the mouth, the second also shows the expansion and contraction of the substance" (*Materialisationsphaenomene*, 537). Schrenck-Notzing claims that this new ability to film materializations "is of the greatest importance" to the scientific investigation of spiritualism. Yet, if this is the case, why did he never film Eva C., the primary focus of his study? Why does he only

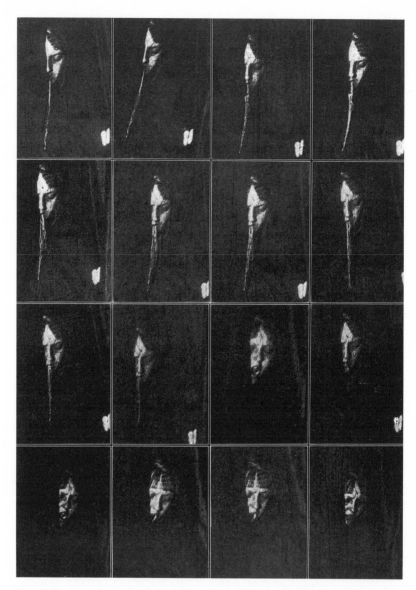

Figure 17. Cinematographic record of Fräulein Stanislawa P.'s materialization, 1913. Reprinted from Schrenck-Notzing, *Materialisationsphaenomene.*

write half a page about the results of his cinematic documentations? And why does he never use the Cinématographe again after this initial attempt? Furthermore, if we look at the images he reproduces from the reel, it becomes clear that film appears again as a "stillbirth." Although the Cinématographe supposedly possesses the ability to represent the temporal sequence of the ectoplasm's appearance and retraction, Schrenck-Notzing chooses to publish not a sequence of images but a selection of individual stills that do not even attempt to give us a sense of the time or process involved in the matter's disappearance (fig. 17). As though wary of exposing cinema's failure to capture the elusive movement of life, Schrenck-Notzing turns the longed-for films back into photographs, perhaps in an attempt to perpetuate the possibility of cinema as he has imagined it. Ironically, cinema must vanish as a medium in order to persist as an idea, and in this sense it can only ever appear as a ghost of itself.

Schrenck-Notzing introduces the Cinématographe into the world of spiritualism with the express intent of proving once and for all the presence of ectoplasm, itself a form of cinema. Instead of documenting the elusive presence of ectoplasm, however, film collapses into the object it seeks and vanishes along with it. But perhaps Schrenck-Notzing is not utterly wrong when he declares that, although the results of his experiment go against all his expectations, they are still of the "greatest importance." For, although Schrenck-Notzing fails to render visible the comings and goings of the immaterial world, his juxtaposition of film with the world of spirit photography illuminates the way cinema can only exist if we repeatedly conjure it into being. Like early film's tireless representations of the vanishing woman, our reinventions of cinema in the wake of its vanishings bespeak an epistemological longing, a desire to understand the limits of our ability to grasp and represent the elusive truth of our own existence. The invention, and reinvention, of photography and film enable us to envision this longing in new ways. These questions are in no way restricted to the ghostly world of visual technology, however, and we find other turn of the century discourses asking similar questions in different ways. In chapter three, then, I turn my attention to the parallel discourse of Freudian psychoanalysis, which, like film, begins with and constantly returns to the perplexing image of the vanishing woman.

3

Mother
Knows Best:
Magic and
Matricide

In "Where Has All the Hysteria Gone?" Juliet Mitchell writes, "Throughout most of the twentieth century it has been supposed in clinical and scientific circles that hysteria has disappeared. According to this pervasive view, hysteria had a late Victorian heyday, a heroic *fin de siècle* moment and, after more than 4,000 years of recorded history, it simply vanished. But *what* exactly disappeared? And what do we mean by 'disappeared'?"[1] Mitchell attributes the disappearance of hysteria within twentieth-century medical discourse to two primary factors. First, she suggests that psychoanalysis feminized hysteria as a disease. Consequently, once cases of male hysteria became prevalent after World War I, the disease itself had to be repressed for fear of feminizing its male sufferers. Second, and perhaps more interestingly, Mitchell argues, "The very notion of a disappearance of hysteria can in part be blamed on the emphasis on Oedipus" (26), claiming that the Oedipus complex, with its almost exclusive focus on parental relationships, has blocked our understanding of the important role siblings play in hysteria. The Oedipus complex, then, plays a crucial role in the disappearance of hysteria as a disease. But this discursive disappearance also mirrors a symptom of the disease itself, that is, the tendency of the hysterical body to vanish and return, as Mitchell acknowledges: "A defining feature of hysteria is that it is mimetic: it may be that its very 'disappearance,' its reappearance in the academies of today and its stop-go characteristic in earlier epochs, are themselves imitations of a condition. . . . Hysteria may have been divided into other illnesses or apparently have lost its appeal on being comprehended, but, endlessly imitative, it has also vanished and reappeared with fashion in an unconscious game of hide and seek" (116). The mimetic nature of the psychoanalytic treatment of the disease establishes a provocative relationship among the disappearing discourse of hysteria, the hysterically vanishing body, and the figure of Oedipus. But how exactly does this complex relationship play itself out? What do hysterical vanishings reveal about the institutional discourse of psychoanalysis?

In the chapter "Emptiness and Possession," Mitchell focuses on the hysteric's vanishing body through an astonishing analysis of "Mrs. Peters." But before we look at how Mrs. Peters disappears we need first to note who "she" is. Mitchell writes: "I propose to amalgamate a number of patients who, despite their different histories, have comparable hysterical responses. This amalgamation I will call Mrs Peters, because, despite a preponderance of women, there are also male patients in the material, and I would like to underscore the bisexuality of the hysterical subject" (226). This "amalgamation" seems quite logical from a practical point of view, allowing Mitchell to present her observations of various hysterics' symptoms succinctly, but I am not convinced that the name she selects effectively conveys the bisexuality of hysteria. Although the surname Peters invokes a male first name, the shift from a male first name to a female surname reenacts the movement of the patronymic, establishing here female identity's indebtedness to the father, rather than conjuring up the figure of "Peter" himself as a hysterical patient. Likewise, the title Mrs. stresses the dependence of the hysterical woman's identity on her husband. In the course of this amalgamation, Mitchell not only inadvertently vanishes the male hysteric all over again, in spite of her express intention *not* to do this, but she also eradicates the only nominal space not inextricably linked to the female hysteric's father or husband, the woman's first name. This textual disappearance of the male hysteric, as well as of the numerous other patients who find themselves crammed into the single hysterical signifier of Mrs. Peters, form only the backdrop to this amalgam's own astonishing vanishing act in the analyst's office. Mitchell writes: "Hysterics often enact their sense of their own presence/absence by 'coming and going' with their therapists. . . . Mrs Peters, however, in one session, rather than missing the appointment without warning or coming so late that she knew I would be worried (she was both accident-prone and had suicidal fantasies), instead perhaps of having a seizure, she 'disappeared' in my company. This is hard to describe but I could see her physically vanishing. First her voice faded, then I found myself wanting to stretch out to stop her falling" (230). In order for the hysteric to recover completely, Mitchell argues, the vanishing hysteric has to learn that she can come back: "If there is to be 'recovery,' then the subject has to disappear completely and then come back. It is the terror of this disappearance, the lack of any sense that one will indeed come back, and at the same time no knowledge that one does not come back from death, that underlies the hysterical reaction in all of us" (230–31). The hysterical subject must learn to disappear in spite of the knowledge, first, that he or she might not come back at all, and, second, that he or she might return as a ghost.

Mitchell treats the relationship between the hysterical vanishings of her patients and the "real" disappearance of hysteria (recovery) quite extensively. But, although she implies a mimetic relationship between hysterical vanishings and the disappearance of the discourse of hysteria, she does not elaborate on how this mimesis plays itself out. In order to think further, then, about the vanishing woman's role in the discursive development of psychoanalysis, this chapter will focus on a number of Freudian texts in which women vanish and return. How, I ask, do hysterical vanishings shape the language and concepts of psychoanalysis? How is vanishing gendered within Freud's writing? And what, if anything, can we learn about discursive disappearance in psychoanalysis through the troubled relationship between the vanishing female body and Oedipus?

In October 1885, as Bautier de Kolta took Paris by storm with his trick L'Escamotage d'une Dame en Personne Vivante, Sigmund Freud arrived in Paris to learn the art of hypnotism with Jean Martin Charcot, who dazzled Freud with his performances at the Salpêtrière. As Peter Gay writes: "Charcot was more than an actor. At once medical luminary and social lion, enjoying unmatched prestige, he had diagnosed hysteria as a genuine ailment rather than the malingerer's refuge. . . . Even more daring, Charcot had rescued hypnosis from mountebanks and charlatans for the serious purpose of mental healing. Freud was amazed and impressed to see Charcot inducing and curing hysterical paralysis by means of direct hypnotic suggestion."[2] For Freud, Charcot was clearly a magician. In his obituary, Freud writes of the "magic that emanated from his looks and from his voice,"[3] and in the second of the *Five Lectures on Psychoanalysis* he admits to having been "completely under the spell Charcot's researches" at the time he and Breuer were working on the *Studies on Hysteria.*[4]

Freud returned to Vienna with the magic of Paris still pulsing through his veins. Ernest Jones recounts: "It was in December 1887 that [Freud] turned to hypnotic suggestion, with which he persevered for the next eighteen months. This often brought gratifying success and replaced the feeling of helplessness by the satisfaction of being admired as a magician."[5] And Freud himself admitted that "there was something positively seductive in working with hypnotism. For the first time there was a sense of having overcome one's helplessness; and it was highly flattering to enjoy the reputation of being a miracle-worker" (quoted in Gay, *The Freud Reader,* 9–10).

In *Studies on Hysteria* (1895), however, we already begin to sense Freud's increasing ambivalence toward the magician's role. On the one hand, he remains entranced by the idea that hysterical symptoms might simply vanish into thin air at the hand of the analyst, rather like Bautier de Kolta's vanishing lady. In the "Preliminary Communication" (1893), Breuer and Freud write: "For we found . . . that each individual hysterical symptom immediately and permanently disappeared when we had succeeded in bringing clearly to light the memory of the event by which it was provoked" (*Complete Psychological Works,* 2:6). And there is nothing more astonishing than the miraculous cure of Katherina (case 4), which Freud conjures up in a single session. But on the other hand the magician's flawlessness begins to falter as Freud discovers that not all of his patients are susceptible to hypnosis. By 1909, he publicly acknowledges that Breuer's theory of the "hypnoid state" has turned out to be "impeding and unnecessary" (11:20). And in 1921 Freud writes perhaps his strongest statement against the violence of the power of hypnosis, the very power that had initially attracted him to the practice: "But I can remember even [in 1889] feeling a muffled hostility to this tyranny of suggestion. When a patient who showed himself unamenable was met with the shout: "What are you doing? *Vous vous contre-suggestionnez!*" I said to myself that this was an evident injustice and an act of violence. For the man certainly had a right to counter-suggestions if people were trying to subdue him with suggestions" (18:89). In spite of this ultimate refutation of the conjurer's powers of hypnosis, however, psychoanalysis remains an inescapably magical field. Hovering in a space between the doctor and the spiritualist, the scientific analyst raises spirits from the past before our eyes, conjuring a psychic phantasmagoria; he reads our minds, helped only by the vaguest of traces. The language of magic saturates Freud's work, even as he tries to dispel it.

Paradoxically, Freud's theory of the psyche, which insists that the repression of that which is most awful to us can only vanish temporarily, always resulting in the return of that awfulness in a more terrifying form, also asks us to believe that analysis has the power to make those ghouls and phantoms truly disappear, never to return. While things that seem nothing to the patient inevitably become something in the course of analysis, only analysis itself, according to Freud, can really turn that something into nothing. And so, like Jacqueline Rose (after Reich), who pursues the question "Where does the misery come from?" I will address the problem of where psychoanalysis claims misery goes in the course of the analytic work.[6] Although Freud would on occasion have us believe that misery truly disappears, as if by magic, the psychic bodies he vanishes return to haunt him and threaten his analytic authority in fundamental ways.

Tempting as it might be to cast Freud himself in the role of magician at all times, the texts I examine resist such oversimplification. Given the inherently ambivalent nature of psychoanalytic authority, power is never in the hands of one person, if anyone within the context of psychoanalysis can ever be "just one person." When the magical mechanism of transference comes into play, which it must if analysis is to succeed, magical authority and power flow in both directions between analyst and analysand. So, as we locate traces of magic in the practice of psychoanalysis, we need to keep asking who wears the magician's robes at any given moment. Who, or what, disappears, and when? Who is the agent of vanishing, and how do we locate that agency in a world of oscillating presence and absence? And, given that the history of disappearing acts is a gendered one in which women usually disappear at the hands of men, how do gender roles play into and transform this destabilizing circulation of power on the analytic scene?

After a brief anecdote from film, which literalizes these questions about the relationship between vanishing and psychoanalysis, and more specifically between vanishing women and Oedipus, I will begin my inquiry into the role vanishing plays in Freud's work by looking at the early writings of Freud and Breuer on hysteria. I first examine the hysterical condition of *absence,* in which not being "all there" becomes a peculiarly feminine affair. After the hysterical patient Anna O. reveals her sexual feelings for Breuer at the end of the treatment, absence leads us inevitably into the confusing world of transference, another site of analytic vanishing. In the final section, I concentrate on Freud's attempts at self-analysis, in which the absence of an "other" draws attention to the ghostly operations of transference. In search of this other, Freud finds his mother, who haunts and obsesses him, simultaneously vanishing and refusing to go away.

Oedipus Wrecks

Perhaps no text illustrates more succinctly the close relationship between nineteenth-century stage vanishings and the oedipal focus of Freudian psychoanalysis than Woody Allen's short film *Oedipus Wrecks* (1989). The "hero," Sheldon Mills, walks into his analyst's office and announces that, in spite of the fact that he is fifty years old and a very successful law partner, he still hasn't resolved his relationship with his mother. "I love her," he tells the analyst, "but I wish she would disappear." This wish proceeds to haunt the rest of the film. Sheldon's mother, Sadie, disapproves of his fiancée, Lisa, a non-Jewish divorcée with three children. In an attempt to pacify Sadie, Lisa organizes a trip to a magic show. The magician, Shando the Great, selects Sadie as his assistant for the Great Chinese Box Illusion. Having crammed her into the box, Shando plunges five sharp swords into Sadie's body, each sword bringing a new smile to Sheldon's face. But his smile soon fades when the magician opens the box and discovers, as if in direct response to Sheldon's earlier wish in the analyst's office, that Sadie has vanished and he cannot bring her back.[7]

Although the loss initially traumatizes Sheldon, the pain soon eases, to the point at which he is able to tell his analyst: "I smile more easily, I'm more energetic at work, and my sex life has never been better . . . and nothing terrible happened, and it wasn't brutal, she didn't die . . . she just mysteriously vanished, you know?" But Sheldon's happiness soon ends when his mother's face appears in gigantic proportions in the skies above Manhattan. Like a monstrous form of the cinematic close-up, this huge maternal visage hovers day and night, revealing to the whole city the secrets of Sheldon's childhood, sex life, and identity (his name is not "Mills," she publicly announces, but "Mill*stein*"). As Mary Ann Doane has argued, the close-up itself can be abhorrent as well as seductive: "The scale of the close-up transforms the face into an instance of the gigantic, the monstrous: it overwhelms. . . . The face, usually a mark of individuality, becomes tantamount to a theorem in its generalizability."[8] Paradoxically, then, that which is larger than life, the "hypervisible," becomes another type of disappearance. The individual becomes a generalization through magnification. Like the Hollywood star, Sadie disappears into her own visual excess. So, although this mother reappears as an uncanny and monstrous form of her previous self, reminding us that permanent disappearance can only be a fantasy, what we see in the sky is in fact all we have ever seen of Sadie Millstein: a caricature of the Jewish mother. Chicken soup, overbearing mothering, and a strong New York accent—Mrs. Millstein was already an enlarged and stereotypical image of the Jewish mother. One might even argue that Sadie, ever "the Jewish mother," can never vanish because she was never really present in the first place.[9] Sadie only decides, "Now I'll come down," after Sheldon has separated from Lisa and become engaged to a maternally approved Jewish psychic named Treva. Like Sadie, Treva embodies a series of stereotypical traits and habits—boiled chicken (which she forces on Sheldon), New York accent, and excessive concern about Sheldon's weight and health. Although Sadie initially seems to disappear as a magician's victim, the film suggests that she discovers at least some degree of agency in her own vanishing and learns how to manipulate the power of her own visible "absence." By vanishing, Sadie takes herself beyond Sheldon's control and influence and puts herself in a position of power over him, dominating his visual and psychic worlds.

Sheldon finds his mother unbearable not, or not only, because of who she is but because of what she knows of her son, of what she reflects back to him and others about his identity, and of his dependence on that knowledge. As an omniscient maternal mirror in whose surface the child sees only his own face, Mrs. Millstein vanished long before she became a magician's assistant. But this reflective quality of the mother's face to the child (who sees his own face) makes matricide unthinkable, at least for the nonsuicidal subject, even if that subject does "wish that she would disappear." Through Sadie, Sheldon becomes visible, albeit too visible, and he resists killing her for fear that he too will disappear. Killing Sadie would be a self-destructive act.[10] Although clearly a comedy, *Oedipus Wrecks* stages an important debate within psychoanalytic theory about maternal vanishing, matricide, and the Oedipus complex. After all, what happens to Sadie Millstein in the magician's box is unclear. She does indeed vanish, later to return, but she is also penetrated with numerous swords, and the dual nature of her eradication, which is simultaneously murderous *and* magical, forces us to consider the relationship between violence and vanishing. But what does Shando the Great's double disappearance of Sadie Millstein tell us about psychoanalysis's treatment of maternal presence? And what do healthy subjects do with their mothers?

Matricide: Our Vital Necessity?

For Julia Kristeva, the psychoanalytic feminist theorist most responsible for bringing the mother back into view in contemporary psychoanalytic discourse, the (symbolic) murder of the mother constitutes an absolute requirement for anyone wishing to enter into subjectivity and language without the burdens of depression and melancholia. Presupposing that loss slips unproblematically into murder, she writes in *Black Sun:* "For man and for woman the loss of the mother is a biological and psychic necessity, the first step on the way to becoming autonomous. Matricide is our vital necessity, the sine-qua-non condition of our individuation."[11] Kristeva argues that those who protect the mother turn the matricidal drive inward upon themselves, leading only to self-hatred and suicide. Establishing a relationship between self-erasure, the mother who should disappear, and the foreign body (a combination of relationships we find first in Freud), Kristeva claims that these patients become depressed, "foreigners in their maternal tongue. They have lost the meaning—the value—of their mother tongue for want of losing the mother" (53). But what does it mean to become a foreigner in the mother tongue? For Luce Irigaray, this sense of estrangement arises not as a result of the mother's continued presence but from the fact that *mother tongue* is a misnomer: "The fertility of the earth is sacrificed in order to establish the cultural domain of the father's language (which is called, incorrectly, the mother tongue)."[12] Perhaps the tongue in question has indeed been wrongly attributed. But we might also ask how one could be anything but a foreigner in the "mother" tongue, a tongue that by definition always belongs to someone else.

While Kristeva argues that the subject disappears because the mother doesn't, Irigaray suggests instead that the mother has always existed in a state of double disappearance, first through a foundational act of matricide and then through a collective refusal to recognize that murder: "When Freud, notably in *Totem and Taboo,* describes and theorizes about the murder of the father as the founding act for the primal horde, he is forgetting an even more ancient murder, that of the woman-mother, which was necessary to the foundation of a specific order in the city" (11). Here, Irigaray draws attention, as will Jean-Joseph Goux, to the striking absence of matricide in the Freudian corpus. Rather than working to further eradicate what's left of this mother, as Kristeva recommends, Irigaray suggests that *all* women need to identify with the mother in order to bring her back into view. She calls us first to recognize the foundational violence toward the mother, then to resist being "accomplices in the murder of the mother" by asserting a matrilineal genealogy. If patriarchy has transformed motherhood into a "desubjectivized social role," she declares nevertheless that "we also need to discover and declare that we are always mothers just by being women" (18). It seems unlikely, however, that all women are in fact mothers. Indeed, as Jane Gallop argues in "Reading the Mother Tongue," the idealized notion of a motherhood outside of culture, society, and politics is in itself "an essential ideological component of patriarchy," making this call for women to identify universally with the mother profoundly problematic for feminists (61).

In *Oedipus, Philosopher,* Jean-Joseph Goux claims that by founding psychoanalysis on the myth of Oedipus Freud, unlike Jung, Lacan, and other later psychoanalytic theorists, avoids altogether the necessary problem of matricide. While classical mythological heroes such as Jason and Perseus have to murder the monster-mother, Oedipus has a purely intellectual encounter with the Sphinx, which for Goux represents the dark and devouring mother of Oedipus. By answering the Sphinx's riddle correctly, Oedipus avoids the bloody combat with the monster, and for Goux this escape from matricide/monstricide makes the myth "deviant." According to him, the foundational use of the Oedipus myth represents Freud's most serious failing because Oedipus's intellectual defeat of the Sphinx in no way constitutes disappearance as a result of heroic action: "If the Sphinx disappears, it is because she does away with herself. Hers is not a physical defeat. . . . The sphinx is not killed, she is offended by Oedipus's answer."[13] It is imperative, Goux maintains, that the encounter between Oedipus and the Sphinx be the place "where the face-to-face confrontation with the Thing ought to take place" (36). The psychic space left behind for the subject by the mother's disappearance is simply not adequate. In Goux's formulation, the hero must vanquish the monster-mother through violent eradication. Within this framework, Oedipus fails, and so does Freud. Goux argues that the Sphinx's vanishing act is *the* blind spot of Freudian psychoanalysis, the place where Freud reveals his failure to get "the monomyth" (his term for the standard myth in which the hero *does* kill the mother), the reason why Freudian psychoanalysis will never be capable of dealing with the monstrous aspects of the mother: "Monstricide is the great unthought element of Freudian doctrine."[14]

Goux employs an impressive arsenal of classical references and anthropological evidence to support his claim that Freud's selection of Oedipus as the foundational myth of psychoanalysis is both unusual and inadequate. Nevertheless, *Oedipus, Philosopher* has two fundamental blind spots of its own. First, Goux repeatedly refers to this striking anomaly in the Freudian corpus as an act of "deviance"; the myth is "an aberrant myth."[15] Polarizing the monomyth and the myth of Oedipus, Goux establishes an extremely problematic notion of an essential and normative masculine desire, arguing that "it is this monomyth (in its amply attested universality) and not the singular history of Oedipus that contains the truth of masculine destiny and desire" (31). More troubling still, he tends to attribute all agency of the production of this binary to the myths themselves, absolving himself of any responsibility in the construction of his own argument: "In the differential relationship between the monomyth and the Oedipus myth, mythic knowledge has already set up the opposition between authentic desire and the desire gone astray" (31). No one disputes that Oedipus's incestuous relationship with his mother is disturbing. *Oedipus, Philosopher* is problematic, however, because it uses the incestuous elements of the Oedipus narrative to advance a problematic and often hidden agenda of heteronormativity. In positing incest as the unacceptable other to "normal" or "authentic" masculine desire that leads the hero to "liberate the bride" who is not his mother, Goux obscures that other "other" of masculine desire, homosexuality (38). Indeed, *Oedipus, Philosopher* constitutes, among other things, an attempt to construct "an entire topology of masculine desire" exclusively within a heterosexual paradigm. Although the desire that emerges within the Oedipus myth may be unusual, it is still based on an assumption of heterosexuality. As Judith Butler argues in *The Psychic Life of Power:* "The oedipal conflict presumes that heterosexual desire has already been *accomplished,* that the distinction between heterosexual and homosexual has been enforced (a distinction which, after all, has no necessity); in this sense, the prohibition on incest presupposes the prohibition on homosexuality, for it presupposes the heterosexualization of desire."[16] In his adamant struggle to establish the deviance of Freud's use of Oedipus, Goux loses sight of what seems to be a crucial question: why does Freud make this selection in the first place? Goux can only suggest that Freud's reading "simply misses the point" (*Oedipus, Philosopher,* 35). But is incomprehension or ignorance really the most interesting and complex reason we can offer for this striking mythical departure in the Freudian corpus? In the pages that follow, I probe further Freud's refusal of matricide. I ask how and why the deviant Freud privileges a model of intellectual engagement over armed and bloody conflict in his negotiations with the monster-mother, displaying an unhealthy fascination with the oscillating vanishings and returns of his mother, his female patients, and himself.

Hysteria: Symptomatic Vanishings and Vanishing Symptoms

The construction of femininity as lack by psychoanalysis has always troubled feminists. Indeed, the female genitals constitute one of the prime sites of vanishing in the psychoanalytic narrative of sexual difference. Either women possess a diminutive penis, the clitoris, a withered version of the male organ, or women once possessed a penis, invisible as it may have been, before an equally invisible castration took place, leaving all women with an invisible wound, otherwise known as the castration complex. The relationship between this version of femininity, which seems, according to the psychoanalytic paradigm, to be anatomically predisposed toward vanishing, and the ultimate goals of psychoanalysis, the disappearance of neuroses, is intricate and complicated. And at times the distance between Freud and his vanishing ladies diminishes in ways that threaten his presence, causing him to assert his difference from them.

In "On Beginning the Treatment" (1913), Freud, through an allusion to Friedrich von Schiller's poem, "Das Mädchen aus der Fremde" (The Maiden from Afar), distinguishes between traumatic neuroses and women precisely on the grounds of their respective "vanishability": "As soon as it becomes a question of the neuroses — which do not seem so far to have found a proper place in human thought — even intelligent people forget that a necessary proportion must be observed between time, work and success. This, incidentally, is an understandable result of the deep ignorance which prevails about the aetiology of the neuroses. Thanks to this ignorance, neurosis is looked on as a kind of 'maiden from afar.' 'None knew from whence she came'; so they expected that one day she would vanish."[17] Here the layperson's assumption that neuroses will vanish into thin air, without the work, time, and effort of a doctor, reveals ignorance, but Freud's suggestion that a foreign female body *might* vanish without a trace seems quite acceptable and goes unquestioned in the analogy. Indeed, the distinction between neuroses and foreign women in this case lies precisely in their differing relations to inexplicable vanishing. But how does Freud come upon this analogy between a vanishing foreign woman and the treatment of neuroses? Why does he defend against the conflation of vanishing women and traumatic neuroses in the first place?

In order to address these questions, we must consider the context of this 1913 analogy. "On Beginning the Treatment" is a guide for the profession, a handbook for practicing analysts, but it is also a justification of the field, a rebuttal of skeptics, and a defense of the analyst's role. Freud alludes to Schiller's poem to demonstrate that psychoanalytic cures demand work and time, just like house building, as he suggests in the preceding sentence: "No one would expect a man to lift a heavy table with two fingers as if it were a light stool, or to build a large house in the time it would take to put up a wooden hut" (12:128). Clearly, vanishing neuroses would undermine the role of the heroic analyst, who would be made redundant by the voluntary disappearance of the deep-seated traumas he must work hard to eradicate. But we can trace the roots of Freud's anxiety about the relative instability of both women and neuroses, and their effects on the analyst himself, to his early work with Breuer on hysteria, in which the vanishing woman makes her psychoanalytic debut.

Freud uses Charcot's French term *absence* to describe a certain type of hysterical attack. The word is apt, not only because the hysteric psychically "disappears" from her surroundings but because the physical symptoms of the illness, such as vomiting and anorexia, contribute to the attrition of female bodily presence.[18] This state of absence marks a loss of consciousness, a second state, a state of confusion; it is also a highly sexualized condition specifically linked to women: "The loss of consciousness, the '*absence*' in a hysterical attack is derived from the fleeting but unmistakable lapse of consciousness which is observable at the climax of every intense sexual satisfaction, including auto-erotic ones. This course of development can be traced with most certainty where hysterical *absences* arise from the onset of pollutions of the female sex" (9:233).[19] As in Victorian Britain, these vanishings emerge in conjunction with an increasingly explicit female sexuality, a sexuality rooted in the realization that women at all levels of society were capable of doing things for themselves, making men, and not themselves, feel redundant.

In describing the effects of psychoanalysis on the disappearing Anna O., Freud and Breuer invoke a notion of permanent disappearance to counter the patient's temporary vanishings. In the preliminary essay to the case studies, "On the Psychical Mechanism of Hysterical Phenomena: Preliminary Communication" (1893), they suggest, paradoxically, that the symptoms can only disappear once analysis renders them truly visible. Just as Eva C.'s ectoplasm vanishes the moment it appears, so hysterical symptoms seem also to vanish upon exposure: "For we found, to our great surprise at first, that each individual symptom immediately and permanently disappeared when we had succeeded in bringing clearly to light the memory of the event by which it was provoked and in arousing its accompanying affect, and when the patient had described that event in the greatest possible detail and had put the affect into words" (2:6). Magically vanishing symptoms permeate the essay: "Stimuli . . . reappear once again with the fullest intensity and then vanish for ever" and "Failure of function . . . vanish[es] in the same way."[20] This language of vanishing symptoms carries over into the case study of Anna O., in which, at least in theory, the symptom (absence) becomes the cure (disappearance of the symptoms) as soon as analysis makes the roots of the symptoms visible. Indeed, one could argue in response to Freud's later discussion of Schiller's "maiden from afar" that "the ignorant" were only taking their cues from Freud's early work, in which hysteric neuroses do in fact ultimately vanish, not unlike the foreign woman. Maidens and neuroses have more in common than Freud would like to admit. But why does he suppress the relationship between hysterics, neuroses, and vanishing and how does the combination of these three factors trouble the newly established profession of psychoanalysis? At the heart of these questions lie complex issues of control and power. Freud points to inexplicable, improbable, and sudden vanishing at those times when he no longer seems to be in control of the analytic scene. But who or what *does* control these narratives? Where can we locate the power of vanishing?

Just as the symptom (absence) seems uncomfortably close to the cure (complete disappearance of the symptom), so the precondition of hysteria resembles the precondition of the treatment in the early phases of psychoanalysis: the existence of a hypnoid state. In 1893, hypnosis is still very much part of Freud and Breuer's work, making Anna O.'s "complete unsuggestibility" especially problematic for the analyst (2:21). As a result of this unsuggestibility, Anna O.'s treatment ultimately depends on her ability to act in the doctor-magician's role and hypnotize herself. During her eighteen months under observation, Freud and Breuer, incapable of hypnotizing her themselves, rely on "the mounting up and intensification of her *absences* into her auto-hypnosis in the evening," after which they can begin their work (2:29).

Anna O.'s "treatment" effectively usurps the analyst's power to put the patient into the hypnoid state: she makes herself disappear. At moments in this case history, however, the magician-analyst attempts to assert the influence of his own physical presence over the absences of his patient. Breuer anxiously differentiates Anna O.'s treatment of him from her treatment of other visitors, claiming that while she makes others vanish from her world he is *always* present to her: "She would soon sink back into her own broodings and her visitor was blotted out. I was the only person whom she always recognized when I came in; so long as I was talking to her she was always in contact with things and lively, except for the sudden interruptions caused by one of her hallucinatory '*absences*'" (2:26). His assertion falters as he admits the exceptions, the absences, which disrupt the stability of his role, indeed of his very existence. When Breuer has to absent himself and go to Vienna, he claims that Anna O.'s self-vanishings become much more severe and extend to the bodily realm: she stops eating altogether. Her physical and psychic states are fatefully tied to the presence of the doctor, or so Breuer contends. But if Anna O. puts herself into the hypnoid state so that *her* words, not those of the analyst, might then cause symptoms to disappear, what role does the analyst actually play? Just who is in control of these vanishing acts? Can hysteria, which we might define as the ability to make oneself disappear, become a position of power or does it, at the very least, mirror the analytic position? And to what extent does Anna O. hand over this power to the analyst by putting her internal traumas into words and making them visible to him? Echoing the exhaustion of Eva C. in the aftermath of her materializations, Breuer tells us that "after [Anna] had given utterance to her hallucinations she would lose all her obstinacy and what she described as her 'energy' " (2:30).

In the midst of this physical and psychic instability, we need to ask ourselves what the hysteric's cure, a disappearance brought about by the externalization of what was concealed internally, reveals about agency. Can we even locate agency during the vanishing acts that occur on the psychoanalytic scene and if not where does this agency go?

Is There Anybody There?

Missing from this discussion is a term capable of describing the oscillating, interdependent comings and goings of both Anna O. and Breuer. Indeed, the problem of fixing the agency of vanishing stems in part from the doctor's own unstable presence during the analytic process, his own inclination toward a type of hysterical absence. But how, if at all, does the doctor's disappearance differ from that of the patient? According to an editorial footnote informed by Freud himself, there is a hiatus in Breuer's text, a vanished narrative moment, and Freud's comment on this omission provides us with the term we have been looking for—the magical mechanism of *transference,* for "when the treatment had apparently reached a successful end, the patient suddenly made manifest to Breuer the presence of a strong, unanalyzed positive transference of an unmistakably sexual nature" (2:40–41, n. 1).

In 1893, when Breuer and Freud were working with Anna O., transference as a concept had not yet emerged, although it had begun to make its "presence" felt. Freud does not, in fact, begin to consider transference carefully until around 1910, after which point it persists as a major theme throughout his work. The doctor's presence on the analytic scene is always questionable, given the physical location Freud recommends for the analyst. In "On Beginning the Treatment" (1913), he explains to an audience of fellow analysts how and why he renders his own body invisible: "I hold to the plan of getting the patient to lie on a sofa while I sit behind him out of sight. . . . I cannot put up with being stared at by other people for eight hours a day (or more). Since, while I am listening to the patient, I, too, give myself over to the current of my unconscious thoughts, I do not wish my expressions of face to give the patient matter for interpretations or to influence him in what he tells me" (12:133–34). Freud insists on this procedure "to prevent the transference from mingling with the patient's associations imperceptibly, to isolate the transference and allow it to come forward in due course sharply defined as a resistance" (12:134). Successful, "sharply defined" transference, then, apparently demands analytic invisibility even before the full effects of vanishing come into play in the form of a series of complex identity projections. By 1912, Freud rejects hypnotic suggestion in favor of the "talking cure." Trying to bury the ghost of suggestion, he encourages the analyst to be "opaque to his patients and, like a mirror, . . . show them nothing but what is shown to him" (12:18). But, although Freud puts aside the practice of hypnosis, we should not assume that he simultaneously gives up his affiliations with the magician's role. If anything, transference, which Freud describes as "conjuring up spirits," is psychoanalysis's most magical feat (20:227). Terry Castle effectively describes the supernatural nature of the transferential moment: "The crucial stage in Freudian analysis is the moment of transference—when the analyst himself suddenly appears before the patient as a ghost: 'the return, the reincarnation, of some figure out of his childhood or past.' At this stage the patient experiences a near-total 'recoil from reality,' and responds to the analyst as a 'reanimated' form of the 'infantile image.' It is up to the analyst to draw the patient out of his 'menacing illusion' and show him that 'what he takes to be real new life is a reflection of the past.' "[21]

Through transference, a patient projects onto the mirror of the doctor "mental attitudes" that he or she has already experienced in relation to someone else, usually the mother or the father. Positive and negative aspects, love and hate, emerge and can constitute either the most forceful resistance to the treatment or the vehicle that makes the treatment possible. The doctor's disappearance into the identity of the spirit conjured up by the patient remains vital to the success of the cure. As we have seen in the case of Anna O., analysis aims to render visible the invisible cause of the symptom. But, unlike the case of Anna O. and much of the other early writing on hysteria, Freud by 1913 no longer writes of simply "vanishing" the psyche's demons, drawing instead on a language of violent battle to describe the analyst's encounter with the neuroses. In the conclusion of "The

Dynamics of Transference," he writes: "It is on that field that the victory must be won—the victory whose expression is the permanent cure of the neurosis. It cannot be disputed that controlling the phenomena of transference presents the psycho-analyst with the greatest difficulties. But it should not be forgotten that it is precisely they that do us the inestimable service of making the patient's hidden and forgotten erotic impulses immediate and manifest. For when all is said and done, it is impossible to destroy anyone *in absentia* or *in effigie*" (12:108). As the struggle between analyst and neuroses intensifies, Freud no longer speaks of the permanent disappearance of symptoms, but rather turns to the idea of a "permanent cure." But try as Freud might to make vanishing disappear in favor of the more reliable, if more violent, process of destruction, the last line of this passage makes us wonder just how successful this turn away from magic has been. How do we understand Freud's claim that "when all is said and done, it is impossible to destroy anyone *in absentia* or *in effigie*"? Freud acknowledges that transference makes the patient's "hidden and erotic impulses immediate and manifest," but the last sentence does not quite follow from this one. Suddenly, the analyst's attention (and aggression) shifts from a series of impulses and symptoms to a person ("anyone"). But who is this person, and does the last sentence assure us of his or her destruction? Even if we are convinced that transference brings people as well as impulses into a type of presence that would belie the "absence" that apparently makes destruction impossible, can we really say that the figures conjured up through the transferential relationship are *not* "effigies"? *Effigy*, from the Latin *effingere* (to portray), suggests the presence of a likeness, a symbolic representation of an absent person, often one who exerts power over others in his or her absence. Although transference does have the power to render absent figures in some way visible to the patient and analyst, is this ghostly "presence" any more substantial than that of the effigy? If "it is impossible to destroy anyone . . . *in effigie*," then perhaps transference can never be a vehicle of destruction and can only effect yet another mode of vanishing in spite of Freud's desire for this not to be the case.

The transformation of magician into warrior is striking and raises a number of important questions for this exploration of the relation between vanishing, violence, and the analytic process. Why must Freud replace the instantaneous and magical cure for traumatic hysteria—the permanent disappearance of the neuroses through hypnosis—with a difficult and sometimes impossible transferential struggle, which, if the analyst succeeds, ends in a fatal act of destruction? Isn't the analyst's transference-induced disappearance from the analytic scene uncannily reminiscent of the hysteric's own unresting oscillation between absence and presence, a state to which Freud suggests women are primarily predisposed? And how does the established link between hysterical femininity and vanishing trouble Freud's experience of transference?

As if these questions don't pose enough problems, we cannot forget the further complications added by countertransference, of which Freud warns his colleagues in "The Future Prospects of Psycho-Analytic Therapy" (1910). In response to the problems of countertransference, Freud suggests that the analyst should analyze himself: "We have become aware of the 'counter-transference,' which arises in [the analyst] as a result of the patient's influence on his unconscious feelings, and we are almost inclined to insist that he shall recognize this counter-transference in himself and overcome it . . . we have noticed that no psycho-analyst goes further than his own complexes and internal resistances permit; and we consequently require that he shall begin his activity with a self-analysis and continually carry it deeper while he is making observations on his patients" (11:144–45). By 1914, however, only four years after writing this, Freud has already begun to recommend that analysts in training undergo analysis with someone other than themselves, having realized the difficulty of self-analysis through his own troubled experiments with the form (11:145, n. 1). Freud's self-analysis constitutes perhaps his most intense engagement with the questions I have posed regarding the relation between female vanishings, neuroses, and psychoanalytic authority and the problem of what to do with your mother if you do not kill her. If we trace these questions through Freud's letters to Wilhelm Fliess from the last few years of the nineteenth century, when Freud was theorizing hysteria, a picture begins to emerge of vanishing as a particularly maternal matter. These letters illustrate that the centrality of Oedipus in Freudian psychoanalysis, which for Mitchell represents the site into which hysteria vanishes, only emerges in relation to the figure of the vanishing woman.

Freud initially mentions his vanishing mother in the same letter to Wilhelm Fliess in which he first declares that the myth of Oedipus has a universal appeal. On October 15, 1897, prior to his discussion of maternal disappearance, he declares: "A single idea of general value dawned on me. I have found in my own case too, [the phenomenon of] being in love with my mother and jealous of my father, and I now consider it a universal event in early childhood. . . . If this is so, we can understand the gripping power of *Oedipus Rex*."[22] The later appearance of the vanishing mother alongside this first mention of Oedipus in Freud's work is striking. Critics and commentators have read this letter with an emphasis on the figure of Oedipus, interpreting the vanishing narrative largely through the lens of the Oedipal myth. I, however, will focus on the moment of vanishing as a useful interpretive lens not only for the myth of Oedipus but for Freud's "deviant" attachment to the myth, which Goux finds so mystifying.

The association between vanishing and femininity that occurs first in Freud and Breuer's work on hysteria erupts forcefully and repeatedly in Freud's self-analysis, this time embodied (and disembodied) in the figure of the mother. Like Oedipus and the Sphinx, or Sheldon Mills and Sadie Millstein, excessive maternal knowledge, bordering on omniscience, constitutes the catalyst for the mother's vanishing. Just as Anna O.'s absences threaten to destabilize the analyst's own authority and presence, so the disappearance of Amalia, Freud's mother, ultimately threatens to usurp Freud's analytic power. Vanishing mothers, I suggest, become *the* privileged metaphor through which Freud articulates his struggles with transference and the search for self-understanding.

Freud cannot access the scene of his mother's disappearance directly. Instead, he comes upon it via a different memory, which he had discussed with Fliess a few days earlier, as a result of a series of dreams about his nurse. On October 3, 1897, Freud identifies his nurse as his "prime originator." "An ugly, elderly woman who told [him] a great deal about God Almighty," Freud's nurse was also his teacher in sexual matters (quoted in Masson, *Complete Letters,* 268). On October 4, Freud has a dream that suggests that he stole zehners (Austrian coins) from his mother to give to the nurse. Incapable of making any sense of this dream alone, he looks beyond the limitations of his own memory and turns to that of his mother: "I asked my mother whether she still remembered the nurse. 'Of course,' she said, 'an elderly person, very clever, she was always carrying you off to some church. . . . During my confinement with Anna (two and a half years younger), it was discovered that she was a thief, and all the shiny new kreuzers and zehners and all the toys that had been given to you were found in her possession. Your brother Philipp himself fetched the police; she was then given ten months in prison'" (271). Mrs. Freud's information corrects Freud's initial assumptions about the zehner incident: he now "knows" that the nurse stole the coins and not he. But this piece of maternal knowledge only leaves Freud with more unanswered questions about how this event, which must have had a huge impact on him as a child, could have vanished from his mind: "I said to myself that if the old woman disappeared from my life so suddenly, it must be possible to demonstrate the impression this made on me. Where is it then?" (271). In the search for this lost impression of his vanished nurse, Freud rediscovers his vanishing mother. Unlike the memory of the nurse, however, Freud's recollection of his mother's disappearance is surreal, dreamlike, with all the bizarre trappings of a nineteenth-century parlor trick: "Thereupon a scene occurred to me which in the course of twenty-five years has occasionally emerged in my conscious memory without my understanding it. My mother was nowhere to be found; I was crying in despair. My brother Philipp (twenty years older than I) unlocked a wardrobe (*Kasten*) for me, and when I did not find my mother inside it either I cried even more until, slender and beautiful, she came in through the door" (271). This scene, so reminiscent of the magician's Vanishing Lady Act, accompanied by the necessary props of a cabinet, a side door, and a beautiful lady, creates a psychic hall of mirrors. One disappearance is recognizable only in the reflection of another. Once she emerges, the vanishing mother, appearing through a strange narrative technique of echo, reflection, and repetition, proceeds to haunt her way through Freud's work for years after the composition of this first letter.[23]

The same memory reappears a few years later in the revised 1907 version of *The Psychopathology of Everyday Life*. While Freud's 1897 account resonates with the emotions and fantastic fears of the child ("I was crying in despair; I was afraid she had vanished from me"), the

1907 retelling reveals a narrator no longer fully identified with his childhood self. In this later account, Freud emerges as a removed observer, watching his early life as if on a movie screen: "I saw myself standing in front of a cupboard (*Kasten*) demanding something and screaming, while my half brother, my senior by twenty years, held it open" (Freud, *Complete Psychological Works*, 6:50). Not only is this account devoid of the immediacy of the child's feelings; it also lacks the object in question, the vanished mother, who has been relegated to a mere "something."[24] Freud continues: "Then suddenly my mother, looking beautiful and slim, walked in to the room, *as if she had come in from the street*" (6:50, emphasis added). The child's sense of relief at his mother's reappearance becomes more complicated in this later retelling, for the mother now looks "as if she had come in from the street," a suggestion that links her separation from the child to maternal promiscuity.[25]

The two accounts differ further in how Freud approaches the act of interpretation. In 1897, his frantic questions in search of meaning reflect the perspective of a child experiencing the disorienting effects of the loss of his mother: "What can this mean? Why did my brother unlock the wardrobe for me, knowing that my mother was not in it and that thereby he could not calm me down?" (Masson, *Complete Letters*, 271). Freud's own answer to these rhetorical questions creates the impression that he arrives at an understanding of the scenario only in the very moment of writing to Fliess: "Now I suddenly understand it. I had asked him to do it" (271). In contrast, there is nothing instantaneous about the 1907 interpretation. In this later text, Freud reaches a calm and rational conclusion as the result of "considerable analytic effort," an explanation that, like Freud's contradictory work on the treatment of traumatic hysterical neuroses, betrays an ongoing tension between the magical instant of vanishing neuroses and the extensive labor of professional analysis. Freud tells us, "I had missed my mother, and had come to suspect that she was shut up in this wardrobe or cupboard; and it was for that reason that I was demanding that my brother should open the cupboard" (Freud, *Complete Psychological Works*, 6:50). In this revision, vanishing itself disappears as a source of the child's anxiety. Here the child, not the mother, becomes the subject of the action, the figure that "is missing," as Freud states quite simply, "I had missed my mother." Longing takes the place of vanishing, a substitution that indicates how closely related these two concepts really are.

The shift from a mother who vanishes to a child missing his mother becomes further complicated as Freud wrestles with the question of "how the child [got] the idea of looking for his absent mother in the cupboard," and at this point he turns to his mother for interpretive help. Here, Freud's younger self, spoken about in the first person until now, suddenly moves into the third person and becomes "the child," a case study rather than a self-analysis. Reluctantly, Freud concedes, "I accordingly resolved that *this time* I would make the problem of interpretation easier for myself and would ask my mother, who was then grown old, about the nurse" (6:50–51, emphasis added). The action of turning to his mother for help is an exception to the rule, Freud suggests, a cutting of analytic corners. Like Sadie Millstein in *Oedipus Wrecks,* the vanished mother returns to haunt the text as the omniscient mother, the keeper of the truth, the one who threatens to usurp her son's authority and replace him as prime agent of interpretation. In trying to work through this memory of his vanished mother alone, Freud encounters the impossibility of analysis without transference, and this later causes him to question the viability of self-analysis altogether. Consequently, he enters into a transferential relationship with his real mother, who occupies the place of the analyst, the subject presumed to know, even as he tries to conjure up the spirit or "effigy" of that mother from his childhood memory. And, while Amalia Freud becomes hyperpresent in the dual role of memory and interpreter, Freud the analyst begins to fade from his own text.

As Freud's commentary progresses, his mother's double presence saturates not only the interpretive process but the memory itself, as if she were always doubly there. Linking the child's bewilderment to an earlier confusion between the nurse's imprisonment (brought about by his older brother) and his mother's confinement, Freud writes: "When my mother left me a short while later, I suspected that my naughty brother had done the same thing to her that he had done to the nurse and I forced him to open the cupboard (*Kasten*) for me" (6:51). Here the singularity of the first person "I" strains as a result of the two quite different perspectives it contains: that of the adult Freud, who sees that his mother had quite simply "left him"; and that of the child, who continues to use a mysterious language of euphemism, "the same thing." To explain this euphemism, Freud briefly refers to his mother's confinement in the 1907 version, speaking once more of himself in the first person: "I now understand, too, why in the translation of this visual childhood scene my mother's slimness was emphasized: it must have struck me as having just been restored to her" (6:51).

Still dissatisfied with his interpretation, however, Freud returns yet again, almost by compulsion, to this same memory. In a footnote added in 1924, he writes: "The wardrobe or cupboard was a symbol for him of his mother's inside. So he insisted on looking into this cupboard, and turned for this to his big brother, who (as is clear from other material) had taken his father's place as the child's rival" (6:51, n. 2). Here Freud firmly establishes his first person "I" as the voice of the analyst, projecting the feelings of his younger self onto the third person "he," while the voice of the mother disappears altogether. But as Mary Jacobus stresses in her study of how this shrink's mother finds herself inside a Schrank, the subject of the memory defies Freud's attempts to relegate the mother to the status of pure content: "The mother is always absent, lost or sequestered, and always doubly inscribed—both contained and container, both the content and the memory and the structure that produces "mother" as its meaning (both what is lost and the representation itself). This game of hide-and-seek for a lost object, or double inscription, is repeated in the form of Freud's narrative. On the one hand, he pursues his self-interpretation by way of associated dream material, in quest of what it contains. On the other hand, he solves the problem of interpretation by asking his mother, now grown old, about the nurse's misdeeds."[26] Just as Mitchell argues that psychoanalysis and hysteria play a perpetual game of hide-and-seek, so Jacobus suggests that Freud's narratives of loss in some way imitate the vanishings and returns of the losses in question. This mimetic quality of Freud's writing enacts the symptoms of hysteria, making the difference between the analyst and patient increasingly hard to discern.

Swan's Way

Fascinated as Freud is by the space opened up by the hysterical oscillation between presence and absence, and by the possibilities for self-analysis that this space allows, such ambivalence undoubtedly also aroused intense anxiety in Freud, as his occasional attempts to re-assert his analytic "I" suggest. The uncertainty created by Freud's appearances and disappearances proves to be deeply troubling not only for Freud himself but for his readers, who, like Jim Swan, must work hard to stabilize Freud's own presence in his text. Swan's suggestive 1974 essay, "*Mater* and Nannie: Freud's Two Mothers," provides an extensive and thoughtful reading of Freud's analysis of his mother's and nurse's disappearances. But interestingly, like Freud's own halting text, Swan's writing falters, almost balks, when it encounters Mrs. Freud in the analyst's chair.

From the beginning of his inquiry, Swan wrestles with Freud's difficult identifications and problematic transferential relationships. Turning to *Group Psychology and the Analysis of the Ego* (1921), in which Freud argues that a boy who identifies with his mother risks homosexuality, Swan contends that Freud avoided maternal identification even within the context of professional transferential encounters: "The struggle appears even in Freud's therapeutic relationships with his own patients. Harold Searles has suggested how, in the transference relationship, Freud probably avoided identifying with the mother projected onto him by patients who needed to work through their primitive oral conflicts."[27] Swan accepts and repeats Freud's privileging of the memory of the nurse as the "genuine ancient discovery" over the memory of the mother, now relegated to the status of a mere screen memory (38). In fact, this distinction provides the foundation for further divisions Swan draws between the two women. Turning to Kleinian theory, Swan maintains that the binary between the women allows mother and nurse to function separately for Freud as the good and bad mother, thus keeping the biological mother pure, asexual, and passive while casting the nurse in the role of seducer and sexual aggressor. But this supposed division is by no means clear if we read Freud's letter to Fliess alongside his 1907 account of the memories of the vanishing mother and the magic cupboard, where, as I suggested earlier, Freud's mother appears as a sexualized, independent woman, looking "as if she had come in from the street."

Swan repeatedly stresses Freud's exclusive identification with the nurse and shies away from any hint of maternal identification. Throughout his analysis of the text, however, Swan himself identifies a little too closely with Freud, and by excluding the possibility of maternal identification from his reading he restricts his interpretation to the limits of Freud's own interpretive act. Consider for a moment the stolen zehners. Freud initially believes that he has stolen the zehners from his mother; but when he asks her if this is true she informs him that it was actually the nurse who took them from him. On hearing this, Freud writes to Fliess, "The correct interpretation is: I = she, and the mother of the doctor equals my mother. So far was I from knowing she was a thief that I made the wrong interpretation" (Masson, *Complete Letters,* 271). Whereas Swan sees only Freud's identification with the nurse, I would suggest that identification operates on two levels. While Freud the analyst identifies with the nurse for giving his patients bad treatment and taking their money from them, Freud the analyst can only access this information by simultaneously identifying with the mother, who at this moment clearly occupies the omniscient, analytic position. Freud's mother here functions not only as the mother of the doctor but as the doctor himself.

Swan's reading attempts to assert a tight distinction between the passive, idealized mother and the aggressive, knowledgeable nurse. In response to the mother's possession of knowledge and Freud's self-confessed debt to that knowledge in his self-analysis, Swan launches into a strangely passionate defense of a purely "analytic" Freud, untainted by conversation with his mother: "How wrong, though, is Freud's original interpretation? How much is it actually corrected by the new information? There is in fact a very important piece of new material supplied by Freud himself and not by his mother" ("*Mater* and Nanny," 41). On two further occasions, Swan triumphantly discredits the mother's contribution to Freud's self-analysis as nothing but an interference, a contamination of the truth of Freud's fantasy life: "But if Freud really did not know she was a thief till later, then it follows that his original interpretation is closer to his own fantasy life, however much it appears to disagree with his mother's conscious memory" (41). Soon after this statement, Swan concludes: "The fantasies can be corrected by someone else's memories of his childhood. Or—to be more exact—the fantasies can be supplemented by memories, and compared to them as a way of confirming their status *as fantasies,* but they cannot be altered or replaced by memories. In an absolutely fundamental way, the fantasies are what is true about Freud more than the actual memories, especially memories supplied by others, his mother in particular" (42). We suspect that something is awry as soon as Swan begins his sentence with, "But if Freud *really did not know.*" After all, the context for this comment is a psychoanalytic reading of Freud's self-analysis, a context that problematizes the idea of ever "really knowing." Indeed, Swan's use of this term, as well as his repeated self-corrections, suggest his desire to find a realm of certain knowledge that psychoanalysis simply fails to provide. Initially distinguishing between fantasy and memory, Swan claims that the memories of others *can* correct one's own fantasies and suggests that memory *is* what we really know— memory is the truth. He then modifies this claim by stating that a comparison of memory and fantasy serves not to correct memory but to verify fantasy's status as fantasy. Finally, in the following sentence Swan suddenly transposes fantasy and memory, so that fantasy holds the place of the certainty for which he strives ("in an absolutely fundamental way") and memory occupies the place of fantastic and supplemental knowledge. As fantasy becomes memory in Swan's attempt to establish a ground of truth, the ambivalent and ungraspable nature of knowledge reveals itself, and we find ourselves concentrating not only on what Freud and his mother did or did not know but on what Swan works to suppress: the vanishing woman's voice.

Swan is troubled less by memory itself than by the memory of Freud's mother "in particular." In his three-tiered hierarchy of truth, maternal memory lies at the bottom of the heap, below fantasy and Freud's own memory. Furthermore, as in the examples we have looked at so far, the figure of maternal knowledge makes itself visible through Freud's own vanishing. When Freud takes account of Amalia Freud's memories, his subsequent dream interpretation has the strange effect of erasing him from the scene altogether, which Swan finds inexplicable: "But Freud, apparently seeking a true 'memory,' interprets the dream as telling how the nurse and not he stole from his mother. Inexplicably, and in spite of the associations, he allows himself to drop out of the scene" (41). Given the necessary frequency of vanishing within the analytic scene, however, is it really so inexplicable that Freud should vanish temporarily from his narrative while conjuring up his memories from the past? And doesn't Swan's struggle to discredit the mother's memory fail to acknowledge that

Freud allows Amalia to be present in his "absence" only to make her disappear again via the memory she revives?

Swan regards Freud's vanishing as a moment of weakness or dis-empowerment and works to repress any identification of Freud with the maternal position that, he claims, Freud avoided at all costs. By foreclosing the possibility of maternal identification within Freud's process of self-analysis, however, Swan marginalizes the crucial role the mother, and metaphors of motherhood, play in Freud's search for self-knowledge in his letters to Fliess. Only through the oscillat-ing presence and absence of both Freud and his mother can Freud negotiate the complicated obstacle of transference in the course of analyzing himself. Absence is not necessarily the space of the dis-empowered, and presence is not always a guarantee of power, as the conclusion to "The Dynamics of Transference" has already dem-onstrated: "it is impossible to destroy anyone *in absentia* or *in effigie*" (Freud, *Complete Psychological Works,* 12:108).

Mother Knows Best

Contrary to Swan's (and Searles's) claim that Freud avoids maternal identification in transferential relationships, I have suggested that it is precisely through maternal identification that Freud pursues his quest for self-knowledge. But why does Freud want to occupy the ma-ternal position? What exactly do mothers know best? In addressing these questions, we need to look at Freud's repeated association of knowledge—the very possibility of knowing—with a maternal sub-ject position, an association that threatens to displace his identity as analyst, as the subject presumed to know. On November 14, 1897, Freud opens a letter to Fliess by announcing: "It was November 12, 1897; the sun was precisely in the eastern quarter; Mercury and Venus were in conjunction—No, birth announcements no longer start like that. It was November 12, a day dominated by a left-sided migraine, on the afternoon of which Martin sat down to write a new poem, on the evening of which Oli lost his second tooth, that, after the frightful labor pains of the last few weeks, I gave birth to a new piece of knowledge" (Masson, *Complete Letters,* 278). This "new" piece of knowledge is not in fact entirely new to Freud. He tells Fliess that "it had repeatedly shown itself and withdrawn again; but this time it stayed and looked upon the light of day" (278–79). A few days later we witness another abortive hiccup in the birth of Freud's baby, a piece of knowledge: the brainchild pops back in again. Interestingly, the catalyst for the retreat is a visit from Fliess's pregnant wife. Freud laments, "Probably it was not an auspicious day, however; the new idea which occurred to me in my euphoria retreated, no longer pleased me, and is now waiting to be born again" (284). Unlike most babies, and quite like Eva C.'s ectoplasm, these epistemological offspring leave and re-enter their "mother's womb" at will in a bizarre game of parturient peek-a-boo, mirroring the oscillation that defines Freud's relationship with Amalia and the maternal spirits they conjure up together. This ambivalence extends to his description of the role his mother and other female relatives play in his process of self-analysis. Only one month after Amalia Freud makes a vital contribution to her son's self-analysis, Freud complains to Fliess that his mother, wife, and sister-in-law, Minna, are all mere obstructions on his path to knowledge, for "they are altogether unfavorably disposed toward anything that seeks to fathom the secrets of growth, toward your affairs as well as mine" (283). Like troublesome sphinxes, these women withhold the solutions to Freud's riddles; as such, they come to embody the riddle itself, the realm of inaccessible knowledge.

Freud's self-analysis involves a series of complex identifications and disidentifications with maternity; the process demands a constant oscillation between birth and vaginal retention, between being the mother and opposing the mother, between conjuring her up and making her disappear. The work of scholars such as Sander Gilman, Marjorie Garber, Daniel Boyarin, and Jay Geller has usefully shown why Freud, as a Jewish male in anti-Semitic Vienna, would have resisted identifying with women. Freud constantly negotiated the stereotype of the Jewish man as feminized and emasculated, but this anxiety became especially pronounced, as Boyarin has argued, during the period of self-analysis when Freud experienced strong homosexual feelings for Wilhelm Fliess.[28] Given these compelling reasons *not* to identify with a female subject position, we might well ask why Freud did it anyway. What role does maternal identification play in Freud's process of self-analysis?

Freud allows himself to fall into the dangerous trap of maternal identification at the moment of maternal disappearance because he realizes that the place of vanishing is also potentially a place of knowledge and power. As Foucault's analysis of Jeremy Bentham's Panopticon illustrates, power must be both "visible and unverifiable."[29] Though a central tower marks the place of power in the prison, the presence or absence of the omniscient one in the tower is hidden from the prisoners through the careful use of architectural design and venetian blinds. Likewise, the power dynamic on the psychoanalytic scene depends, at least in part, on the physical layout: the doctor sits behind the patient's head, invisible.

Commenting on the spatial arrangement of the analytic scene, Irigaray, in "Body against Body," correlates the dynamic between patient and analyst with that of a child and its mother: "The analyst in therapy generally sits behind the analysand, like the mother toward whom the analysand is forbidden to turn. The patient must look forward, ahead, out, by forgetting the mother. And if he did turn around, perhaps she might have disappeared? Perhaps he has annihilated her?" (14). *Who* might have been annihilated? *Who* might have disappeared? Deliberately ambiguous, Irigaray's language points to the danger for both the analyst and the mother he or she mimes in this psychic game of hide-and-seek. As a result of the oscillation, Freud the analysand suffers an increasingly serious dose of motion sickness with each retelling, becoming more and more invested in fixing his presence and authority once and for all. The ambivalence of vanishing haunts the scene of self-analysis, in which the analyst is simultaneously the analysand, and in which, in Freud's case, the analyst's mother temporarily occupies the analyst's position, with all the power, presumed knowledge, and "vanishability" that this position entails. In order to gain control over the vanishing mother's power, Freud must put someone else in the position of analysand so that he can finally vanish *himself* as the analyst in the course of transference. This substitution act finally succeeds in the now famous fort-da narrative in the second chapter of *Beyond the Pleasure Principle* (1920), in which Freud manages to turn his loss into somebody else's game.

Fort-Da

Like the story of the mother in the cupboard, the description of Freud's grandson's fort-da game illustrates a child's attempt to give meaning to and take control of the traumatic separation from his mother. Pushing the similarities beyond the point of mere comparison, I want to suggest that the fort-da story not only describes Ernst's—the grandson's—game but simultaneously retells and reworks Freud's early experiences with his own vanishing mother. In this last version, however, Freud introduces a third subject to play the part of the vanishing mother's son onto whom he projects his own maternal anxieties. Recognizing the way in which Freud implicates himself in this story of Ernst, Jacques Derrida comments in "Coming into One's Own" that "This text is auto-biographical, but in a completely different way from what was believed before. First, auto-biography is not exactly the same as self-analysis. Second, it will force us to reconsider the whole topography of the *autos,* the self."[30] The repetition, which becomes both the mode of writing and the subject being written in *Beyond the Pleasure Principle,* turns to the vanishing mother as the ultimate emblem of subjectivity itself.

Elisabeth Bronfen also reads the fort-da narrative as an autobiographical text, but she places the death of Sophie—Freud's daughter, Ernst's mother—at the center of her interpretation. She writes, "While many critics have elaborated on the notion of fading or absence and its necessary precondition for symbolisation, as this is enacted in the child's game, the discussion in general has doubled Freud's own gesture of severing theory from historical event, at least in respect to an occultation of Sophie Freud's role. What I will do instead is privilege the fourth piece in this game of disappearance and re-presencing, which binds a child, a spool, and a chain of signifiers (*fort, da*)—the absent mother."[31] The problem with Bronfen's formulation is that it suggests the accessibility of "historical events." We learn, however, from both Freud's earlier attempts to capture personal "history" and Jim Swan's efforts to distinguish the "truth" of that history from the story of the mother, whose narrative intrusions threaten to undermine the very possibility of history, that we may only be able to access the "event," particularly the event of death, through "theory," or what Barbara Ehrenreich calls "a story about something else."[32]

Although Sophie's death does make an appearance in Derrida's essay, autobiography emerges less as a history of a particular life than as the writing of the movement of the self, especially as it emerges in imitation of the movement of the mother (Derrida, "Coming into One's Own," 137). The self in question in *Beyond the Pleasure Principle* can never be fixed, with each pronoun simultaneously signifying multiple identities—"he" being the grandfather, Freud, the observer-analyst, the (absent) father/son-in-law, and the grandson himself (who ultimately "becomes" the mother). In the endless movement between these pronouns, the self writes itself. And, like the frustrated photographers and cinematographers trying to capture the moving image of the ghost, Freud finds a way of documenting this movement of the self, not through "his" story, but through the re-presentation of "her" story, "she" being, of course, the figure of the vanishing (and endlessly returning) mother, of which Sophie Freud is only one of many iterations.

Undoubtedly, there are striking differences between the stories of Sigmund and Ernst and the way their mothers vanish. While Freud has to negotiate the double loss of two mother figures, Amalia and the nurse, while Freud initially articulates the figure of the disappearing mother through a double maternal presence, he goes out of his way to emphasize, even idealize, the singularity of his grandson's maternal experience: "He was greatly attached to his mother, who had not only fed him herself but had also looked after him without any outside help" (*Complete Psychological Works,* 18:14). At the beginning of this tale, Freud minimizes the "oscillation factor" of his daughter, Sophie, Ernst's mother, emphasizing that she exists firmly within the mother-child dyad. She never displaces herself or swaps places with a figure from "outside."

One wonders, then, about Freud's earlier claim that this eighteen-month-old child was "a very good boy," who "above all . . . never cried when his mother left him for a few hours" (18:14). This statement highlights a gap in the text and signals Freud's desire to suppress the "other" caretakers in his grandson's life in order to fix the absolute singularity of the child's experience of the mother. After all, if Sophie did leave Ernst for a few hours at a time who looked after him if she never employed "outside help"? Someone must have been there for Freud to know that the child never cried. Perhaps it was even Freud himself, and if this is the case the boundary between the analyst and the mother suddenly slips, suggesting yet again that "I" equals "she." Also important, Freud idealizes Ernst's own response to the absence of the mother, a striking contrast to the young Freud, who, though a year older than Ernst, screamed and cried in despair when his mother left him.

Having provided these details of Ernst's usual behavioral patterns, Freud recounts his observations of this eighteen-month-old child, who plays a game of throwing away a spool. Ernst accompanies this action with the long sound "o-o-o," which Freud, again relying on the mother's interpretive skills, understands as the German word *fort* (gone). The child then pulls the spool back with an attached string, accompanied by the sound *da* (there). In a victorious moment of exegesis, Freud explains: "The interpretation of the game then became obvious. It was related to the child's great cultural achievement — the instinctual renunciation (that is, the renunciation of instinctual satisfaction) which he had made in allowing his mother to go away without protesting. He compensated himself for this, as it were, by himself staging the disappearance and return of the objects within his reach" (18:15). Whereas Freud could only articulate his experience of loss to Fliess in 1897 from the perspective of a still mystified child who had no idea how or why his mother vanished, he attributes the idealized child of this 1920 retelling with all the powers of a magician. Ernst not only manages to *make* the mother symbolically disappear and reappear but he conquers the trauma of that loss in the very moment of disappearance. Indeed, by collapsing the child's loss into the moment of his mastery over that loss, Freud transforms this narrative into a double fantasy of disappearance in which mourning itself vanishes along with the mother. The collapse recalls the earlier confusion between the vanishing "Mädchen aus der Fremde" and the disappearance of traumatic neuroses, a confusion that Freud, defending the analyst's "labor," is keen to resist. In representing the disappearance of the mother, however, the work of analysis and the work of mourning must themselves vanish in order, paradoxically, for the analyst to emerge.

The absence of maternal mourning raises the question of how we can relate *Beyond the Pleasure Principle* to Freud's earlier work on the painful process of loss. After all, in "Mourning and Melancholia" (1917), loss, even in the form of "normal mourning" (as opposed to "abnormal" melancholia), temporarily results in the subject's inability to adopt a new love object and in a loss of interest in the world.

Melanie Klein goes so far as to argue that the child not only experiences feelings comparable to adult mourning but that all later grief can be traced back to the early mourning for the mother.[33] How, then, can Ernst experience maternal loss as exclusively enabling and progressive, something that moves him into language, culture, and the desire to be grown up himself? Why does loss cause this child to progress temporally and linguistically while the mourner regresses into the past and silence? Why, in other words, has mourning vanished?

Mourning only disappears from this scene if we read it solely as Ernst's story. If we read it as yet another narrative attempt to work through Freud's own trauma of maternal loss, mourning reappears. Read in this light, the familiar and repetitive tale becomes itself the site and work of mourning. Within this act of repetition, Freud reproduces his childhood self through the insertion of his grandson Ernst into his own vanishing mother story, a doubling that ultimately allows him to disidentify with the subject experiencing the loss. Mourning may vanish as content from this narrative, but it persists as form in the repetition of retelling.[34] By adding Ernst to his story, Freud frees himself to occupy the analyst's chair, from which he constructs an interpretation of loss that hovers between memory and fantasy. While traces of Freud's own memory reveal themselves (e.g., in the theatrics of maternal disappearance), Ernst's game stages a fantasy of traumas and neuroses that vanish like maidens, instantaneously and completely, at the moment in which they are experienced.

Although Freud here finally seems capable of holding his analytic ground, the moment of interpretation still remains a joint effort between the mother (this time Ernst's mother, Freud's daughter) and the analyst himself. When the child utters the sound "o-o-o," apparently signifying the mother's absence, his mother is not only (paradoxically) present but she is one of two key interpreters, as Freud acknowledges through a strange and crucial grammatical construction: "His mother and the writer of the present account were agreed in thinking that this was not a mere interjection but represented the German word *'fort'* [gone]."[35] In a startling act of self-erasure, Freud, who otherwise refers to himself as "I" throughout the narrative, disappears into a third-person construction at the very moment when the mother emerges as an interpretive figure and the magician-child utters the word *gone.*

Is this yet another moment of Freud's filial disempowerment in the face of the omniscient mother? Possibly. But given the complexity of the relationship between disappearance and analytic power this vanishing act demands a more nuanced reading. Transference depends precisely on the presence of "a third person," the analyst, who functions as a screen onto which the patient can conjure up and project an other, usually a parent. But Freud's oscillations between the positions of analysand and mother constantly arrest his self-analysis and call out for a third person. Not until the fort-da narrative does Freud finally occupy this third-person position of analyst. By 1920, the vanishing mother story ensures that the powerful figure of the interpreting mother, whose oscillation and omniscience so threaten Freud in his self-analysis, now has no choice but to be present, a witness to and interpreter of the very game that enacts her annihilation. Stripped of her double—the nurse, or "outside" mother—this "inside" mother finds herself trapped in her own singularity, robbed of agency in her own disappearance, and forced into a state of presence until her child decides otherwise. Freud further celebrates the child's triumph by describing in a footnote how Ernst, in another period of maternal absence that belies Freud's insistence on her constant presence, not only gains mastery over his mother's evanescence but appropriates her powers of self-erasure. Although the mother now only disappears at the behest of the child, the child has learned to vanish himself from the mother at will: "One day the child's mother had been away for several hours and on her return was met with the words 'Baby o-o-o!' which was at first incomprehensible. It soon turned out, however, that during the long period of solitude the child had found a method of making *himself* disappear. He had discovered his reflection in a full-length mirror which did not quite reach to the ground, so that by crouching down he could make his mirror-image 'gone'" (*Complete Psychological Works,* 18:15, n. 1). Ironically, only the mother remains in this staging of her own disappearance. And Freud, successfully vanishing himself through the reproduction of his childhood image, finally attains a position of analytic power.

Within Freud's writing, psychoanalytic authority works itself out in relation to the vanishing body of both the hysteric and the omniscient mother. We might read the disappearance of hysteria on which Mitchell focuses her attention as an ongoing attempt on the part of the psychoanalytic institution to distance itself from the blurred line that has always existed in this discourse between doctors and hysterics and their respective vanishings. Mitchell rightly notes the relationship between the disappearance of the discourse of hysteria and the centrality of Oedipus in Freudian psychoanalysis. But I have tried to suggest in this chapter that female vanishing, most explicitly embodied by the hysteric, is not displaced as a result of the Oedipus myth but actually stands at the center of Freudian psychoanalysis as a result of Freud's decision to focus on this rather than another myth. Although the institution endlessly enacts the desire to "disappear" the vanishing female body and the threat it poses to psychoanalytic authority, the vanishing lady repeatedly and unavoidably reemerges with every oedipal utterance. Mitchell frames psychoanalysis's focus on Oedipus as a displacement of both lateral (sibling) relations within the family and of hysteria itself. However, in Freud's letters to Fliess, Oedipus makes his psychoanalytic debut in the context of a vanishing woman story that is all about sibling rivalry, and in many ways we cannot read one without the other. In choosing vanishing over murder, Freud ensures the possibility of return for knowing women, often to his own chagrin, offering feminism a compelling deviation from the paradigm of necessary matricide. Although the "verlorene Spuren" (lost traces) of Schiller's "Maiden from Afar" suggest that women do indeed disappear for good, psychoanalysis as an institution—almost in spite of itself—fundamentally opposes this suggestion, relying as it does on the belief that things may vanish but never without a trace.

4

Violent Vanishings:

Hitchcock, Harlan,

and the

Politics of

Prestidigitation

Two vanishing woman mystery-melodrama films appeared in 1938 on the eve of World War II—Alfred Hitchcock's last British film, *The Lady Vanishes,* and the National Socialist director Veit Harlan's *Verwehte Spuren (Footprints Blown Away).* Each tells the story of an older woman who disappears mysteriously in the presence of a visually vigilant younger woman. The issue of vanishing permeates these films in multiple guises, forcing a number of important questions. Why does the vanishing lady appeal across ideological lines, drawing British and German attention alike? What do the narrative and cinematic differences between these two remarkably similar films, both made on the brink of the war, reveal about the politics of disappearance? And how do these disappearances of women relate to the effacement of other "others" at this historical moment?

Slavoj Žižek, in a discussion of *The Lady Vanishes* and other "vanishing woman" films, suggests that the woman who disappears is always the "woman with whom the sexual relationship would be possible, the elusive shadow of a Woman who would not just be another woman."[1] But Žižek's desire to prove filmic romance's affirmation of the idea that "the Woman does not exist" blinds him to a crucial fact in Hitchcock's film, the fact that the woman who disappears is not the object of the hero's desire, is not a femme fatale but a middle-aged spinster. *Verwehte Spuren* is one of the other rare exceptions to the pattern outlined by Žižek. As I will argue later, the romance plot in these two films does not rely on the hero's renunciation of the "Other Woman" but on the heroine's loss of an older female figure (in Harlan's case, the mother of the heroine), a loss that enables the progression of romantic love.

In *The True Story of the Novel,* Margaret Anne Doody describes this enabling loss as a "breaking trope," which we are likely to find in the first paragraph of many novels. She compares this beginning with "a kind of birth, the plunge into another existence, the cutting of the umbilical cord," and draws our attention to the fact that this "cut," which gets the whole thing going, is often the death of the mother.[2] Both *The Lady Vanishes* and *Verwehte Spuren* feature a middle-aged woman who fails to die in the cinematic equivalent of the first paragraph, and because of this delayed breaking trope, both films must contend with the problem of getting the story going. That the romance plot cannot begin until these women are forcibly cut out of the picture means that at some level we, the spectators, are *relieved* by the excision. And it is in this complicated relationship between the cut, the plot, and audience expectations that I wish to trace the ideological appeal of the story of the vanishing woman.

Through my analysis of these two films, I will continue thinking about the issues raised by the vanishing woman's appearances in early cinema and the relationship between these short films and the narrative-enabling cinematic techniques that emerge out of them. For instance, Méliès's *Escamotage d'Une Dame Chez Robert-Houdin* (1896) represents one of the earliest examples of the technique of stop-action camera, a process in which, after shooting a couple of frames, the camera stops, the scene is adjusted, and more frames are shot, resulting in an illusion of continuity repeatedly exploited by the early makers of "trick films" like Méliès.[3] Tom Gunning argues against conflating the editing devices that further a film's narrative with the "dramatic trick work" of the early filmmakers: "In parallel editing the 'magical' switches from one line of action to another are not the product of a Méliès-like prestidigitator, nor indications of a marvelous overturning of the laws of space and time. . . . In contrast to Méliès and others, Griffith's 'trick work' is in the service of the drama, a narrativizing of the possibilities of filmic discourse."[4] On one level the difference between these two techniques is clear: while the narrative film works to subordinate the "trick" of the editorial moment to the coherent story, Méliès aims to make a spectacle of this trick and its ability to overturn "the laws of space and time." But in spite of this distinction both narrative and magical forms ultimately exploit the illusions that these editing techniques make possible. Continuous narrative *is* a trick. Indeed, it is precisely in the complex relationship between the filmmaker's "dramatic trick work," both blatant and disguised, and the construction of narrative continuity that I locate some of the most slippery and problematic ideological questions raised by the spectacle of the vanishing woman.

In this chapter, I investigate how both a National Socialist filmmaker and a British filmmaker in the late 1930s came to articulate their prewar politics through the figure of the vanishing woman. I ask not only why it is a woman who vanishes but what kind of woman in this period is most in danger of vanishing into thin air. To equate the stakes of an individual, "magical" vanishing with the larger political agenda of National Socialism would be to fall into the trap constructed in *Verwehte Spuren,* a film that repeatedly attempts to dissolve the boundaries between the individual and the social body, between the real and the fictional. Even so, it remains essential not only to recognize the way in which National Socialist ideology operated through popular, apparently innocuous media but to determine why particular narratives, such as that of the vanishing woman, were more compelling than others to these filmmakers.

Although neither Hitchcock nor Harlan seems to have been aware of each other's films, both construct their plots around the same purportedly true story that Hitchcock later describes in an interview with François Truffaut: "The whole thing started with an ancient yarn about an old lady who goes to Paris with her daughter in 1880. They go to a hotel and the mother is taken ill. They call a doctor . . . who tells the girl that her mother needs a certain kind of medicine, and they can send her to the other end of Paris in a horse drawn cab. Four hours later, she gets back to the hotel and says, 'how is my mother?' and the manager says, 'What mother? We don't know you. Who are you?' . . . Anyway, the woman came from India, and the doctor had discovered that the mother had bubonic plague . . . if the news got around, it would drive the crowds who had come for the exposition away from Paris."[5] Hitchcock moves the tale away from the Paris Exhibition of 1880 to a contemporary moment in a fictional central European country named Bandrika, ruled, as an offstage voice tells us, by a dictator.[6] The action takes place aboard a train full of British tourists returning from a Bandrikan holiday, among them Iris (the heroine) and Gilbert (the hero), who together will search for Miss Froy, an elderly English governess (actually a British spy in disguise) who vanishes mysteriously early in the film. Other passengers include the Bandrikan minister of propaganda and his wife; Dr. Hartz, a brain specialist; and Signor Doppo, an Italian magician who specializes in the Vanishing Lady Act.[7] These latter characters represent the anti-British villains of the story. Although Hitchcock emphasizes almost to the point of caricature the national traits of each passenger onboard, he only explicitly identifies the nationality of the British characters. Dr. Hartz's name suggests a German identity (conflating the German for *hard* (*hart*) and *heart* (*Hertz*) within the name of a geographical region of Germany), as do the Germanic uniforms of the soldiers who come to his aid toward the end of the film; yet when he introduces himself to Gilbert he declares, "I am Doctor Egon Hartz of Prague." In this way, the film avoids overt typecasting of the German as a villain. But, needless to say, any confusion of German and Czechoslovakian identity would be highly overdetermined in 1930s Europe. As Sam P. Simone writes in *Hitchcock as Activist: Politics and the War Films,* "In 1938, Austria and Czechoslovakia, as autonomous nations, had 'vanished' from the continent of Europe. Chamberlain gave Czechoslovakia to Germany to buy time for England."[8] Through references to these two nations, Hitchcock inscribes central European politics into the fabric of the film's narrative.

Hitchcock aims his main political critique throughout the film at British passivity rather than German aggression, although the former necessarily evokes the latter. With the exception of Iris and Gilbert, the British passengers onboard—an illicit couple and two obsessive cricket fans named Caldicott and Charters—refuse to involve themselves in the search for Miss Froy, each quiescent for their own particular reasons. The illicit pair, posing as a honeymoon couple, must avoid a scandal because the man, "Mr. Todhunter," is a respected barrister. And the cricket fans fear that any inquiry into Miss Froy's disappearance might result in their missing the test match. Hitchcock implies that this political passivity relates directly to the characters' cultural isolationism. In striking contrast to Caldicott and Charters, with their jingoistic passion for English cricket, stand two of the most politically active characters in the film: Miss Froy, who loves Bandrika, its music, and its language; and Gilbert, a collector and preserver of world folk songs. The other British passengers onboard view these two with suspicion because of their "unhealthy" interest in foreign culture, and in this way Hitchcock reveals to his audiences that Germany is not alone in its hatred and fear of the other.

In spite of what seem to be obvious political references, neither the actors who played in the film nor most of the contemporary critics regarded *The Lady Vanishes* (originally entitled *The Lost Lady*) as a film with a serious political agenda. Googie Withers (who played Blanche, one of Iris's two friends) revealed in a personal interview that politics was the last thing on the mind of the young actors during the making of the film. According to Withers, they were all simply glad to have a part in a film with such a "jolly good story."[9] In 1938, *Variety*'s reviewer wrote that, *The Lady Vanishes* "flits from one set of characters to another and becomes slightly difficult to follow, but finally all joins up and becomes the kind of hooey to which the popular picture-going public cottons."[10] Similarly the *New York Post* and the *New York Herald Tribune* both praised the film as a "top notch mystery melodrama." Only William Whitebait in the *New Statesman* notices the pertinence of the film's political subtext, but even he gives the impression that the film's historical relevance is accidental: "to complete our pleasure, the film contains a number of lines rendered almost embarrassingly topical by the events of the past few weeks."[11]

Later Hitchcock critics do gloss the political parallels, but they still prefer to focus on the clever, entertaining, and ultimately superficial plot. Raymond Durgnat regards it as "one of the most comfortable and least substantial films" of the English era, adding that "if the plot is hardly convincing, the film is sufficiently cheerful to carry its absurdities gracefully."[12] Even Sam P. Simone, whose explicit topic is "Politics and the War Films," writes that "it is perhaps wrong to overstate the political context. . . . *The Lady Vanishes,* if it is political, is remarkably balanced and discreet for a polemic."[13]

Why do critics resist the political dimension of this film? Perhaps their reluctance arises from reading "serious" politics into a romantic comedy-thriller based on a popular yarn. Yet the film carries an ideological message not, as critics like Simone have tried to show, in spite of the uneasy juxtaposition of international politics with conjuring and romance but because of it. At a moment when the British Board of Film Censors was blocking any film that overtly criticized foreign governments, Hitchcock employed a familiar and superficial plot to make a striking though subtle commentary on the state of Europe in 1938. As Hitler and Chamberlain negotiated over Czechoslovakia and Poland for the sake of "peace in Europe," Hitchcock pointedly presented not the familiar version of the yarn he recounted to Truffaut but a variation on that theme, highlighting the tale's parallels with contemporary politics.

Explicit anxiety over Hitler's disregard for national borders in Central Europe only appears at the boundaries of the film itself—the publicity still. External to the film strip, the staged publicity still doesn't quite belong to the "whole" of the film. And yet as a publicity still this spare part must somehow encapsulate the film in a single snapshot. Forcing the limits of the whole, such photographs become the site of excess, the space in which we, the spectators, glimpse the eruption of the film's repressed material. One such publicity still from *The Lady Vanishes* shows Gilbert reading a newspaper. Its partially visible headline appears neither in English nor Bandrikan but in German: "Hitler erzählt . . ." (Hitler says . . .). A fragment excluded from and pointing beyond the whole, the publicity still provides a space in which *The Lady Vanishes* openly connects itself with the burning question of Anglo-German relations, although the film itself never refers to this taboo topic. The movie spectator's eye might miss such a subtle trace if it flashed by within the film itself. As Walter Benjamin remarks, "at the movies, this position [of critic] requires no attention. The public is an examiner, but an absent-minded one."[14]

But the photograph, like the painting, clipped and suspended in time, allows for closer examination: "The painting invites the spectator to contemplation. . . . Before the movie frame he cannot do so. No sooner has his eye grasped a scene than it is already changed" (241). The stasis of the still asks the "absent-minded" spectator of the movies to be still and pause momentarily on the name of Hitler.

If the illusion of continuity in film is historically intertwined with the Vanishing Lady Act, we perhaps need to disrupt that illusion in order to reveal the agency behind the vanishing process. Like the publicity still, the editorial cut exists in the borderland of the whole film. The cut, the film's site of disappearance, hides from our view the "faces on the cutting room floor" as well as the work of dissection that paradoxically produces the complete picture.[15] While the cut implies incision, penetration, and forceful separation, its effect is that of a magical sleight of hand, creating a smooth whole out of violently extracted bits and pieces.

We must understand the cut as both real and illusory. In *The Lady Vanishes*, Hitchcock suggests that public acceptance of political violence relies upon its alliance with the magician, master of illusion. The public tolerates the state cutting away unwanted members of the national body on the condition that it will provide the public with a means of believing that this violent erasure never really happens. Hitchcock exposes this illusion, however, by revealing the secret partnership between Dr. Hartz, the German-Czech brain surgeon, and the vanishing lady specialist, Signor Doppo, who work together to make Miss Froy imperceptibly disappear.[16] By exposing this alliance, Hitchcock uncovers a key factor of the workings of ideology — the mystification of the moment of violent incision.

Throughout the 1930s, surgical images permeated fascist rhetoric. As David Forgacs argues in "Fascism, Violence, and Modernity," Hitler and Mussolini repeatedly employ a language of violence to describe their roles in "healing" the national body. Paradoxically, the act of cutting away promised to make the nation whole. Mussolini declares that it is necessary "to use the scalpel to take away everything parasitic, harmful, and suffocating."[17] Other Mussolini speeches invoke the drip, the needle, and the cauterizing iron as essential instruments of healing. Hitler, too, utilizes a discourse of surgical removal, in spite of the fact that the most prominent metaphor of illness in

Mein Kampf represents the Jews as a plague or bacteria infecting the nation, forms of disease that by their very nature cannot be cut away. Early in *Mein Kampf,* he writes, "If you cut even cautiously into such an abscess [any form of filth or profligacy], you found, like a maggot in a rotting body, often dazzled by the sunlight—a kike!"[18]

In *The Lady Vanishes,* a film steeped in the politics of Britain's relationship with Germany and central Europe, "the cut" becomes crucial both in its narrative and cinematic function. Hitchcock employs a variety of fragmenting camera techniques to draw our attention to the hidden incisions of the editorial cuts. In doing so, he challenges the period's norms of film editing and of the finished product—the idea of a film as whole. In Nancy Naumburg's 1937 guide to the workings of a motion picture studio, Anne Bauchens, the film editor or "cutter" for Cecil B. De Mille of Paramount Pictures, writes: "And now that the editor's job is over, he hopes that he has told the story as effectively as possible . . . so that the audience will be utterly unaware of his work. The story should flow smoothly and the various shots should match perfectly. . . . The moment the audience is aware of the various cuts and devices used, the story will suffer. . . . We must maintain the whole greater than the sum of its parts" (Naumburg 214–215).[19] But at what cost must we protect the uninterrupted smoothness of the story, and what is the surplus value that makes the whole more than the sum of its parts? Jean-Louis Baudry suggests that the ideological effects of cinema reside precisely in this concealed locus of the cut, which represents the work that separates the film product from "objective reality": "Cinematographic specificity thus refers to a *work,* that is, to a process of transformation. The question becomes: is the work made evident, does consumption of the product bring about a 'knowledge effect' [Althusser], or is the work concealed? If the latter, consumption of the product will obviously be accompanied by ideological surplus value."[20] Knowledge resides in the cut, and by drawing our attention to those cuts Hitchcock forces knowledge on the spectator, knowledge of the illusion of cinematic wholeness, of the hidden surgical process through which images (or women) come to be "lost" or discarded, and of the fiction of disappearance itself. In forcing this awareness on the spectator, Hitchcock's political critique moves beyond his most obvious target of British isolationism, both cultural and political, and begins to expose, with the legerdemain demanded by this period of rigorous censorship, the machinations of an ideology like National Socialism, which employs the illusion of disappearance to disguise the violent excision of that which is other than its own self-image. But in doing this Hitchcock simultaneously exposes the potential violence of the cinema itself.

Keeping in mind the cut's historical and theoretical contexts, we can now return to the film itself to examine more closely Hitchcock's representation of the "disappearance" of Miss Froy. After talking briefly with Miss Froy in their train compartment, Iris falls unconscious as a result of a knock on the head she received before boarding. Like Iris, we spectators see nothing of Miss Froy's disappearance, which occurs during Iris's sleep. Through this major narrative cut, Hitchcock aligns us with Iris by rendering us unconscious as well. While she sleeps, we see nothing but a hypnotic "montage of shots [that] helps convey the passing of time and miles. There are shots of the engine, telegraph wires, railway lines repeated rapidly," much in the style of a dream sequence.[21] When Iris awakes, we must work along with her to reconstruct the events that led to Miss Froy's disappearance.

After finally convincing Gilbert, an English collector of folk tunes, of Miss Froy's existence, Iris and her newfound ally search the train for clues. Only on their arrival in the luggage carriage do they find their first piece of evidence: Signor Doppo's magical equipment. Gilbert unrolls a poster and reads: "The Great Doppo. Magician, illusionist, mind reader. . . . See his fascinating act, The Vanishing Lady." After a comic scene with costumes and trick cabinets, Iris and Gilbert try (and fail) to make sense of why the magician would have made Miss Froy disappear. Is it for practice or publicity? Their speculations don't get them very far.

With the discovery of Miss Froy's spectacles (it's no coincidence that the enemies of a spy would first disable the vision of this woman, who sees and knows too much), the scene suddenly takes on a more serious dimension. Gilbert and Iris notice the broken glass in Miss Froy's spectacles, perhaps an oblique reference to another older woman's smashed glasses in an earlier film that famously made editing techniques visible for ideological purposes, Eisenstein's *The Battleship Potemkin* (1925). This image of fractured vision is followed immediately by the first in a series of obvious and rapid cuts, revealing Signor Doppo's hand forcing the spectacles out of the hand of Iris, who has inherited this damaged visual aid from the vanished woman. The camera proceeds to cut back and forth between the ensuing fight and the rest of the carriage; a calf in a wicker basket and three white rabbits interrupt the continuity of the scene and remind us of the magical backdrop to this scene of violence. These cuts, of which the audience, according to Anne Bauchens's theory of editing, should be unaware, here arrest our attention and force us, through the erratic and fragmenting movements of the camera, to recognize the violence behind the smooth illusion of the uninterrupted narrative.

When the magician, artist of legerdemain, suddenly pulls out a knife, the illusion of mystery fades and exposes the true violence of Miss Froy's disappearance.[22] Following this, the scene disintegrates into another series of verbal, cinematic, and bodily fragments. First the camera cuts to a close-up shot of Signor Doppo's hand holding a knife as Gilbert shouts, "Try to get a hold of it before he cuts a slice off me." When Iris stands on a suitcase to reach for the knife, the camera pans to show only her feet and legs, dramatically severing her at the waist. Thus, amid the magician's paraphernalia, Hitchcock imitates another favorite trick in the magician's repertoire — sawing a woman in half.

This shot recalls an earlier moment of severance at the Bandrikan hotel, when Iris stands on a table in her lingerie to renounce, in the presence of her friends and the waiter, her identity as Iris Henderson, a woman who will "disappear" into Lady Charles Fotheringail when she marries on her return to England. As she announces her own demise, the camera cuts between the waiter's face, Iris's legs, and the faces of her two friends. At the moment when she declares her loss of identity, her face vanishes from sight and the frame severs her body in half for the first time. Her anxiety about her own fading, combined with the ocularity of her name, make her the ideal person to search for Miss Froy. As Gilbert tells her, "You haven't any manners at all, and you're always seeing things." This last statement reconfigures the relationship between really seeing and having delusions, an important theme throughout *The Lady Vanishes*. The delusional woman — especially an ill-mannered one — turns out to be the only one who sees things as they really are, and her habit of relentlessly announcing what she has witnessed, specifically the disappearance of another woman, makes her the next victim of the disappearing act. In *The Lady Vanishes,* Dr. Hartz the brain specialist, with the help of Signor Doppo the magician, must make this verbose witness disappear as well if they are to get away with the abduction of Miss Froy.

At first, Hartz attempts to disavow the reliability of Iris's vision by questioning her mental stability. Smoothly moving into the role of the psychoanalyst, which straddles the positions of surgeon and magician, Hartz suggests in front of the other passengers, "There is no Miss Froy. There never was a Miss Froy. Merely a vivid subjective image . . . some past association." Failing in his attempts to erase Iris psychically by implying that she is not "all there," Hartz then tries a more direct, corporeal approach. He begs Gilbert to allow him to take Iris to the National Hospital in Morsken to "rest," where no doubt she will meet with the same fate as that planned for Miss Froy, whom they eventually discover, wrapped from head to toe in bandages. With an evil twinkle in his eye, Hartz admits: "Yes, the patient is Miss Froy. She will be taken off the train at Morsken in about three minutes. She will be removed to the hospital there and operated on. Unfortunately the operation will not be successful. Oh, I should perhaps have explained, the operation will be performed by me."

Step by step, the plot uncovers the illusion of innocence collectively woven by the magician and the surgeon, behind which lies the fatal incision. However, in a rare moment of subversion within the history of the vanishing woman, Miss Froy exploits her own vanishability, disappearing into the forest under the noses of the Bandrikan soldiers and escaping to the embassy in London, where she must deliver a coded message in the form of a song, which she teaches to her assistants before she departs. With the exception of Iris and Gilbert, the British passengers on board stand exposed as failed witnesses, a blatant challenge to Britain's policy of nonintervention and blindness in the year of Chamberlain's peace negotiations with Hitler.

Like Hitchcock's rendition of the vanishing woman yarn, Veit Harlan's *Verwehte Spuren* has resisted political classification in its reception history. Veit Harlan himself has not. As Norbert Grob writes in *Cinégraph,* "Die Nazis und das Kino: Damit verbinden sich vor allem zwei Namen—Leni Riefenstahl und Veit Harlan" (The Nazis and cinema: two names in particular are connected with these—Leni Riefenstahl and Veit Harlan).[23] The popularity of Harlan's films with

Hitler and Goebbels remains undisputed. Describing the successful reception of *Verwehte Spuren,* which premiered on August 26, 1938, in Munich and Hamburg, Harlan writes in his autobiography: "Nun trat der seltene Fall ein, daß ich keiner einzigen Szene etwas verändern mußte. Hitler war so begeistert von dem Film, daß er Goebbels befahl, mir seine Anerkennung auszusprechen" (The rare event of not having to change a single scene now occurred. Hitler was so enthusiastic about the film that he asked Goebbels to pass on his praise to me).[24] This is not the first time that Hitler had acknowledged Harlan's work. One year earlier, on May 1, 1937, Harlan received an award from Hitler for *Der Herrscher,* giving him the opportunity to stand before Hitler and gaze into his eyes. Harlan's autobiographical description of this moment is striking, not only because it demonstrates Hitler's power to entrance Harlan like a magician but because Harlan chooses to cast Hitler in the role of an Indian magician. This fact becomes particularly interesting in the context of *Verwehte Spuren,* in which, as we shall see, India comes to signify the idea of a contaminating national threat.[25] Harlan writes: "Es war mehr als bedrückend, in Hitlers Augen zu sehen. . . . Ich hörte plötzlich auf meinen Atem, aber auch auf dem Atem Hitlers. Er wirkte wie ein Fakir, der sich der Macht seines Atems bewußt war" (40) (It was more than oppressive to look into his eyes. . . . I suddenly listened to my breath, but also to Hitler's breath. He appeared like a Fakir, who was aware of the power of his own breath).

After the war, Harlan, never actually a member of the Nationalsozialistische Deutsche Arbeiterpartei (NSDAP) became notorious, primarily for his 1940 anti-Semitic film *Jud Süss.*[26] After his Hamburg trial in 1949 declared Harlan innocent of crimes against humanity, a wave of newspaper articles pondered the question of whether German moviegoers should boycott his new films. Demonstrations took place; headlines denounced him as the "Regisseur des Teufels" (the devil's director).[27] Nevertheless, critics, while focusing their attention on the overtly anti-Semitic works, redeemed a handful of "nonpropaganda" films, one of which was his "vanishing woman" film, *Verwehte Spuren.* In the 1966 afterword to Harlan's autobiography *Im Schatten Meiner Filme,* H. C. Opfermann writes: "Alle von ihm 1938 und 1939 geschaffenen Filme: *Verwehte Spuren, Die Reise Nach Tilsit,* und *Pedro Soll Hängen* zeigten keine staatspolitische Tendenz und waren, vielleicht eben deshalb, bis auf den letzten Film, sämtlich überwältigende Publikumserfolge im In- und Ausland" (261) (All of his films made in 1938 and 1939: *Verwehte Spuren, Die Reise Nach Tilsit,* and *Pedro Soll Hängen* showed no sign of state politics and were, perhaps because of this, except for the last film, overwhelming successes at home and abroad). But how can we reconcile this opinion with the fact that the *Gleichschaltung* process, which brought every aspect of life—religion, culture, education, and bureaucracy—into line with the National Socialist revolution, had been in operation since 1933 and was firmly established by 1938? In order to answer this question, we first need to define exactly how *propaganda* was understood in 1930s Germany. In *Mein Kampf,* Hitler states that "the function of propaganda is to attract supporters, the function of organization is to win members" (581). The difference between supporters and members is quite clear. Being a supporter "requires only a passive recognition of an idea, while membership demands active advocacy and defense" (581).

The propagandistic nature of *Verwehte Spuren* lies in the suggestion of a particular idea, the idea that the sacrifice of individual "contaminating" bodies is unquestionably necessary for the sake of the health of the national body, an idea that, in its obliteration of the individual as such, is as insidious as any political message propounded by National Socialism. I will argue that the film seduces the spectator into becoming a "passive supporter of the idea" through the illusion of a familiar and ultimately banal romance plot, which serves to distract the spectator away from the idea itself. Like all illusions, the success of Harlan's film is predicated on the disappearance of its operational method—its cinematic magic.

While Hitchcock strives, in spite of censorship restrictions, to implicate the key nations involved in the peace negotiations of 1938, Harlan tries to obfuscate the whole question of German national identity by locating his story in nineteenth-century Paris, although his France is constantly haunted by German specters. *Verwehte Spuren* opens to the sound of a military march. A close-up of a painted drum informs us that this is the Paris Exhibition of 1867. The city houses two million people, a title declares, before the words dissolve into a flag-lined street procession, full of cheering people, brass bands, and floats, a scene that, given the historical moment, cannot help but recall Nazi rallies. "Europa" leads the procession. Naked and smiling, she rides her bull through the streets of Paris, a visual testimony to the unity of Europe and in stark contrast to Hitchcock's Europe, full of spies, intrigue, abduction, and murder. The cry of a Wagnerian horn announces the next float—a female personification of beautiful Paris, who, with her long braids and pale skin, has all the traits of the Aryan female archetype. Through an implicit act of usurpation, this German National Socialist drama plays itself out in the streets of Paris, leaving explicit references to Germany conspicuous largely by their absence.

The floats of America, Africa, Australia, and Asia follow Europe, and for a brief moment the film directly displays its anxiety about the limits of national and continental identity. The United States appears first as a Native American chief in full headdress, standing with arms folded to the tune of "Yankee Doodle," then as an African American dressed in top hat and tails, waving the Stars and Stripes, and singing "Old Folks at Home." Africa appears as a smiling tribesman, dressed in a loincloth, chanting, and rubbing a long stick between his palms. Australia follows in the guise of an africanized Aboriginal, dressed in a grass skirt and gold hoop earrings and carrying a leather shield. Asia closes this line-up of "others" in the form of a Chinese man and woman, dressed in long silk robes, smiling, and bowing to the momentarily orientalized version of the military theme tune. Thus, Harlan personifies each continent as a nonwhite, racially stereotyped other. Europe—the important exception—is a naked, white, Germanic woman.

Suddenly the camera cuts to the faces of the crowd. Four urgent brass chords, each higher and louder than the previous one, announce a series of rapid close-ups of generically costumed North African, Chinese, Indian, and Arab male faces in the crowd. As the fifth chord sounds—the climax of the crescendo—the camera cuts to the white faces of Mrs. Lawrence and her daughter Seraphim, the two Canadian women at the heart of the story. With their heads pressed together, this double gaze pierces the camera from a shared viewpoint. The moment is unique. After this point, the topic of race never emerges explicitly again. These five shots also stand out as Harlan's most pronounced fragmentation of the cinematic whole. From this moment on, he saturates the film with editing techniques that disguise the editorial cut and force the illusion of continuity—primarily through fades and dissolves.[28] Numerous critics, including Marc Ferro and Karsten Witte, have noted that the dissolve is the privileged cinematic technique in Nazi film.[29] As Eric Rentschler writes in "The Elective Other": "The dissolve can travel back in time and evaporate history. . . . The dissolve can turn limp human shapes into waving flags and marching mass ornaments, as we witness at the end of *Hitler Youth Quex*. In a dramatic dissolve, the womb of the expired artiste Caroline Neuber gives birth to the future German national theater (G. W. Pabst's *Komödianten/Traveling Players*, 1941). Repeatedly in films of the Nazi era, we see dead bodies dissolve into death masks, gravestones, monuments, and paintings" (161–62).

At the conclusion of this anxious and discontinuous camera work, two white females, the fifth in a series of racially marked faces, become the screens upon which Harlan projects all the horror associated with race within National Socialist Germany: disease, social disruption, contamination. Rather than make a film explicitly about the extermination of non-Aryan bodies at a historical moment when anti-Semitic propaganda had not yet succeeded in gaining a firm foothold in the population as a whole, Harlan uses the familiar yarn of the disappearing female body as a "visible-invisible," an apparently harmless mystery insidiously saturated with National Socialist ideas, to exercise his ideological legerdemain.

Having identified these two heretofore unknown women as racially contaminated (by placing them fifth in a series of four racial others at a historical moment in Germany when proximity to non-white bodies means contamination), the film then shows Mrs. Lawrence and her daughter Seraphim sitting in a carriage, unable to make their way through the throngs of people in the streets of Paris. Feeling unwell, Mrs. Lawrence becomes increasingly irritated. Seraphim attracts the attention of Dr. Moreau, a young man in the crowd, who raises his hat to her. As their eyes meet to the strains of romantic violins, which transform the military march into a love theme, Dr. Moreau mesmerizes Seraphim with his piercing gaze—love at first sight. Unlike Hitchcock's Dr. Hartz, Harlan's doctor will occupy the space of the romantic hero in spite of the instrumental role he will play in the eventual disappearance of Mrs. Lawrence. But Harlan fails to repress entirely the darker side of this romantic medical practitioner, who is specifically *not* a surgeon, for the name Moreau cannot help but recall H. G. Wells's exiled vivisectioner—an uncomfortable eruption of repressed violence in Harlan's romantic narrative.[30]

As Moreau helps the Lawrences through the crowd, Seraphim literally makes a spectacle of herself, screaming out her precocious knowledge at the top of her high-pitched voice. Although this is her first visit to Paris, she recites the history and layout of the city without hesitation. As she recognizes each monument she stands up in the carriage, points, and shrieks piercingly, "Sieh doch da!" (Look there!) or "Da ist die Straße, die führt zum Arc de Triomphe!" (There's the street that leads to the Arc de Triomphe!). When Moreau asks how she knows all this, her crucial reply is "von Mama." As in *The Lady Vanishes,* the heroine's special ability to "see things" is intimately connected with the knowledge and visual prowess of an older woman who will disappear in the course of the film. The mother's eventual disappearance only encourages Seraphim to look harder and shout louder. Mrs. Lawrence echoes her daughter's gestures when she sees the hotel des Deux Palombes, where she has made reservations. She, too, stands up, points, and shouts, "Da ist es!" (There it is!). Clearly, these women both know, see, and speak too much. Nothing escapes their attention as they watch with a double gaze. Seraphim tells Moreau that she has never spent a day apart from her mother in her life. Each one sees everything the other sees, as the camera has emphasized from the beginning of the film by repeatedly showing mother and daughter staring into the lens, head to head. They habitually announce what they see, making them particularly dangerous and undesirable citizens in this world, which depends upon the erasure of traces.

On their arrival at the hotel, the manager informs Mrs. Lawrence that he never received her reservation and he has only a single employee's room in which to accommodate her. At this point in the film, the severity of Mrs. Lawrence's illness begins to manifest itself. Sweat beads appear on her brow, and as she tries to find her room with Seraphim her misperception that it is too dark to read the numbers on the doors suggests that her eyesight is fading. This last detail marks an important parallel with *The Lady Vanishes;* in both films the woman's loss of vision precedes her own disappearance. Hitchcock's Signor Doppo removes Miss Froy's spectacles, and Harlan's Mrs. Lawrence goes blind. Before each woman disappears from sight, her own sight vanishes, removing her entirely from the sphere of vision.

Figure 18. *Verwehte Spuren* (Veit Harlan, 1938). Publicity still. Courtesy of the British Film Institute.

The producers of *Verwehte Spuren* advertised the film with a photographic still from this hotel lobby scene. As before, the repressed ideological content of the film returns in the publicity still, exceeding the official borders of the finished product. In the film itself, the hotel lobby reverberates with the sound of people speaking different languages, reminding us that Paris is full of guests from around the world who have come to the exhibition. But none of the figures in the frame are marked as racially other. This cosmopolitan world is, in spite of its linguistic diversity, a world of pure, white bodies. In fact, most of the scene focuses on the faces of four main characters: the hotel manager, Mrs. Lawrence, Seraphim, and Dr. Moreau. However, the publicity still from this scene has one striking addition. Opposite Mrs. Lawrence stands, like a mirror image, an Indian woman in full Indian dress, reinforcing the suggestion early in the film that the whiteness of these women has in some way been contaminated (fig. 18). If we recall the yarn narrated by Hitchcock earlier, the woman who disappears in Paris turns out to have visited India and contracted the bubonic plague, which, as we only discover at the end of the film, has also happened to Mrs. Lawrence. In this still, the photographer conflates the internal, invisible disease carrying "foreign bodies" of the plague with a visible female body from India.[31] Through a dangerous act of metonymy, the Indian woman comes to stand for the plague itself. Slowly and subtly, the film implants the idea that the extermination of race *as* a disease is a difficult but necessary role of the state. Once again, the photograph, the fragment beyond the illusory whole, provides the site where we can read the traces of "invisible" National Socialist propaganda.

Seraphim puts Mrs. Lawrence to bed, then goes out on the town for a romantic evening with Dr. Moreau. When she returns to her hotel, she enters her bedroom and immediately opens her locket to reveal a photograph of her mother. A close-up of the photograph of Mrs. Lawrence encased in the silver trinket hauntingly suggests that the mother is already a memory, as if a consequence of Seraphim's first experience alone. As Eduardo Cadava suggests, "Rather than reproducing, faithfully and perfectly, the photographed as such, the photographic image conjures up its death. Read against the grain of a certain faith in the mimetic capacity of photography, the photographic event reproduces, according to its own faithful and rigorous *rigor mortis* manner, the posthumous character of our lived experience. The home of the photographed is the cemetery."[32] Doubly entombed, first in the photographic image, then in the coffin-locket, whose lid allows even the visual memory to disappear at the viewer's will, Mrs. Lawrence "dies" as she becomes an image in her daughter's eyes, and this is the "breaking trope" that romance demands if the heroine is ever to fall in love. As the photograph dissolves into a shot of the seriously ill Mrs. Lawrence lying in bed, bathed in sweat, her death in Seraphim's psyche literalizes itself in the body of a dying woman. Through this confusion, Harlan posits the "loss" of the mother as a normal step in the romance plot. A gentle dissolve back to the scene of Seraphim's room, accompanied by more romantic violin music, draws our attention back to the scene of love. In a metacinematic moment, Seraphim witnesses her own temporary vanishing as she looks in the mirror to discover her reflection slowly vanishing and dissolving into an image of Dr. Moreau. Whereas Iris's romantic involvement with Gilbert saves her from vanishing into

Lady Charles Fotheringail, Seraphim's love for Moreau brings about her disappearance in this scene. The mirror becomes a movie screen on which we, with her, view the memory of their intimate evening of dancing together. Now that her mother is buried in the photographic cemetery, Seraphim can no longer stare out into the camera, head to head with her mother. Transported to the other side of the screen, she becomes a passive spectator as her evening plays itself out before her, and us. Her gaze is here brought into line with the dominant order of the camera; instead of looking into the lens, she now sees through its eye. As the image of the couple fades back into an image of herself, she whispers, "Vernant, Vernant" (Dr. Moreau's first name). Unlike Hitchcock, Harlan avoids dramatic cuts and instead relies repeatedly on romantic dissolves, which slowly ease Mrs. Lawrence into nothingness. There is no end cut, no final moment in Mrs. Lawrence's life—only a gentle fading—or so the cinematography would have us believe.

As Seraphim's enchantment with the doctor deepens, the mother disappears not only from the physical world but from the screen of her daughter's memory. In spite of her mother's sickness, Seraphim oversleeps the next morning, and by the time she gets to her mother's room it is too late. The hotel staff claims never to have seen or heard of Mrs. Lawrence. Seraphim, in her usual declamatory manner, runs all over town shrieking at the top of her voice, "Ich will meine Mutter wiedersehen" (I want to see my mother again), but no one responds. Finally, a journalist agrees to publish her story, but before he succeeds the authorities censor his article. He explains to Seraphim, "Die Stadt hat eine Interesse daran, daß das Verschwende dieser Engländerin nicht aufgeklärt wird. Wahrscheinlich ist es irgendeine Spionage Sache" (The state has an interest in keeping the disappearance of this English woman quiet. Probably a spy thing). But Mrs. Lawrence's threat is not that of the disguised eyes of the enemy spy (although her identity as a member of the British Commonwealth in 1938 would certainly play on this anxiety). Rather, her plague-infested body represents the image of the internal threat to National Socialist ideology, the hidden, unrecognizable disease carrier that contaminates the whole nation. In this sense, her body enters the same circle of meaning as the Jewish body; both exist in the context of a discourse of the plague. Neighboring and assisted by this film world of symbolic disappearances, saturated with the language of elimination, lies a world in which people really disappear.

Verwehte Spuren powerfully participates in the political rhetoric of the Nazi period, rhetoric that figured Jewishness as a "godless plague," a disease contaminating the body of Germany.[33] In *Mein Kampf,* Hitler regards the nation's specifically sexual problems of prostitution and syphilis, which he also calls "the Jewish disease," as key factors in the downfall of the German people. In an attempt to solve the problems of this "plague" Hitler argues that such threats to the health of the national body necessarily obliterate the rights of the individual for the sake of the collective. And it is precisely this purportedly humane idea that lies at the heart of the film's ideological strategy. Hitler writes:

> We must do away with the conception that the treatment of the body is the affair of every individual. . . . The right of every individual recedes before the duty to preserve the race.
>
> Only after these measures are carried out can the medical struggle against the plague itself be carried through with any prospect of success. But here too, there must be no half measures; the gravest and most ruthless decisions will have to be made. It is a half-measure to let incurably sick people steadily contaminate the healthy ones. This is in-keeping with the humanitarianism which, to avoid hurting one individual, lets a hundred others perish. (254–55)

When Moreau, the "good" doctor, asks the city officials whether the disappearance of Mrs. Lawrence had to happen in such a cruel manner, the officials employ Hitler's logic of necessity, a logic of sacrificing the part for the whole, to justify their actions. An elderly bureaucrat tells him, "Wir kennen so gut wie Sie die Gesetze der Nächstenliebe und Menschlichkeit; aber es ist besser grausam gegen eines, als gegen eine ganze Stadt" (We know as well as you the laws of brotherly love and humanity. But it is better to be cruel to one than to a whole city). The officials may be content with their rationalization of cruelty, but they still have to deal with the problem of Seraphim, the witness, who becomes increasingly hysterical in the course of the film, shrieking, slapping people, and dragging women about by the hair. When she finally discovers a trace of evidence—her mother's highly bejeweled necklace—she demands to know the truth. The woman wearing the necklace mutters, "Sie war ja längst tod" (She was long dead), but the facts around the death remain concealed from the spectator. Harlan never reveals what happened. In contrast to Hitchcock, the lost parts of the narrative never disclose themselves, even though the film goes through the motions of a revelation process. The officials deny murdering Mrs. Lawrence, but when asked where her body is they answer with a chilling prefiguration of the National Socialist final solution, "Sie ist . . . verbrannt" (She's incinerated).

The utterance of these words, revelatory of the violence that Harlan tries so hard to conceal, produces momentary chaos in the film. Seraphim runs into the street screaming, and a horse and carriage run her over, putting an end to both her screams and our ability to see the violence of the mother's vanishing. But the film carefully manages this crisis, reimposing the order of the romance plot. As the chaos dissolves smoothly into the following scene, we see Seraphim in bed, emerging from an unconscious state, whispering, "Die Pest. Meine Mutter. Die Pest" (The Plague. My mother. The Plague). An elderly official explains to her that she must sign a form, declaring that she came to Paris alone, in order to prevent panic from spreading throughout the city. He adds, "Es ist das Vaterland Ihrer Mutter den Sie diesen Dienst erweisen" (You're acting in the service of your mother's fatherland). In signing the form, she shifts her primary loyalty from mother to father(land), effecting the "normal" transference of loyalty that characterizes the marriage plot, behind which Harlan attempts to hide the violence of the state's demands. Seraphim's signature obliterates the final traces of her mother's existence and publicly undermines her own agency, her status as witness, possessor of knowledge and reliable perception.

As Seraphim signs the form, Harlan's camera zooms in to give us a close-up of her piercing eyes. Slowly the repressed returns as we see two superimpositions between Seraphim's eyes, first the image of naked Europa, a visual echo from the opening procession and then of mother and daughter looking into the camera together, head to head. Just as the superimposition threatens to dissolve Seraphim's face entirely, the heterosexual relationship reasserts its control, and the mother-daughter image disappears to leave Seraphim's face alone. The violins play a romantic theme, while Moreau sits at her bedside and gazes into her eyes. "Vernant," "Seraphim," they whisper to each other. Through this union of the protesting witness with the complicit doctor-magician, so deeply implicated in the cremation of Mrs. Lawrence, Harlan attempts to induce the film's spectators to lose themselves in the happy ending of romance. The final shot in this film returns once more to the photographic portrait of Mrs. Lawrence in Seraphim's locket, a capsule of memory. To the tune of the violin love theme, *Verwehte Spuren* ends with a long, slow fading of this maternal image. As though dissatisfied with the existence of even one small reminder of the woman's existence, the film cannot end before the mother's body, along with the memory of that body, is erased, a violence once again portrayed as a gentle fade-out.

Our collective blindness to the violence enacted against the figure of the mother, heterosexuality's own easy acceptance of the necessity of "matricide," becomes a screen that renders the insidious nature of this film's politics so difficult to perceive. Consequently, the disappearing, diseased mother becomes an ideal medium through which to advocate an ideology founded on the state's absolute right to erase the "foreign bodies" that purportedly contaminate the nation. Like the faces of the four "others" at the film's opening, which appeared, strikingly never to reemerge, Mrs. Lawrence's face simply vanishes from sight. In order to resist the illusion of *Verwehte Spuren,* we must illuminate and challenge the implicit violence of the romance plot, the acceptability of which makes it so compelling for ideological appropriation.

Both *Verwehte Spuren* and *The Lady Vanishes* rely heavily upon the form of the romance plot, which demands that the mother be obliterated in order for the heterosexual relationship to begin. Hitchcock subverts the form, in that the older woman is *not* a mother but a spinster, and, although her disappearance does enable Iris and Gilbert to come together, they do so not to obliterate Miss Froy but to rediscover her and eventually save her from a gruesome end. Although the spinster's dependence upon the heterosexual couple has its own problems, Gilbert and Iris's relationship still develops through the process of uncovering the violent illusions of the "plot," and in this sense the film challenges its own form. This self-reflexivity extends beyond the plot to the cinematography, through which Hitchcock repeatedly draws the spectators' attention to the complicity between cinematic magic and romance, disrupts the illusion of continuity, and refuses to allow the spectators a passive role.

In contrast, Harlan fully exploits the complicity of the romance plot and the cinematic illusions of continuity to disseminate the National Socialist idea that the state has the right to annihilate its unwanted others. The ease with which Harlan succeeds in convincing even postwar spectators of the apolitical nature of *Verwehte Spuren* is a frightening testimony to the entrenchment of romance, a testimony that challenges us to question the ethics of a plot that persistently relies on the obliteration of a woman. The "story" of narrative film has its roots in this same pattern, as the early works of Méliès and Edison show. And, while we may not be able to rewrite that story, we can at least begin to question our own willingness to accept illusions at face value and become attuned to the vanishing bodies on which our own stories and histories depend.

Aside from becoming more aware of the complexity and depth of the political rhetoric in these two films, I hope that my discussion will also alert us to the dangerous ambivalence of the metaphor of disappearance. Unlike the cases of vanishing women described by Žižek, sexually driven romantic "heroes" display little interest in uncovering the fate of these disappeared, middle-aged, culturally contaminated women. The detective labor is left in the hands of women like Iris and Seraphim, who work to show that magical disappearance is not always mere entertainment. As Diana Taylor writes in *Disappearing Acts*, "What do cheap theatrics and magic shows have to do with human annihilation? Too much, unfortunately."[34]

5

Shooting Stars, Vanishing Comets: Bette Davis and Cinematic Fading

We find one of the most compelling icons of the cinema's relationship with the vanishing woman in the figure of the Hollywood star. Although the metaphor of the star as a particularly brilliant type of performer has been in usage since at least 1779 (according to the *Oxford English Dictionary*), this sense of the word concretized itself in the studio systems of the American movie industry. Hollywood addresses the relationship between the star and the cinematic medium most explicitly in the narratives that depict the fortunes of the fading female star, of which Billy Wilder's *Sunset Boulevard* (1950) is the best-known example. At the end of *"Sunset Boulevard:* Fading Stars," feminist film critic Lucy Fischer condemns the fading star genre for its dismissal of mature women: "If Hollywood had worshipped the actress, in youth, for her glamor and beauty, its only use for her in maturity was mercilessly to divest her of those very traits, conducting a prurient, onscreen 'striptease' at the very site of her former triumph. For aging woman then—the situation has somewhat changed now—was viewed by man only as a site of profound loss. And her sunset years stretched out as bleakly as the desolate Hollywood boulevard that presciently opens the film."[1] For Fischer, *Sunset Boulevard* presents the mature star as nothing other than a pathetic spectacle of loss. Indeed, at the level of plot almost all of these films work to denigrate the identity of the older woman. They punish the economic and artistic success of the younger star who "has-been" both by domesticating her within the narrative (e.g., turning her into a wife and/or mother instead of a star) and by cruelly exposing the humiliations of age.

Why, then, would any feminist inquiry turn its attention to such a problematic genre in the first place? Feminist film theory has long preoccupied itself with the problem of visual excess in the Hollywood cinema, and before we consider how these films represent the fading female star we need to revisit briefly the debates of the 1970s and 1980s in order to retain a historical awareness of how discussions of women's presence and absence have emerged to date. Laura Mulvey suggested in 1975 that the hypervisibility of the Hollywood female star repeatedly functions not only as a form of excessive presence but as a marker of absence. The female figure "connotes something that the look continually circles around but disavows: her lack of a penis, implying the threat of castration and hence unpleasure. . . . Thus the woman as icon, displayed for the gaze and hence the enjoyment of men, the active controllers of the look, always threatens to evoke the anxiety it originally signified."[2] Excessive visual pleasure always implies an absence or lack, Mulvey argued, echoing Claire Johnston's earlier claim in "Women's Cinema as Counter-cinema" (1973) that "despite the enormous emphasis placed on woman as spectacle in the cinema, woman as woman is largely absent."[3] Feminist film theory was quick to spot the problems within its own critical paradigms, and as early as 1978 B. Ruby Rich highlighted the way in which Mulvey and Johnson, while raising important issues, reenact an exclusion of women that directly parallels the exclusivity of the cinematic codes they criticize: "The Mulvey and Johnston articles are both 'positive' film criticism, yet what you are left with from each piece is very negative. According to Mulvey, the woman is not visible in the audience which is perceived as male; according to Johnston she is not visible on the screen. She is merely a surrogate for the phallus, a signifier for something else. . . . Likewise, the cinematic codes have structured our absence to such an extent that the only choice allowed us is to identify either with Marilyn Monroe or with the man behind me hitting the back of the seat with his knees."[4] Since the late 1970s, film theorists have moved beyond the "negative" consequences of this rigidly gendered paradigm of presence and absence in significant ways. Most importantly, perhaps, feminist filmmakers have responded to the problems of classic Hollywood cinema by conceiving of alternative forms of female on-screen representation. By creating new paradigms of "presence" for female actresses and audiences alike, these filmmakers offer feminist film critics different narratives through which to think about the possibilities (and constraints) of the medium. Numerous theorists, and queer theorists in particular, have highlighted the operations of cross-gender identification and same-sex desire, forcing us not only to read female star texts in new ways but to pay attention to male stars and the way in which Hollywood frames them, too, as objects to be looked at and consumed.[5] Others, remaining within the heterosexual paradigm, have noted that Marilyn Monroe is not, in fact, the only "type" of identificatory object available to women, stressing that Hollywood film also creates strong female role models, particularly within the genre of the "woman's film." Critics have also noted that Mulvey's paradigm limits itself exclusively to questions of gender, pointing out that race functions in equally problematic ways. Here strategies of resistance such as bell hooks's formulation of an "oppositional gaze" and Richard Dyer's attention to the construction and fetishization of whiteness have played a crucial role in expanding the boundaries of the debate.[6] Just as presence has to some extent been reframed as something other than the woman as spectacle, so our discussions of "absence" have become increasingly complex and interesting. Terry Castle's *The Apparitional Lesbian,* for example, illuminates both how lesbianism is perceived as a type of absence and how physical presence never guarantees visibility. She writes: "When it comes to lesbians—or so I argue in the following chapters—many people have trouble seeing what's in front of them. The lesbian remains a kind of 'ghost effect' in the cinema world of modern life: elusive, vaporous, difficult to spot—even when she is there, in plain view, mortal and magnificent, at the center of the screen."[7] Patricia White further develops Castle's discussion of absence in her *Uninvited: Classic Hollywood Cinema and Lesbian Representability,* in which absence in Hollywood film repeatedly reveals itself as a trace of lesbian desire.[8]

Through the metaphor of the star, a celestial body whose own presence can only be illusory, I will continue to pursue the question of what modes of existence we might begin to imagine through film's own (im)materiality. This ectoplasmic medium has always been haunted by the problem of corporeal presence, as the vanishing women films of Edison, Méliès, and others illustrate. But turning my attention to classic Hollywood cinema, I will suggest in this chapter that the vanishing female body haunts narrative film, providing a potentially productive space for thinking about and beyond the difficult question of cinematic identification.

The fading star genre endlessly wrestles with the ambivalence of a medium in which the body always hovers between absence and presence. Rather than providing us with simple misogynist stories about the redundancy of "old" female stars, these films might instead be read as sites of resistance to the very ideal of youthful femininity they initially seem to support. In the case of Bette Davis, who chose to appear repeatedly in this fading role, thereby making it an integral part of her star persona, these films work to demystify the illusion that the woman on screen exists only as a fantasy of the male gaze, a fantasy that shines brightly and momentarily, then permanently disappears. Instead they offer us a forceful vision of the spectacularly vanishing woman as a figure who, though sometimes in danger of being done away with, utilizes her visibility in order to resist the very problems that arise out of that spectacular state of being.

We can, of course, never tie the phenomenon of cinematic vanishing exclusively to the body of the *female* star. Describing the actor's experience of making a silent film, Luigi Piradello, for example, writes: "With a vague sense of discomfort he feels inexplicable emptiness: his body loses its corporeality, it evaporates, it is deprived of reality, voice, and the noises caused by his moving about, in order to be changed into a mute image, flickering an instant on the screen, then vanishing into silence."[9] Male "stars" do fade, and fade repeatedly, as happens in the multiple remakes of *A Star Is Born*. These men are part of a story that is related to that of the vanishing lady, but it is not quite the same story.[10] In *A Star Is Born,* Norman Maine, the male star, is indeed past his prime, though more because of his drinking habits than his age. He discovers a rising star, Esther Blodgett, who can only achieve stardom by changing her name to Vicki Lester (another form of vanishing), and her career soon overtakes his. He continues to drink, but when he hears that Vicki plans to abandon her successful career in order to take care of him he walks into the ocean and drowns himself. Rather than fading away, as the older actress seems to, Norman Maine turns his back on his still interested fans and does away with himself. When Vicki appears before an audience after Norman's death, she declares, "Good evening everyone. This is Mrs. Norman Maine," another name change that emphasizes the fact that the female star always appears at the site of her eradication. In contrast to the active self-destruction of the male star, the story of Hollywood's fading female star and the anxiety she produces can be traced back directly to film's early magic tricks and their projection of the medium's metaphysical crises onto the body of women. Male stars do not fade in the same way that their female counterparts do, nor are they susceptible in the same way to a rhetoric of falling. Male faces never need "lifting" in the way that female faces do, a gravitational immunity stemming largely from a misogynist mythology of age that suggests old men remain desirable while old women do not. But it also reflects a more specific association of female sexuality with downward motion, with falling, even (and here I think about the oblique biblical reference in *All about Eve*) with "the Fall" itself.[11]

Given these negative associations with the fading female star, why did Bette Davis allow herself to be cast, and in some cases even push to be cast, in the role of the has-been? Rather than reading these films as further examples of Hollywood misogyny, I want to suggest that Davis's embrace of this genre allows us the chance to contemplate further the political potential of spectacular vanishing. As the stars of these films fall out of full visibility and into something more ambivalent, we enter the space Phelan describes as "the unmarked," a space of potential agency and freedom. What becomes visible, we need to ask, when we read the repetitious comings and goings, rises and falls, of a star like Bette Davis alongside each other? What does

Davis, through her performances in the fading star role, which she embraced no less than four times in the course of her career, illuminate about the permutations and limitations of gendered stardom, age, film spectacle, and the vanishing body? These narratives, I will argue, offer potential moments of feminist resistance, in that they present elusive vanishing and reappearance as alternatives to finite disappearance. As such, they provide us with strategies not only for surviving a particular conception of female surplus but for surviving—through the very states of visibility that only film makes possible—the medium of film itself.

The interest of these films for feminism lies less at the level of plot or audience identification than in the degree of attention they pay to the metaphor of the star itself.[12] When former star of the silent screen Norma Desmond turns to scriptwriter Joe Gillis, declaring, "Here's the chart from my astrologer," clear evidence that the time is ripe to present her unwieldy *Salomé* script to Mr. DeMille, she establishes a relationship between the metaphor of the cinematic star and its celestial point of reference, a relationship that has received remarkably little attention within the discourse of contemporary "stellar studies."[13] The connection between stars and photography has, however, been carefully considered by Eduardo Cadava, and his discussion of celestial matters in Walter Benjamin's work usefully sheds light on the ontological and representational crises that stars can provoke: "This [star]light, which in a flash travels across thousands of light-years, figures an illumination in which the present bears within it the most distant past and where the distant past suddenly traverses the present moment. This emergence of the past within the present, of what is most distant and closest at hand, suggests that, like the flash of similarity, starlight appears only in its withdrawal. . . . Like the photograph that presents what is no longer there, starlight names the trace of the celestial body that has long since vanished. The star is always a kind of ruin."[14] The star presents us with the spectacle of a body that has either already vanished or is in the process of vanishing, making the idea of a fading star somewhat tautological. With stars, temporality and materiality enter into crisis mode, as past, present, and future constantly collide. Pure presence becomes a temporal and material impossibility. Through the metaphor of the fading star, repeatedly embodied as female, we find ourselves having to confront the relationship between gender, materiality, and time itself. The star bespeaks the space of vanishing at every utterance. And as we try to think about how vanishing impacts Hollywood's use of stars we need not only to pay attention to the issues of identification and commodification, as star theorists such as Richard Dyer, Barry King, Jackie Stacey, and others have so usefully done to date. We must also contemplate how stars resonate with the medium of film and how this resonance might open up radical spaces for feminist film theory.

Why and how stars shine remains inseparable from the possibilities and problematics of female cinematic presence, and we might begin to consider the philosophical implications of the shining stars of Hollywood by thinking about them alongside Martin Heidegger's discussion of "shining" in *An Introduction to Metaphysics*. In a chapter entitled "The Limitation of Being," Heidegger introduces us to the distinction between *being* and *appearance*. He argues that, although these terms seem to delineate the difference between the "real in contradistinction to the unreal; the authentic over and against the inauthentic," the apparently conflicting meanings of *"Schein"* are actually variants of each other.[15]

> The sun, as it shines (scheint) seems (scheint) to move around the earth. The moon which shines seems, but only seems, to measure two feet in diameter, that is only an illusion (Schein). . . . On closer scrutiny we find three modes of Schein: 1) Schein as radiance and glow; 2) Schein and Scheinen as appearing, coming to light; 3) Schein as mere appearance or semblance (Anschein). But at the same time it becomes clear that the second variety of "Scheinen," appearing in the sense of showing itself, pertains both to Schein as radiance and to Schein as semblance, and not as a fortuitous attribute but as the ground of their possibility. The essence of appearance (Schein) lies in the appearing (Erscheinen). It is self-manifestation, self-representation, standing-there, presence. . . . The stars shine: glittering, they are present. Here appearance (Schein) means exactly the same as being. (99–100)

The fading star genre *seems* to portray the failure of the movie star to shine and glitter, where shining and glittering apparently constitute the only ways to be, and in this sense the genre threatens an uncomfortable encounter with the prospect of *nonbeing,* which Heidegger defines as "to withdraw from appearing, from presence" (102). Yet this genre deals not only with the disappearance and imminent death of subjects but with the refusal of less than shiny (or sometimes much too shiny) stars to go away. And when we place Davis's four fading star films together other ways of reading Hollywood female stardom become possible. While Heidegger defines *nonbeing* as the withdrawal from appearance, which would seem at first sight to describe the fate of the fading star, the essence of appearing, a constitutive element of being, actually includes withdrawal, although only when it occurs in combination with "coming on the scene": "The essence of appearing includes coming-on-the-scene and withdrawing, hither and thither in the truly demonstrative, indicative sense" (102).

Western philosophy has tended to place "woman" in the category of linguistic, physical, and visual other, resulting in the spectatorial habit of transforming the female body on-screen into a fetish or substitution for the phallus. I want to suggest, however, that particular features of Davis's repeated performance of the fading star resist this mode of spectatorial fetishism, forcing us to devise new articulations of the possibilities of cinematic viewing. First, some of Davis's fading star films present us with the spectacle of the old or "dowdy" female body, a body that deflates the illusion of the cinematic woman as eternally young by making a spectacle of that body's wrinkles, weight, and so on. But more than the age of Davis's body in these films, that body's ostentatious performance of its resistance to presence, appearance, and visibility within the diegetic space, its repeated and often bellowing announcement of that body's tendency to vanish allows it to resist spectatorial fetishization without completely "withdrawing from appearing." This genre seems to present us with narratives that link Davis's star image to both failure and disappearance, yet when we read her four fading star films against each other their repetitions and alterations of gestures and their reiterated but always ambivalent resistance to certain conventional notions of appearance — such as Joyce Heath's refuge under her hat at the edge of the frame in the opening scenes of *Dangerous* (Irving Rapper, 1935) — offer us new ways of thinking about female visibility in the cinematic context.

Through its explicit engagement with the image of the star, the genre forces us to contemplate how film itself produces anxiety about temporality, materiality, and repetition, all key components of the vanishing woman's story. Like the magician's vanishing lady, Freud's vanishing mother, or Hitchcock's vanishing spy, Miss Froy, the star remains caught in a repetitious cycle of disappearance and return because of the endlessly porous nature of that star's temporal boundaries. If the star we see only shines when it has already vanished, then that star's earthly presence remains inextricably linked to its celestial past; similarly, its celestial presence remains inseparable from its earthly future. Each disappearance points forward to an appearance, and each appearance in turn points backward to an earlier disappearance.

Bette Davis versus Gloria Swanson

Most people would choose Gloria Swanson's depiction of Norma Desmond as the obvious text through which to explore the figure of the fading star, but I have taken Bette Davis as an alternative figurehead for this inquiry for a number of reasons. First, and perhaps most importantly, Davis literalizes the star's endless cycle of vanishing and reappearing by playing a fading star no less than four times within the course of her career: in *Dangerous* (Alfred E. Green, 1935), for which she won an academy award; *All about Eve* (Joseph Mankiewicz, 1950); *The Star* (Stuart Heisler, 1952); and *Whatever Happened to Baby Jane?* (Robert Aldrich, 1962). Although vanishing and repetition exist in a symbiotic relationship, Gloria Swanson adamantly refused to "repeat herself" after *Sunset Boulevard,* perhaps because this film suppressed the possibility of vanishing more successfully than did Davis's films in this genre. By the end of *Sunset Boulevard,* we know that Norma Desmond is a "profound site of loss," that she will not make a come-back, and that this star is no longer a star, unlike Margo Channing, who "never was, or will be, anything less, or anything else." Lucy Fischer writes in *"Sunset Boulevard:* Fading Stars,": "For years after that, scripts arrived at [Swanson's] door containing imitations of *Sunset Boulevard,* 'all featuring a deranged superstar crashing toward tragedy.' As [Swanson] commented: 'I could obviously have [gone] on playing [the part] . . . until at last I became a sort of creepy shadow of myself, or rather of Norma Desmond—a shadow of a shadow' " (111).

Davis was no stranger to the real possibility of professional disappearance. In September 1962, soon after the completion of *Baby Jane,* she placed an ad in the Hollywood trade papers, stating: "Mother of Three—10, 11, and 15—divorcee, American. Thirty years' experience as an actress in motion pictures. Mobile still and more affable than rumor would have it. Wants steady employment in Hollywood. (Has had Broadway.) Bette Davis. References on request."[16] Dorothy Kilgallen responded in her Hollywood column by condemning Davis's agent for allowing her to appear as such a "broken-down 'has-been,'" yet Davis herself seems to have been determined to embrace the condition of fading stardom, returning to it even at the peak of her career. After winning the American Film Industry's Lifetime Achievement Award (the first woman ever to do so), Davis drew public attention to her flagging career, commenting, "If something positive careerwise doesn't happen now, it never will."[17] Given Davis's penchant for fading, it comes as no surprise that one of the first roles she receives in the wake of this award is the repetition of an earlier vanishing, the title role in Anthony Page's 1979 remake of Hitchcock's 1938 film, *The Lady Vanishes.*[18] Davis ultimately turned down the role, which then went to Angela Lansbury, but the proximity of her star identity to the cinema's vanishing lady remains unmistakable. The starlight of Bette Davis repeatedly illuminates the ambivalent space of vanishing and return, a space in which both vision and visibility are strained and unstable. Through these four Davis films, which span the length of her career, this chapter will investigate the relationship between the star metaphor and fades and comebacks, vanishing and returning, and temporality and materiality. Ultimately, I will suggest that Davis's star image, as enacted through this character of the fading female star, refuses to vanish silently and instead emerges as a force that reshapes the vanishing woman's relationship with the medium that made her so visible in the first place.

Dangerous (1935): Fading and Falling

Alfred Green's *Dangerous* (1935) tells the story of stage actress Joyce Heath, who has fallen from greatness because of a "jinx." After Heath's leading man dies on an opening night, everyone associated with her is "haunted by failures, divorces, suicides, scandals." Don

Bellows, a successful architect and fiancé of the high-society Gail Armitage, discovers the alcoholic Joyce Heath in a seedy bar, Jerry's Joint, and when she falls unconscious he falls in love. Bellows breaks off his engagement, invests his fortune in a play that will be the vehicle of Heath's comeback, and asks her to marry him. Heath, already secretly married to a man who won't divorce her, tries to free herself from him by driving herself and her husband into a tree. The husband ends up paralyzed but not dead, while Heath is hospitalized, unable to open the play. The play's failure ruins Bellows but allows him to win Gail back. Heath condemns herself to a life of nursing her husband, and, although she eventually does reopen the play, she does so not as a star but as a wife who needs to provide for the husband she owes.

At the opening of *Dangerous,* Mr. Farnsworth, a minor character, passes Joyce Heath on the street. Hidden behind a hat and lurching from side to side in a manner that is clearly not typical of Heath (although this swagger is very typical of Bette Davis), she evades the viewer's gaze and belies her own presence. Farnsworth hesitates momentarily, then arrests the star: "I beg your pardon, but aren't you Joyce Heath?" From under her hat, at the very edge of the frame, Heath replies, "No, you've made a mistake." This denial of her own name serves as an important moment of protest, of disidentification with the star image that, while not allowing Heath to escape the position of woman as spectacle, does place her in a strategic, confrontational relationship with that role. As Judith Butler writes of the Althusserian moment of interpellation: "Imagine the quite plausible scene in which one is called by a name and one turns around to protest the name: 'That is not me, you must be mistaken!' And then imagine that the name continues to force itself upon you, to delineate the space you occupy, to construct a social positionality. Indifferent to your protests, the force of interpellation continues to work. One is still constituted by discourse, but at a distance from oneself."[19]

Farnsworth's fleeting encounter with the former female icon produces a lengthy discussion of Heath's disappearance in the exclusively male space of his gentleman's club. Columnist Ted Henley declares: "She was too brilliant, too startling for a star. She was a comet, which appeared suddenly, fell spectacularly, and disappeared completely. . . . Last time I saw her she was on a cheap vaudeville tour, and then she vanished, like the magician's lady." Why does Henley shift Heath's celestial status from a star to a comet? What's the difference between the two? Deriving from Aristotle's description of this celestial body as *kometes*, meaning "wearing long hair," Farnsworth's renaming of Heath emphasizes Hollywood's concern with vanishing as a particularly female phenomenon.[20] The comet appears brilliantly only in relation to its own death, falling stars being the visible evidence of the comet's demise.[21] By renaming Heath as a comet, Henley places her in a celestial discourse of the spectacle of death, of disintegrating female beauty.

Ted Henley works hard in this scene to reassure us that Joyce Heath has gone for good. After recasting her as a comet, he tells us three times of her disappearance: she fell spectacularly, disappeared completely, and then vanished like the magician's lady. But the repeated iteration of Heath's "final" disappearance fails to convince us of the star's demise. On the contrary, every new declaration of her absence raises the threat of her return. First, and most obviously, the spectators already know that Joyce Heath exists to be seen right outside the door of the gentleman's club, even though she may deny that she is herself. After Henley tells us that Heath disappeared "completely" following her spectacular fall, he goes on to admit that he has since seen her on a cheap vaudeville tour. Although Heath may have vanished from the star stages of Broadway, she does not disappear completely but rather reemerges in a different venue, a venue that disrupts Henley's certainty and provokes him to insist yet again that she then "vanished, like the magician's lady." Henley tries to do away with Heath's presence once and for all in this final statement, but he merely reopens the possibility of her return through his comparison of her with the magician's lady. For, as I have argued in previous chapters, the vanishing lady does not disappear completely but constantly reappears as a physical presence, and this reappearance constitutes an essential component of the spectacle of vanishing. Any failure to reappear provokes a collective crisis, as it does in Woody Allen's *Oedipus Wrecks*.[22] To vanish like the magician's lady is not to disappear but to partake in a particular kind of spectacle that self-reflexively puts the woman *as* spectacle into question, and this is precisely what happens in Davis's fading star films.

When Don Bellows (played by Franchot Tone), the architect, recounts his life-changing encounter with Heath (he saw her once, and her creativity inspired him to become an architect, just as it will later ruin him), it comes as no surprise that he, like a modern day Dorian Gray, falls for her in the role of Juliet, an intertextual reference that takes us straight to the stars. Perhaps no other literary character resonates as strongly with the metaphor of the stars, their shine, and the semblance inherent in that shining. From the very beginning of *Romeo and Juliet,* Juliet emerges as a figure of shining light. In act 1, Benvolio assures Romeo that Juliet only seems fair to him because he has not yet compared her with other women: "But in the crystal scales let there be weigh'd / Your lady's love against some other maid / That I will show you shining at this feast, / And she shall scant show well that now seems best" (1.2.98–101). But obviously Juliet does outshine the other maids, even, according to Romeo, outshining light itself: "O, she doth teach the torches to burn bright. / It seems she hangs upon the cheek of night / As a rich jewel in an Ethiop's ear" (1.5.43–45). By the opening of act 2, scene 2, however, this shining has become specifically stellar. "Juliet is the sun" (2), declares Romeo. But within a matter of lines Shakespeare develops an extended and endlessly complex conceit on Juliet's relationship with the stars. A former sun, Juliet soon emerges in imitation of the stars, shining so brightly that the birds, mistakenly perhaps (for earlier she *was* the sun), think that it is the sun, not the stars, that shine.

> Her eye discourses, I will answer it.
> I am too bold. 'Tis not to me she speaks.
> Two of the fairest stars in all the heaven,
> Having some business, do entreat her eyes
> To twinkle in their spheres till they return.
> What if her eyes were there, they in her head?
> The brightness of her cheek would shame those stars
> As daylight doth a lamp. Her eyes in heaven
> Would through the airy region stream so bright
> That birds would sing and think it were not night.
> (12–22)

Juliet begins as a spectator of the stars, not a passive spectator but an active interlocutor in the visual realm ("Her eye discourses"). The stars at which she directs her gaze are naturally vanishing stars, stars that disappear from view, promising to return. Having business else-where, they call on Juliet's eyes to take their place in the heavens. These eyes begin by seeming (*scheinen*) more authentic than the stars they replace and then go on to appear so bright that they make the birds believe they are in fact the sun. Like Heath, Juliet is "too bril-liant, too startling" for a star. While one becomes a comet, the other transmutes into the sun itself.

This double movement of vanishing and returning seems to be a female prerogative, and those who fall for the star are in danger of falling with her, without any guarantee of rising up again. Reaching for brilliance, these stargazers all too often end up dead or ruined. Directly echoing Romeo's own stellar imagery in act 3, scene 2, Juliet declares

> Come gentle night, come loving black-brow'd night,
> Give me my Romeo; and when I shall die
> Take him and cut him out in little stars,
> And he will make the face of heaven so fine
> That all the world will be in love with night,
> And pay no worship to the garish sun.
> (20–25)

But the "little death" on which Juliet puns here is hers alone, for Romeo cannot vanish, cannot be "dead before" then "warm," as Juliet can (5.3.195–96), but only dead. Nor can he shine in such a way as to produce the illusion of the sun but only turn attention away from the sun. Semblance belongs to Juliet, the star, and this ability to "schein" proves fatal for those who fail to recognize, like Romeo, the difference between semblance and truth.

Consolidating the film's association between Juliet and the fad-ing star, Heath performs a drunken excerpt of the balcony scene for Bellows in Jerry's Joint, then collapses onto a nearby chair, only the first of several associations of Heath with the act of falling. The next morning she falls out of bed in Bellow's country house. Her language is saturated with downward motion; she speaks of going "over the cliff" and "off at the deep end" and fears that no one will let her in-side a theater because "they'd be afraid it would fall down." Bellows works hard to distance himself from her gravitational pull. "I can't fall down," he insists. "I've waited too long to flop." As he compares himself with Heath, her transience serves only to set off his own immunity to falling and fading: "You and I are both artists. I deal in permanence, things that last. You in emotions, moments, things that flame, burn and leave ashes, so we're not the same."

But Heath fails to deliver even the Pater-like moment of the transient burning flame, for she crashes her car, landing herself and her husband in the hospital. She misses the opening night and ruins Bellows financially. In a stifling final scene, Heath waves up at her husband's hospital window with an armful of flowers, apparently indicating to the audience that she is no longer a star but a wife. We might read this ending as the sign of a successful narrative of containment, successful in the sense that the woman's propensity for vanishing and returning has finally been brought under control. But in spite of the gestures the film makes in this direction Heath ultimately transcends the star's disappearance into the role of invisible wife. Once out of hospital she does realize her sins and she does submissively acknowledge that she has "debts to pay," both to Bellows and to her husband. Yet, if the fading star film is supposed to assert the star's demise, this film fails. A certain spectacle of loss accompanies the enslavement of the glorious star to her paralyzed husband. But even as Joyce waves to the bandaged Mr. Heath, we note visual echoes of the vertical distance established between lovers in the earlier balcony scene. Heath as Juliet does fall down before reaching the end of her speech at the film's opening, but she returns in this final scene in the space of Romeo down below, playing the male lead. After leaving hospital, Heath visits her producer (alone), telling him that she must reopen the play in order to pay off her debts. Although the film suggests at one level that Heath returns to the stage not as a star but as a working wife, we cannot help but think that she transcends her punishment simply by refusing to disappear. At the end, we are left with a woman who decides to go back on the stage in order to become the financial provider for not one but two hopeless and ruined men.

Joyce Heath's returnability is not bound by the limits of the film *Dangerous,* for she makes a feminist comeback in Yvonne Rainer's 1985 film *The Man Who Envied Women,* which explicitly addresses the problematic relationship between the female actress and cinematic visibility. Trying to undo the visual accessibility of the female star, Rainer casts two people in the role of the main female protagonist, Trisha.

While Trisha Brown produces the voice, Kate Flax provides Trisha's elusive body, a body that is only ever fleetingly available to the camera's gaze, thereby disrupting the possibility of any simple identification with a single cinematic image. And, as I will later point out, this technique of separating the body and the voice of the actress finds an ancestor in another Davis fading star movie, Robert Aldrich's *Whatever Happened to Baby Jane?* Toward the middle of Rainer's film, we see Jack Deller, the main male protagonist, in a therapy session. As he sits on a chair facing away from a screen that hangs behind him, Trisha's voice-over discusses the dominant paradigms of the heterosexual relationship: "In our culture woman is sexually desirable only as long as her sexuality can also inspire fear. For the heterosexual male, woman is dangerous because she menstruates. . . . Sex for most heterosexual men is by definition an enactment of power, the kind of power over a woman that is intended to demean her whether or not she engages with that aspect of it. . . . Good grief! And here I've been thinking all these years that sex was fun."[23] In the course of this monologue, Bette Davis appears on the screen behind Jack Deller in the role of Joyce Heath, cued by Trisha's reference to our culture's view of the sexual woman as "dangerous." "You may never love me," Heath tells Bellows, "but you'll find you'll always come back to me. And each time you return it'll cost you more and more until you've spent your career, your ambitions, your dreams. Oh, I'm bad for people." At one level, this return to Heath (and she reminds us that we *will* keep returning to her, even if we try to leave her, perhaps as independent feminist film tries to leave the paradigms offered by Hollywood cinema) illustrates the stereotype of the dangerous woman Trisha rejects. But a more nuanced reading of this citation might also note a certain continuum between Trisha and Heath. Like Trisha, Heath refuses to present herself as an object-to-be-looked-at in the film's opening scene. Asserting her agency over the passive fading of the falling star, an agency that allows her to refuse then reclaim identity at will, she turns her face away from the camera, hides at the edge of the frame, and disidentifies with her own name, telling Farnsworth, "No, you've made a mistake." She also embodies the metaphor of the star in her constant oscillation between the states of absence and presence, visibility and invisibility, states that are always contaminated by the more ambivalent space of vanishing.

Hollywood's double focus on the fading star in 1950 with Billy Wilder's *Sunset Boulevard* and Joseph Mankiewicz's *All about Eve* provides us with two quite different modes of stellar demise. Both films open in temporal crisis, beginning at the end. Mirroring the time of the celestial stars, these films create a present that is always inexorably bound up with both the past and the future. Addison DeWitt's voice-over introduces us to Lloyd Richards, a playwright, stressing that the only function of the writer is "to construct a tower so that the world can applaud a light, which flashes on top of it. And no brighter light has ever dazzled the eye than Eve Harrington. Eve . . . but more of Eve later, all about Eve in fact." Although Margo's stardom should precede that of Eve chronologically, it is with Eve's dazzling shine that this film begins before the future-present of this moment moves forward into the past of Margo's shining. As DeWitt repeats the over-determined name of this female star in the context of these temporal confusions, we are forced to contemplate the relationship between time and Eve. And we are not surprised when he tells us that there will be "more of Eve later," for "eve," is always, even in its present, the moment before, is therefore always, at some level, "l'Eve future."

Immediately following this encounter with the thrice-named Eve, DeWitt turns his and our attention to Margo, this time repeating not her name but her condition as a star. The beginning of *Sunset Boulevard* reveals the dead body of the screenwriter, guaranteeing not only that Norma Desmond will never make a comeback but that she will be swallowed up by one of two institutions of disappearance—the mental asylum or the prison. By contrast, the voice-over of Addison DeWitt lingers on metaphor of the star and insists not only on the star's past but on her present and future as well: "Margo Channing is a star of the theater. She made her first stage appearance at the age of four in *A Midsummer Night's Dream*. She played a fairy and entered, quite unexpectedly, stark naked. She has been a star ever since. Margo is a great star, a true star. She never was, or will be, anything less, or anything else." Although Lucy Fischer has suggested, rightly, that the genre of the fading star film works to dispose of the mature woman, *All about Eve*'s opening scene (the endpoint of the narrative) complicates Fischer's reading by insistently drawing attention to the star's inseparability from the play of tenses. True star presence, DeWitt suggests, remains tied to both the star's past and future. There can be no escape from this temporal oscillation, and the film's recognition of Margo's place within the temporal complexity of the star metaphor fundamentally separates her from Norma Desmond. Indeed, the primary difference between *All about Eve* and *Sunset Boulevard* lies in the distinction between the vanishing woman who returns and the woman who permanently disappears. This is not to say that *All about Eve* has no truck with the permanent disappearance of women. As Patricia White argues in her astute reading of the inhabitants of the visual landscape of *All about Eve,* women do disappear in the course of the film, and these disappearing women are marked as lesbian: "Inexplicably, Birdie disappears about midway through the film, her function made redundant by that of Eve, a less benign personal assistant" (*Uninvited,* 176). Although this is ostensibly a narrative about the displacement of Margo by Eve, White correctly suggests that "in the film's memory it is Margo who displaces Eve, and Bette who displaces Anne Baxter, not the other way round" (213). We might well attribute Margo's persistence in the film's memory to her decision to embrace "womanhood" and leave the queer world of female stars and fans behind her. But despite the heteronormativity of Margo's continued visibility, that is, despite her ability to remain the object of the camera's interest at the apparent "end" of her story (the film's opening), as Eve fails to do at the end of hers (the film concludes by focusing on the endlessly multiplied images of "Phoebe," a member of the Eve Harrington fan club), the portrayal of Margo in the fading star role still offers important examples of Davis's disruptive and iconoclastic relationship with the fantasy image of the female star.

Both Norma Desmond and Margo Channing appear as mute in these opening scenes, which look forward to the films' endings, the narrative being controlled by disembodied male voices.[24] But, while Desmond has disappeared completely from view by the beginning/end of Wilder's narrative, Margo Channing remains an object of interest for the camera's gaze. At the Sarah Siddons Society dinner, Eve Harrington, an ambitious young actress who has usurped Margo's place on the stage, will receive an award for distinguished achievement in the theater, which, in the words of Addison DeWitt, "was originally intended for Margo Channing." Although Eve has supposedly displaced Margo by this point in the story, the camera yearns for a close-up of Davis in these opening moments, perhaps to expose the humiliation of the aged star in the moment of her deposition but more likely to capitalize on the face of a still-shining star.

Feminist criticism has long been troubled by the close-up. As B. Ruby Rich points out, filmmakers like Chantal Ackerman have worked extensively with the alternatives of medium and long shots in order to free the female character "from the exploitation of a zoom lens and to grant her an integrity of private space usually denied in close-ups, thereby also freeing the audience from the insensitivity of a camera barrelling in to magnify a woman's emotional crisis."[25] Whereas Norma Desmond is "ready for her close-up" to the very end, everything about Margo Channing resists the triple appeal of the camera for a direct gaze at the space of loss, offering the spectator nothing but a series of sidelong glances.[26] Her body remains diagonally positioned away from the camera's lens, and the cut of her dress only serves to emphasize her pulling away, her active resistance to visibility. The strong diagonal cut of her dress's off-center V neck provides an arrowlike indicator away from her cleavage and underscores yet again the asymmetry of her posture for anyone who fails to notice how this body literally gives its audience the cold shoulder. As she shoos the waiter away with a flick of her hand, we cannot help but think that she does the same to us. At this moment of supposed disappearance, Margo is neither completely absent nor present, hovering instead in a space of active vanishing. When she finally does turn to face the camera, her bulging eyes challenge, even affront the viewer. They look back *too* directly and pressure us to look away. "What demands they make on us!" writes Charles Affron, in another context, of Davis's eyes. "Their power is frightening."[27]

These early shots of Margo contrast strikingly with our first full shot of Eve Harrington (Anne Baxter), the rising star, which is accompanied by DeWitt's second series of repetitive utterances of Eve's name: "Eve. Eve the golden girl, the cover girl, the girl next door, the girl on the moon. Time has been good to Eve. Life goes where she goes. She's been profiled, covered, revealed, reported, what she eats and what she wears and whom she knows and where she was and when and where she's going. Eve. You all know all about Eve." Eve is on good terms with time. But, although her past and future seem relatively certain, her presence is more elusive. We may know where she's been and where she's going, but it becomes hard to tell where she is in the "now" of the film (which is in fact the film's future) as the camera struggles to present her to us. Proudly occupying center screen, flanked on either side by an admiring male spectator, Eve appears to offer exactly what the camera demands: a full frontal gaze, face reaching out to its fans, a centrality and symmetry complimented by her dress, with its neckline plunging into her cleavage rather than away from it.

But the rising star's relationship with the camera and visibility itself suddenly becomes more complicated. As Eve reaches out to accept the award that will (supposedly) confirm both her star status and Margo's fall, press cameras flash so brightly that even hyperspectacular Eve, who moments earlier seemed to be the ideal object of the gaze, disappears into the light. And at this moment of Eve's bodily disappearance, which is markedly passive in contrast to Margo's active turning away, we remember that, although this story ostensibly deals with stars of the stage, the rhetoric is distinctly cinematic.[28] The flash of the camera may result in bodily absence, but projected on the oil painting behind Eve we see her shadow, recalling nothing so clearly as the shadows of Norma Desmond's celluloid self projected nightly onto the home movie screen behind a different oil painting in the former star's mansion. Prefiguring Eve's own displacement by the multiplicitous Phoebe at the end of the film, this moment suggests the inevitability of female disappearance within the space of photographic reproduction. Yet the images of Davis defy this luminous fade-out, and her face and voice persist, not least because of their stubborn and confrontational relationship with the image ideals themselves.

Shining Stars

Ask Richard Dyer, one of the founding theorists of stardom, why (white female) stars shine, and he might well answer that they don't. In *White,* Dyer argues: "Idealized white women are bathed in and permeated by light. It streams through them and falls on to them from above. In short, they glow. They glow, rather than shine. Shine, on the other hand, is light bouncing back off the surface of the skin. It is the mirror effect of sweat. . . . Dark skin, too, when it does not absorb the light, may bounce it back. Non-white and sometimes working-class white women are liable to shine rather than glow in photographs and films."[29] But if white female stars usually do not shine we need to ask ourselves why Margo shines conspicuously at different points in *All about Eve* in a way that other stars (Celeste Holm and rising star Marilyn Monroe, for example) never do.[30] Margo first shines in the dressing room scene that immediately follows the Sarah Siddons award ceremony, the scene in which she meets Eve, the fan. The camera moves in on Margo's face (still the face of a star at this point, though we have already seen the film's (failed) attempt to show her after her fall), trying to capture a close-up. But Margo resists the intrusion of the camera by smothering her face in cold cream (or "vanishing cream," as this type of invisible face cream is sometimes called), shielding herself in a slick shiny surface that bounces the gaze right off. Her forehead, nose, and cheeks all reflect the light so thoroughly that the features themselves disappear, rendering the face only partially visible, a mottled spectacle of presence and absence. Again, Margo the star appears as the agent of her own vanishing, defiantly applying the shine that throws a spanner in the works of the vision machine. Her face not only refuses to be visible; it also exposes the supposedly hidden apparatus of cinema that attempts to construct the illusion of the star's luminous presence in the first place. The lights in Margo's dressing room are behind her, but her mirror face reflects the glare of the studio lights that try to make her glow. This vanishing lady, with her patchwork presence, reveals what she should conceal and conceals what she should reveal.

Margo's shine dares us to try to idealize her through the mask and seems to disrupt the possibility of any spectatorial identification with or desire for the star. Roland Barthes, for example, would not lose himself in this human image, as he did in the face of Garbo, being more likely to find his own reflection in its shiny surface.[31] It effectively resists (white) stardom and the conventions of female beauty that belong to it. Like the grotesque mask of makeup worn by Baby Jane, a mask whose "ultrawhiteness" again distinguishes her as "not white" (or "not Blanche"), this "junkyard's" shine complicates the operations of identification and desire. In rejecting, or failing to access, the conventions of white beauty, Davis repels rather than invites the kind of identification that Barthes remembers.[32] Yet in Davis's embrace of this not whiteness an interesting space of something akin to cross-racial identification, or, to speak more accurately, cross-racial identification with Davis's disidentification, begins to emerge. In *The Devil Finds Work* (1976), James Baldwin writes: "So, here, now, was Bette Davis, on that Saturday afternoon, in close-up, over a champagne glass, pop-eyes popping. I was astounded. . . . For here, before me, after all, was a *movie star: white:* and if she was white and a movie star, she was *rich:* and she was *ugly.* . . . Out of bewilderment . . . and also because I sensed something menacing and unhealthy (for me, certainly) in the face on the screen, I gave Davis's skin the dead-white greenish cast of something crawling from under a rock, but I was held, just the same, by the tense intelligence of the forehead, the disaster of the lips: and when she moved, she moved just like a nigger."[33] Although Margo's shine, her deliberate self-vanishing, makes it impossible for "one" to "lose oneself" in her face, Baldwin here seems to find not himself but something not unlike himself in this space of the not white, precisely as a result of the disidentificatory stance Davis adopts. In her excellent reading of *The Devil Finds Work,* Jane M. Gaines writes, "What [Baldwin] does is quite extraordinary—making out of Davis something like and not like himself, something to aid identification as well as to prevent it absolutely—to ward it off. . . . Think what is accomplished by producing Bette Davis as green! She inhabits the world of mixed-race society; she is alien to it. She is a frog. She is a lizard."[34] Clearly, Baldwin's complex relationship with the color of Davis's skin reveals that he has "discovered something about the arbitrariness of race," as Gaines suggests (30). However, we need also to note that Baldwin's discovery is in part made possible through Davis's active ambivalence toward the whiteness of the female star, emerging here in the form of excessive shine. Although Baldwin's production of Davis as green is certainly a startling move in its own right, Davis makes herself open to this "strange" color both through her failure to occupy the space of whiteness and through the awareness of the constructed nature of whiteness that her failure provokes. In the presence of her ultrawhiteness and brightness, the white "ideal" repeatedly eludes us. As Dyer has argued in *White,* "Whiteness as an ideal can never be attained, not only because white skin can never be hue white, but because ideally white is absence: to be really, absolutely white is to be nothing" (78).

Margo's face cream bends the conventions of Hollywood makeup to the breaking point. Instead of creating the illusion that the perfect (but artificial) surface is the face of the star, the excessive shine of Margo draws attention to the gap between the painted mask and the surface of the face, a gap that can be utilized for the purpose of establishing a degree of agency in the visual field. When stars shine, they do so in excess of themselves, and this excess can be both the cause of their downfall and the source of their resilience.

The Star (1952)

Only two years after *All about Eve,* Davis played Margaret Elliott, a fallen star role apparently modeled on Joan Crawford.[35] Davis told *Playboy* in 1983 that she "adored that script," the role brought her her ninth Oscar nomination, and the film was generally well received by the press. *Time*'s critic declared: "Her performance as an ex-first lady of the screen is first rate. . . . It is a marathon one-woman show and, all in all, proof that Bette Davis—with her strident voice, nervous stride, mobile hands, and popping eyes—is still her own best imitator."[36] Although the 1952 return of Davis to the fading star role, received by this reviewer as an imitation of herself, clearly belongs in a continuum with her three other films in this genre, Stuart Heisler's *The Star* has in many ways a closer relationship with Wilder's *Sunset Boulevard* than *All about Eve.* At first glance, Heisler tries to present the older star as a "profound site of loss" in the style of Norma Desmond rather than perpetuating Mankiewicz's notion of the star as a figure who will never fade. If *All about Eve* establishes the futurity of the star, her resilience to complete disappearance, *The Star* works to clarify the ambivalence and uncontainability of Margo Channing. Although nowhere near as sophisticated as *Sunset Boulevard, The Star* resembles Wilder's film in that it adamantly refuses the ambivalent presence of the older female star, going to extreme and sometimes violent measures to ensure the impossibility of her comeback. In the course of this one film, the former queen of the silver screen is jailed for drunk driving and subsequently humiliated in the press; she works as a sales clerk in a department store; her landlords evict her from her apartment; she goes bankrupt; and toward the end of the film Jim, her lover, slaps her to her senses and throws her across the room. However, in spite of the overwhelming odds Elliott faces, she, like the fading stars who precede her, comes to embody the star persona of the fearlessly resilient Bette Davis, who has by this point made the fading star role a key vehicle for her professional success. Consequently, if we read each of Davis's star films in relation to the other three, it becomes possible to regard even the most dejected of female stars as a site of ambivalent visibility rather than a further example of the eradication of the older woman.

In the opening scene, we see former star Margaret Elliott walking down the street in a depressed manner that cannot help but recall Joyce Heath's opening street walk in *Dangerous* seventeen years earlier. But we also remember an earlier spectacle of female vanishing when Elliott stops abruptly before a show window to regard a photograph of herself as a young star on display. This image appears in the window of an auction house because the "personal effects" of Margaret Elliott are up for sale. "She *used* to be your favorite star," we hear the auctioneer cry. "Show Margaret Elliott you haven't forgotten." Just as L. Frank Baum's Chicago storefront staged the spectacle of female vanishing as a mode of profit making, here, too, the sight of the vanishing star aims to lure shoppers into the auction house. Just as Baum's window display marketed the necessary accoutrements of femininity, so this shop window presents the trappings of female stardom, the material objects that supposedly make the star what she is, the things that, when absent, render her nothing more than a site of vanished presence. The star emerges here as a collection of things, material fragments, and when Elliott's agent, Harry, emerges holding a chandelier lamp that once belonged to her, the film implies that even the star's shine can be detached and sold. As Harry stops to explain to Margaret his participation in this metaphorical act of dismemberment, we hear the auctioneer utter for the first time what will become a leitmotiv of the film: "Going, going, gone." Although these words emerge ostensibly in relation to the items on sale within the building, they metonymically implicate the star herself in the fantasy of a woman who will not only vanish but will disappear for good. We might, however, simultaneously read the reiteration of "going, going, gone" as symptomatic of the *impermanence* of vanishing, something that the star persona of Davis dramatically emphasizes. The characters within the film continue to remind us that the star is in the process of vanishing, and will ultimately disappear, only because this star—Davis—so persistently comes back.

The Star challenges the somewhat tragic aura that usually surrounds the figure of the falling star not only because of the impact Davis's persona has on the "disappearing" role but as a result of the ambivalent responses of the "viewing public" as they emerge in the course of the film. Harry takes Margaret to a nearby café, where she begs him first for a chance at another part and finally for money. Pleading her case, she insists, "I was a star, Harry." Rather than strengthening her claim, however, Elliott's statement, with its unfortunate employment of the past tense, seems to confirm her belief in her own demise, even in the moment she attempts to assert her continued presence. Soon after, the waitress brings the check to Harry; turning to Elliot, she asks, "Say, aren't you Margaret Elliott?" When Elliot affirms her identity (in a way that Joyce Heath will not do, responding "No, you must be mistaken"), the waitress continues, "that's what I told Bill back there . . . but he bet me you wasn't." Elliot turns to Harry and declares, "You see, the public remembers," but this statement can only be half true. Offering a gendered representation of both stardom and spectatorship, the film depicts the male spectator, Bill, as being unable to recognize Margaret Elliot once she has lost the material trappings of stardom. He "bets" accordingly, but by choosing to assert his way of seeing through the *bet,* a verb that unconsciously recalls the star persona who plays the role of Margaret—Bette—who has found fame through her repetition of spectacular female fading and return—we know immediately that Bill will lose this one. He asserts quite simply that "she wasn't," a grammatical error implying that when the male spectator no longer recognizes the female star she not only "never will be," but "never is," and "never was." In contrast, the female spectator—embodied not only by the waitress but later by the elderly female shoppers in the department store where Margaret briefly works—has no trouble recognizing Elliot without the star's accoutrements, suggesting that there must be more than one way for a star to be visible and for spectators to look at the stars.

Unlike many other fading stars, Margaret Elliott is also a mother, and throughout the film maternity and stardom intertwine. After talking with Harry, Elliott visits her daughter Gretchen, played by rising star Natalie Wood, at the mansion of her former husband's new family.[37] And as the new wife Peggy informs her, Margaret lost her husband and child as a result of her exclusive attention to her star career. Interestingly, Gretchen emerges as a figure determined to establish the truth of her mother's star presence or absence. She persistently interrogates Elliott about the grammar of her stardom, whether it belongs in the past or the present tense. First, she asks her mother whether she can come to live with her, to which Elliot replies "mother is gone most of the day." In speaking of herself here as a mother, Elliott loses the ability to use the first-person singular, as though the "I" disappears in the space of the maternal, just as *mother* disappears in the space of the (star's) working day: "mother's gone." Gretchen pushes her for details, using a present tense formulation that makes this a question both about where Elliott spends her days and where she is right now, suggesting that, although she stands before her daughter and talks with her, her presence is radically in doubt: "But where are you?" "At mother's studio," Elliott responds curtly. Later in the scene, Gretchen asks suspiciously, "You *are* a big movie star, aren't you?" She then goes on to explain that the kids at school say Elliot is a has-been and that Janie Marx says her father, a writer, "told her mother that you were all washed up."[38] Insisting again on her continued presence, Elliott states, "You tell this Janie Marx that your mother *is* a star." But Gretchen will not let the star be. "I know you *were,* but *are you now*?" Lacking an Addison de Witt to assert on her behalf that "she never was, and never will be anything less or anything else," Elliott must insist herself that "if you're a star, you don't stop being a star," a statement that reflects a change from the beginning of the film when, we remember, she insisted to her agent, "I *was* a star." Dissatisfied still with her mother's protestations, Gretchen states simply, "Well, they say you'll never make another picture," forcing Elliott to lie about shooting a new movie in three weeks, and with this lie Gretchen finally ends her inquisition.

Traumatized by this temporal exposure, Elliott picks up her Oscar from her tiny apartment and takes him out in the car to get drunk. She makes a toast to "absent friends," and we suspect that the missing mutual friend she and Oscar honor is the star herself. Elliot takes Oscar on a guided tour of the Hollywood mansions, stopping only at the former home of Margaret Elliott, to whom she again refers in the third person. Adopting a maternal stance toward the statue of the Oscar, perhaps because of the star's absence, Elliot cries, "I remember the day you came home. That was a day! Going, going, gone." With these words, which function like an incantation designed to enact the disappearance they describe, the star seems to recede further still; yet, although these words describe the star's demise, the fact that Elliott speaks them means that she still has a voice. As she careens through the Hollywood streets, she muses aloud, "Wonder where I am?" suggesting that she has lost her self as well as her way but also that she is actively in search of a sense of her own existence. The space of living repeatedly eludes the fading star, making life itself seem impossible. First, she loses her mansion and the family that makes it a home. Then, as a result of her drunk driving, she finds herself in jail, although her real crime seems to be, like Norma Desmond's, the fading star's refusal to disappear, which constitutes a fundamental threat to the society she inhabits. Jim Johannsen, a former actor turned shipbuilder, who has himself turned his back on spectacular male visibility, pays Elliott's bail and takes her home to her "tiny apartment," but even this diminutive living space has been repossessed by her creditors, leaving her with no choice but to accompany Jim back to his place. Having lost everything, including, it appears, her right to make decisions about her own habitat, Jim tells her, "You're going to stay here a few days, and then we'll decide where you're going," to which Elliott can only respond, "Going, going, gone." A voice on the radio confirms the disappearance she suspects: "Since she was released on bail, efforts to locate Miss Elliott have been without avail. Where she is, nobody knows."

Although the Hollywood star does seem to have vanished, Jim encourages Elliott to think of life beyond pictures and suggests that she apply for a job as a sales clerk in a department store, reminding us again of the interrelationship between these two institutions of spectacular yet evanescent femininity. Although Elliott does briefly work as a clerk in the lingerie department, she soon walks out and returns to her agent to demand a new part, any part. Harry manages to get her a screen test for the role of an older sister, but Elliott secretly hopes to be cast as the younger sister by refusing to "look old" during the test. Margaret "fails" the screen test within the narrative, yet her excessive performance also constitutes a moment of triumph for the older female spectators the film has already presented to us in various forms. These spectators (and their like) continue to recognize Elliott in spite of her losses, and for them Elliott's portrayal of the older woman as highly sexualized, though censured and mocked within the narrative, offers female spectators a different kind of viewing plea-sure, one that acknowledges an alternative to an age-based sexuality in women. Toward the end of the film, a young director approaches Elliott at a party and offers her the role of a fading star: "It's a Holly-wood story, but it might have happened anywhere," he (wrongly) tells her, adding that the woman could be, among other things, the head of a department store. The character "has been on a sleigh ride, but she can't face the fact that it's over." When Elliott asks how the director intends to get sympathy for the character, he replies, "Not sympathy, Miss Elliott, pity. This is a great tragedy. My character was denied the privilege and the glory of just being a woman." Refusing pity, Elliott drives to the home of her former husband to pick up Gretchen, then on to the home of Jim. They rush into the arms of Johannsen, thanks to whom Elliott will presumably be able to bask in the privilege and glory of being not just a woman but a wife and mother, too. But can we really trust the young director's assessment of how audiences will respond to the falling star figure? Is pity a sure bet on his part? The falling star films of Bette Davis suggest otherwise. Although we may never hear of Margaret Elliott again, Joan Crawford and Bette Davis, two older stars whose own life stories helped to produce the story of Elliott's ultimate demise, return with a vengeance ten years later to insist once more that, although stars may vanish, they do not completely disappear.

Whatever Happened to Baby Jane? (1962)

Robert Aldrich's 1962 fading star film opens with what might well be the creepiest song in film history. Baby Jane Hudson steps onto the vaudeville stage in her baby doll dress and blonde ringlets and be-gins to sing the following song, accompanied by her father on the piano: "I've written a letter to daddy, / His address is heaven above, / I've written dear daddy we miss you, / And wish we were with you to love. / Instead of a stamp I put kisses, / The postman says that's best to do. / I've written a letter to daddy, / Saying 'I love you.'" As if the incestuous undertones of this little ditty weren't enough to set the appropriate mood for any horror film, Baby Jane's theme tune also invokes a distinct sense of necrophilia. This opening scene marks the peak of Baby Jane's career, the star at her brightest. Things only go downhill from there. Yet this, the darkest of Bette Davis's fading star films, reminds us that a star is born always in death, appearing only against the backdrop of "heaven above," home of the dead father. The star's macabre essence announces itself explicitly after the performance when a young boy carries a stiff, corpselike reproduction of the shining star. Meanwhile, the shameless father pimps his daughter to the audience, encouraging them to purchase their own "original" Baby Jane doll, complete with "real hair"—a detail that evokes hordes of cropped, or, worse, dead, little blonde girls.

The camera then cuts to the lobby where these dolls are lined up in coffinlike boxes. At one level, we might read this appearance of the entombed star body as a successful fantasy of the faded star in miniature, as a narrative of female containment and disappearance. But, although this child star masquerades as a prepubescent virgin dressed in white, easy to do away with, her closest relative is not in fact her dead daddy, whom she longs to join in heaven, but the vampire, the transgressively sexual, endlessly reproducing undead, who, like the stars, only comes out at night. In their rows of coffins, these dead girls resemble nothing so much as Dracula's brides. Hovering between coffin and stage, absence and presence, this star reproduces herself vampirically not only through the dolls but through the spectatorial identification she invites: be like me.

Baby Jane disturbs not because she is dead but because she seems dead. And we can locate the source of this troubling semblance primarily in her relationship with the process of embodiment. As Michel Chion points out in *The Voice and Cinema*, sound film is fundamentally dualistic split down the middle between body and voice. Although talkies work to restore voices to bodies, the match is never seamless and the sound film itself marks the site of the suture. Most films try hard to hide or disavow this dualism. Indeed, Chion describes the successful "embodiment" of the voice as one of the defining ideological features of French and American cinema: "More than others, these cinemas seem obsessively concerned with synchronization that has no detectable 'seams.' "[39] But, he goes on to argue, "In French, the term *embodiment* (mise-en-corps) is reminiscent of *entombment* (mise en bière) and also to *internment* (mise en terre)" (140), implying that the felicitous embodiment of the voice always, at some level, invokes the spectacle of death. The extent to which Aldrich's film manages to embody Jane's voice determines the success of her entombment, and a close analysis of this opening scene reveals that her embodiment is anything but complete. When Jane sings her opening song, we feel disturbed, not only because she addresses her love song to her dead father but because her big voice does not fit her little body. The maturity of the voice signals to the spectator/listener that this voice does not belong to the child star Julie Allred, who lip-synchs the song, and the film's titles confirm that the singer is not Allred but Debbie Burton.[40]

Through this mismatch of body and voice, this intrusion into the illusion of the star's bodily integrity, the sound technology that contributes to the production of the star enters the spectator's consciousness, just as Margo Channing's shiny face cream inappropriately rendered visible the presence of the studio lights in *All about Eve.* But further, and more importantly, this disjunction ruptures the "wholeness" of the star's presence, leaving us instead with two vanishing stars, neither present nor absent, a body without a voice and a voice without a body. Although this fragmentation of the star body initially seems to threaten the possibility of "presence," the fundamental elusiveness of these stars ultimately makes them far more resilient to the process of disappearance. If the voice is never properly *mise-en-corps,* how can it ever be successfully *mise en terre*? Although the film shows us a series of entombed Baby Janes in the opening shots, something is missing from these dolls, and that something is the voice without a body, which will certainly come back to haunt us.

If French and American cinema rely so profoundly on the ideological operations of synchronization, then the disruption of this illusion of unity obviously presents us with one strategy of resistance to dominant institutional practices. Yvonne Rainer mobilizes this separation of body and voice in *The Man Who Envied Women,* as does Marguerite Duras in *India Song* (1974). Chion, in *The Voice and Cinema,* writes: "Marguerite Duras coined the idea that the contemporary cinema stringently requires voices to be *nailed down* to bodies.

It's this nailing, which for her is a form of cheating, that she tries to break with in *India Song*. Here she unfastened the voices and allowed them to roam free. "Nailing down" nicely captured the rigidity and constraint in the conventions that have evolved for making film voices appear to come from bodies" (130). In *The Acoustic Mirror*, Kaja Silverman similarly draws attention to feminist filmmakers' pursuit of "a vocal itinerary": "Rather than forging closer connections between the female voice and the female body, Bette Gordon, Patricia Gruben, Yvonne Rainer, and Sally Potter have all experimented boldly with the female voice-off and voice-over, jettisoning synchronization, symmetry, and simultaneity in favor of dissonance and dislocation" (165).[41] In *Whatever Happened to Baby Jane?* desynchronization, the disruption of the star's identification with her image, occurs not only through the body's separation from the voice but through a process of "unnailing" the body from time itself. But the successful melding of body and voice founders with this temporal incoherence, the term *synchronization* coming from the Greek for *together* and *time*.

Although *Baby Jane*'s primary box office selling point was that it offered spectators the chance to see the notorious and aging rivals Joan Crawford and Bette Davis play opposite each other in the role of has-beens, the film frustrates the viewers' desires by perpetually deferring the promised spectacle of these mature star bodies. The first few scenes of the film jump from 1917 to 1935 to "yesterday," leaping from one star body (or, in the case of Baby Jane, two) to the next, offering us a paradigm of viewing that is always deferred and disrupted. As fragmentation becomes the dominant spectatorial mode *within* the film, the various viewers become increasingly less passive, entering interactively into the spaces that emerge between the star fragments. Cutting from the disjointed double presence of the "original" 1917 Baby Jane to 1935, we catch our first glimpse of Bette Davis. We are, however, doubly disappointed to find that she appears on screen alone and that we see not the fallen face of a fifty-three-year-old Davis but a twenty-four-year-old Davis in her role as an unemployed typist in Alfred E. Green's B movie *Parachute Jumper* (1933). The camera cuts between the faces of the young Davis and two producers, who are clearly unhappy with these rushes of the latest Jane Hudson movie. "She stinks," complains one producer, shifting Jane momentarily out of the audiovisual and into the olfactory realm. Just as Baby

Jane's stage performance evokes an uncanny awareness of the mismatch between body and voice, so Jane Hudson's movie raises the question of vocal authenticity. "She's got a southern accent like I got a southern accent!" complains one producer, echoing the original reviews of *Parachute Jumper*, which noted Davis's southern accent in quite ambiguous terms.[42] When the projectionist asks the producer if he will want to see the movie again, the producer, belying the star's inevitable return, declares, "No one's ever gonna want to see that movie again."

Another confusing temporal leap takes us simultaneously backward and forward in time to "yesterday," where we encounter Crawford's image for the first time. Like the celestial star, this mature actress presents herself to us not as she is but as she was, appearing, like Davis, first as a citation from an earlier film, a television rerun on the neighbors' screen. The neighbors, a mother and daughter, seem enraptured by the return of the young Blanche Hudson in their living room, but again the film disrupts the possibility of viewing pleasure for spectators in living rooms and movie theaters alike. Stopping abruptly in the middle of a romantic love scene, the film gives way to an advertisement for "Iliad" dog food. But even as this interruption frustrates the viewer, vanishing the star from our screens just as identification seemed possible, the disruption makes space for a different type of pleasure, the pleasure of moving out of the position of silent spectator and into that of interactive observer. The television presenter opens the discussion by telling the viewers how wonderful he thinks Blanche Hudson is, but the mother and daughter continue to converse about the future visibility of the star on the screen who also happens to be the star next door.

A final cut takes us into the house of the Hudson sisters, where the same rerun plays on Blanche's television screen. When we do finally encounter the mature face of Joan Crawford, it is not, or not just, the face of a star but also the face of a spectator. Embodying the position of the narcissistic female spectator that feminist film theory has reacted so strongly against, Blanche's glowing expression reveals the extent to which she finds herself rapt in her own younger image. In the kitchen below, we see Davis's grotesquely made-up face for the first time, an ugly face that affronts the viewer. As she slugs back a drink (obviously not her first of the day), we note the poster that hangs on the Hudson sisters' kitchen wall, a zodiacal chart whose presence reminds us that the story of these two sisters, like that of Norma Desmond with her astrologer's chart, has everything to do with the temporal life of the celestial stars. Jane lurches up the stairs, enters Blanche's bedroom, takes a look around, and switches the television off immediately, actively disrupting her sister's narcissistic pleasure. Blanche, incapable of intervening because she is bound to a wheelchair, protests, "I was watching that." Jane replies simply, "Then you're an idiot."

Child stars become voiceless bodies and bodiless voices, voiceless bodies become dead dolls, dead dolls become film failures, and film stars become crippled spectators. In these opening scenes, the body of the star is anything but stable. And, although this, the last, most excessive, and most violent of the four Davis fading star films, seems determined to do away with this endlessly returning star, we realize that the narrative possibility of the star's total disappearance founders on the prior impossibility of true star presence. Whereas *The Star* more successfully establishes the illusion that Margaret Elliot was once a real presence, a presence that makes her ultimate disappearance imaginable, *Whatever Happened to Baby Jane?* begins by undermining the metaphysical terms on which the genre of the fading star film depends. Unlike the more stable Margaret Elliot, whose trajectory from "favorite star of the silver screen" to has-been the film ostensibly delineates, stars in *Baby Jane* have always oscillated in the space between absence and presence. The ambivalence of vanishing is their domain, and this gives them a degree of resilience to disappearance that Margaret Elliot does not have.

Not content with the return of Blanche Hudson on her television screen, the nosy neighbor decides that she must see the aging Blanche in person and goes round to the Hudson house with an armful of freshly cut gladioli. Once again Jane refuses to permit the pleasure of looking, telling the neighbor: "Mrs. Bates . . . my sister doesn't ever go out. She's not fit to receive visitors." When Blanche asks who was at the door Jane informs her dismissively, "Only that nosy Mrs. Bates going on about your picture last night." Blanche, ecstatic, exclaims, "Oh really? Did she like it?" Repulsed by her sister's desire to be looked at, Jane adopts a grotesque smile, a pantomime imitation of Blanche's joy, echoing her words and throwing them back in her face:

"Oh really? Did she like it?" This moment marks another fundamental tear in the fabric of the film's narrative, for the voice that emerges out of Jane's mouth is neither Davis's own raspy voice nor an imitation of Crawford but Crawford's own unmistakable smooth, deep tones. Just as the child star sang with someone else's voice, here, too, Jane becomes a body without a voice, a cipher for the free-floating voice of another.[43]

The catalyst for this detachment of voices from bodies is the mother next door, Mrs. Bates, an ironic and complicated recall of another Mrs. Bates, who had haunted the screen two years earlier in Alfred Hitchcock's *Psycho,* a film that explores precisely this territory of what Michel Chion calls "the impossible attachment of a voice to a body" or "impossible embodiment" (*Voice and Cinema,* 140). "Real embodiment," claims Chion, "comes only with the simultaneous presentation of the visible body with the audible voice, a way for the body to swear 'this is my voice' and for the voice to swear 'this is my body.' It must be a kind of marriage with a contract, consecrating the bonding of the voice to the habitat of the body, defusing and warding off the acousmetric forces. Which doesn't happen [in *Psycho*]" (144). For Chion, not surprisingly, Hitchcock's refusal to allow the voice and body to come together in the first Mrs. Bates constitutes a disturbing return to the magician's Vanishing Lady trick: "We expect de-acousmatization to happen here; Hitchcock gives it to us only halfway, like a magician at once showing it and conjuring it into thin air. The disappearing act consists, of course, in using the extreme high-angle shot that makes it hard to see, and also in fading out before we've been able to see or hear much of anything—just at the moment when we'd hoped we could have both voice and body *together*" (145–46). Of course, in *Baby Jane* we do have voice and body together, but it is the wrong voice, a voice that cannot declare in good faith "this is my body," and through this unfixing of the voice from the body Jane and Blanche align themselves with the magician's vanishing lady.

In *Baby Jane,* however, the person most closely associated with Norman Bates's dead mother is neither the grotesque Jane, who was in her youth already undead, nor Blanche, whose incarcerated immobility and shadowy presence in the window does resemble that of *Psycho*'s Mrs. Bates. Rather, Mrs. Bates makes her comeback in 1962 most explicitly in the form of the "nice" neighbor, Hollywood's ideal consumer of the "woman's film," a mother who loves to watch Blanche Hudson reruns with her daughter. While the first Mrs. Bates is in fact a silent stuffed puppet, brought to life only through the voice of the "psycho" son who so violently silences his mother, *Baby Jane* transforms this dead silent figure into a chatty critical spectator who shares her viewing space and thoughts with her daughter. Within the narrative of the film, the fading star enables and provokes the mode of critical and curious spectatorship that Mrs. Bates performs. Furthermore, the film implicitly presents this spectator as an intimate relation of, even a double of, the difficult and obstinate Baby Jane Hudson by casting Bette Davis's own daughter, B. D. (whose real name suggests that she is indeed another version of Davis), in the role of the neighbor's daughter. To be the mother of the daughter in this film, then, is to be both Mrs. Bates and the mother of Bette Davis's daughter, and in this sense the film works to reduce the distance that traditionally exists between viewer and spectator without collapsing one into the other. Playing with the memory of *Psycho,* in which the woman in the house next door is actually the same as the psycho in the building that is the primary spatial focus of the film, *Baby Jane* forces us to think carefully about the definition of passive and active spectatorship vis-à-vis the "actor" being watched. Just as the spectator-neighbor encroaches upon the identity position of the (fading) female star, so both former stars, Baby Jane and Blanche, repeatedly appear in the position of spectator, watching and commenting on movie reruns, performing before mirrors, and watching each other. But while *Psycho*'s Mrs. Bates—a dead woman whose voice is actually that of another and whose face horrifies us with its empty eye sockets—can do nothing "except just sit and stare like one of his stuffed birds," the Mrs. Bates we encounter in *Baby Jane* has eyes and words of her own. Deconstructing the opposition of star and spectator, this film opens a space where women appear on-screen as viewing figures rather than as mere objects to be viewed, presenting spectatorship itself as a mode of acting, which is in turn both a performance that shapes identity and a form of agency. No longer silent, the real mother of the fictional daughter of Mrs. Bates—Bette Davis—performs, mimics, and mocks with a voice that bellows throughout the film.

Baby Jane repeatedly stages scenes of watching again and, more specifically, of watching again, critically, in the company of others. Indeed, part of the pleasure we gain from this movie derives from joining a tradition of critical spectatorship that begins within the diegetic space. Watching, in *Baby Jane,* takes place not in the dark and hushed space of the cinema but in the living room, where people view movies together in broad daylight, finding time to discuss their reactions with each other in the critical gaps provided by commercial breaks and now by the option of pausing a video or DVD. Through its use of clips, this film forces us to experience the act of re-viewing, even if we only watch *Baby Jane* once. It offers us the pleasure of watching familiar clips again *with* the characters, but it simultaneously encourages us to think critically about the act of watching again, even in the moment when we do. The ambivalent pleasure of female spectatorship here does not require us to be "stuffed birds," and does not, or not only, come at the price of one's own disappearance, although we may at times find ourselves vanishing into a variety of Hollywood personae. These fading star films ask us to watch again, to watch critically, and to think about the consequences of this type of watching, making me think that, contrary to Jane's suggestion, we may not be idiots for watching old movies after all.[44]

As we approach the end of this inquiry concerning the proliferation of spectacular female vanishing that begins in the mid-nineteenth century and continues to appear throughout the twentieth century, we need to consider what kind of theory of vanishing we might begin to articulate in the wake of such diverse appearances and disappearances. Clearly, any theory of vanishing must necessarily also be an ambivalent theory. The vanishing body hovers between the ostensibly more stable sites of absence and presence, fundamentally disrupting the security and limits of both of these terms in useful ways. Vanishing, then, teeters on the brink of both absence and presence, refusing properly to resolve itself into either one or the other; consequently, these terms repeatedly haunt the space of vanishing, threatening to overtake it and undo its destabilizing force. As the *Oxford*

English Dictionary tell us, vanishing might be one of many things. To vanish might be (1) to disappear from sight or become invisible; (2) to disappear by decaying, coming to an end, or ceasing to exist; or (3) to cause to disappear or become invisible. Throughout the book, I have wrestled with the vexing question of how we move between each of these definitions and to suggest ways in which we might avoid unconsciously equating the space that allows a feminist exploitation of the power of invisible subjectivity with the space into which subjects (often marked female) are forcibly "vanished" at the hands of another, a space in which vanishing subjects may not only decay, come to an end, or cease to exist but may also do so invisibly. In the course of trying to make these distinctions, it has proved largely impossible to delineate a mode of vanishing that always works in benevolent ways. Vanishing will always be haunted by the specter of death, but this does not mean that we can do nothing with it. On the contrary, the fact that the spectacle of vanishing forces us to think simultaneously about our own freedom and power in relation to the possibility of another's death or injury seems to be where its theoretical usefulness resides. As I argue in chapter one, although the "success" of the magician's trick ostensibly depends upon our acceptance of the idea that seeing is believing, the person watching a magic act knows that he or she is being tricked, and part of the pleasure of this mode of spectatorship lies in trying to find the visual traces that exceed what we must see in order to believe. Magic provokes critical spectatorship through its self-acknowledged performance of undisclosed activity. In watching more closely, we notice both the traces of other bodies that disappear along with the lady and fail to return and the possibility that the lady herself functions all too often as a passive screen for these other disappearances, at times even becoming an active accomplice of the magician, perhaps in order to guarantee her own return. The spectacle of vanishing is politically useful because it provokes the viewer into a heightened state of visual awareness, arousing anxiety and curiosity about the status of the bodies of others. Two key questions arise out of the experience of repeatedly and critically watching the spectacle of vanishing. At what cost do we witness the return of the vanishing subject? Whose lives do we trade (invisibly) in order to guarantee our own survival?

The dubious political potential of the vanishing lady remains inextricably linked to the persistence of formal repetition in this figure's history. On the one hand, the repetitive quality of the narrative—the woman who disappears and returns only to disappear and return again—suggests that these are stories about resilience and survival, about coming back, or comebacks, and in many ways they are. But this repetition also works to hypnotize the spectator, so thoroughly familiarizing the once magical and ominous spectacle that it becomes uninteresting and predictable, allowing us to stop paying full attention because we think we know the routine. These moments of comfort and inattentiveness become the danger zones, the spaces where vanishing as eradication might most easily occur. So it is not enough for those of us who might feel threatened by the temporary and spectacular vanishing of the white woman, for example, to celebrate her return with a sigh of relief. For if the woman who knows what it means to vanish is to emerge as a useful figure in the realm of visual ethics she must do more than vocally reassure us with her assertion of presence: "here." Rather, we must use the voice that becomes available to us as well as to her in the context of the public performance to pose the questions: Here, but how? At whose expense? And where is "there"? Hovering on the border between female agency and female vulnerability, this figure has everything to gain from posing the question—loudly—of how the possibility of being seen again relates to the act of leave-taking, as in "see you," or "Auf wiedersehen." To whom or what do we happily say goodbye in order to see ourselves represented as present?

This book argues that the proliferation of spectacles of female vanishing coincides with the rise of precinematic visual spectacles and later with the invention of cinema, partly because filmmakers project their own anxieties about the insubstantiality of film onto the bodies of women in order to distance that medium from the transience that always haunts it. This projection does not occur randomly but grows out of the misogynist fear of women's reproductive capacities, a fear that resonates with and becomes inseparable from anxieties surrounding the technologies of visual reproduction. Consequently, as I argue in chapter two, this evanescent medium maintains a powerful investment in the survival of its female doubles in spite of its apparently insatiable desire to make these women go away. I have tried to unravel some of these projections without destroying, or suggesting that we need to destroy, the close relationship that exists between the vanishing woman and the medium of film. For, while critical analysis of this relationship allows us to look more closely at, and hopefully intervene in, the violence that often occurs in less than spectacular ways, the woman's survival does seem to depend at some level on the medium's identification with her. To fundamentally disrupt this identification would be to lose an important window onto how a particular mode of violence operates, and perhaps, as we begin to understand the operations of this violence better, both the medium and the violence it discloses may begin to change.

The vanishing woman's ability to resist complete eradication seems, in the context of the various examples I have examined, to be inextricably linked to the female voice and its strange relationship with the body that produces it. But, like the vanishing woman herself, the voice eludes full presence in spite of the fact that cinema seems capable of capturing and fixing this voice as presence. Kaja Silverman warns us in *The Acoustic Mirror* that "The notion that cinema is able to deliver 'real' sounds is an extension of that powerful Western episteme, extending from Plato to Hélène Cixous, which identifies the voice with proximity and the here and now—of a metaphysical tradition which defines speech as the very essence of presence."[1] Through a turn to Lacan, Silverman goes on to suggest the extent to which the voice belongs to the space of absence: "Lacan emphasizes . . . that speech produces absence, not presence. He also reminds us that the discoursing voice is the agent of symbolic castration—that at the moment the subject enters into language, he or she also undergoes a phenomenal 'fading' or 'aphanisis' " (43–44). In this last reference to Lacan, however, it becomes clear that the subject's linguistic entry into language occurs in conjunction with the experience not of full absence but of aphanisis or "fading." And although, as I have pointed out, the word *aphanisis* is etymologically indebted to a language of violent eradication, it speaks of something less certain than absence; it speaks of vanishing. Vanishing becomes the condition for speech, and this voice in turn enables the body to vanish without completely disappearing. Mademoiselle Patrice asserts her return by calling out from the space of the audience, "Here." Anna O. not only rediscovers her "mother tongue" through her self-induced absences but also (as Bertha Pappenheim) becomes a leading voice in the German feminist movement, though not until she ceases to be an object of examination for Breuer and Freud. The disappearances of the elderly women in Hitchcock's *The Lady Vanishes* and Harlan's *Verwehte Spuren* give rise to the loud and sometimes shrieking voices of the younger women who are left behind. And in the case of *The Lady Vanishes,* which names its vocal young woman Iris, the link between seeing and being heard becomes quite explicit. Similarly developing the relationship among the vanishing woman, the active spectator, and the critical female voice, Bette Davis's four fading-star films repeatedly present the star in the role of a vocal spectator, commenting on either her own performances or the performances of others. Although the films seem initially to represent the inevitable disappearance of the older female star, when read alongside each other they suggest not only that this disappearance is never final but that it provokes and enables the emergence of critically curious and unusually talkative female spectators. These spectators want to know what happens when women get old, they have an investment in the continued existence of the no longer visible female star, and they are not afraid to bang on doors and interrogate those around them.

They might be us.

Notes

Introduction

1 Baum describes the display in his 1900 guide to window decorating: "It occupied but a small space in the center of the display, showing the bust and head of a pretty young woman, supported on a thin pedestal with a large bowl top. From the waist down the young woman was invisible, at the same time one could see all around the pedestal, which produced a startling illusion. At short intervals this young woman would disappear right into the pedestal (or so it would seem), and presently would reappear with new hat, waist, gloves, etc." (L. Frank Baum, *The Art of Decorating Dry Goods Windows and Interiors: A Complete Manual of Window Trimming* [Chicago: Show Window Publishing Company, 1900], 83).

2 Ibid., 83–4. As Stuart Culver has noted, the show window represents the "eruption of theater into the centers of commercial activity," which Baum hoped would transform the "passive throng" into "an audience of absorbed specta-

tors." Baum's vanishing lady actually belongs to a series of "illusion windows," all recycling what Culver calls "the hackneyed tricks of would-be Barnums" ("What Manikins Want: *The Wonderful Wizard of Oz* and *The Art of Decorating Dry Goods Windows,*" *Representations* 21 [winter 1988]: 107).

3 Baum had become interested in trick photography and film on a trip to Paris, and his illusion windows clearly mirror Georges Méliès's early trick films, not only in their subject matter but in their positioning of a particular kind of spectator. Susan Wolstenholme writes, "During a trip to Paris Baum, always fascinated by technology, grew interested in the film industry there and in trick photography, as developed by George Méliès; and in 1907–8 Baum produced a series of films to advertise his books" (L. Frank Baum, *The Wonderful Wizard of Oz,* edited by Susan Wolstenholme [Oxford: Oxford University Press, 1997], xx). For further discussion of Baum's own films, see Anne Morey, " 'A Whole Book for a Nickel'? L. Frank Baum as Filmmaker," *Children's Literature Association Quarterly* 20.4 (winter 1995–96): 155–60. The conflation between the woman who disappears and the mannequin found here still haunts contemporary cinema. In Ray Lawrence's *Lantana* (2001), when a prominent psychotherapist disappears on an Australian back road, detectives erect a mannequin, dressed in the clothes the vanished woman was wearing that night, at the site of her disappearance.

4 Anne Friedberg has usefully drawn a correlation between three related sites of looking: the mirror, the shop window, and the screen. She writes, "Baum's conception of the show window seems to bear a clear analogy to the cinema screen. The window frames a tableau; placing it behind glass and making it inaccessible arouses desire. . . . From the middle of the nineteenth century, as if in a historical relay of looks, the show window succeeded the mirror as site of identity construction, and then—gradually—the shop window was displaced by the cinema screen. Window shopping becomes an apt paradigm for cinematic and televisual spectatorship" ("Cinema and the Postmodern Condition," in *Viewing Positions: Ways of Seeing Film,* edited Linda Williams [New Brunswick, NJ: Rutgers University Press, 1994], 65).

5 For further discussion of the relationship between the cinema and the show window, see Jane M. Gaines, "The Queen Christina Tie-Ups: Convergence of Show Window and Screen," *Quarterly Review of Film and Video* 11 (1989): 35–60; and Charles Eckert, "The Carole Lombard in Macy's Window," in *Fabrications: Costume and the Female Body,* edited by Jane M. Gaines (New York: Routledge, 1990), 100–121.

6 It's perhaps not surprising that we find some of the most explicit critical engagement with the figure of the vanishing woman in the field of romanticism. In *Keats and the Silent Work of Imagination,* Leon Waldorff argues that for Keats "La Belle Dame sans Merci" transcends the problem of "women," suggesting that in this poem the vanishing woman comes to stand for the difficulty of the relationship between truth and imagination. After quoting a letter written by Keats while aboard the *Maria Crowther,* waiting to set sail for Italy, in which Keats says of Fanny Brawne, "I eternally see her figure eternally vanishing,"

Waldorff writes: "Keats had already been forced to awaken from a long love dream into a state of almost unrelieved melancholy, and here, at the end of his life in England, as at the end of so many episodes in his poems, the unresolved relationship of imagination to truth again presents itself in the image of a vanishing woman" (*Keats and the Silent Work of Imagination* [Urbana: University of Illinois Press, 1985], 90). Feminist readers of this poem have approached romance's vanishing women with more circumspection. Karen Swann, for example, writes that a feminist critic "might conclude that 'romance' is at least as fatal to the lady as the knight. Not only does its logic work toward her disappearance from the scene, romance blinds most readers to the woman's point of view—a point of view from which the exchange between the lady and knight looks less like a domestic idyll or a fatal encounter and more like a scene of harassment" ("Harrassing the Muse," in *Romanticism and Feminism,* edited by Anne K. Mellor [Bloomington: Indiana University Press, 1988], 89). Just as romance "disappears" the vanishing woman's point of view, so here, too, we have no access to the perspective of the woman who repeatedly vanishes "without a word." "The Haunting" represents one interesting exception to Hardy's representation of the vanishing woman as a silent figure. In this poem, the woman's ghost speaks from beyond the grave, reassuring the mourning lover of her continued presence, in spite of the fact that he, unlike the reader, cannot hear her. Strikingly, this vanished woman criticizes as well as reassures. She reminds the reader that these poems tend to eroticize the dead and points out that she never received the kind of attention in life that she now receives in death: "When I could let him know / How I would like to join in his journeys / Seldom he wished to go. / Now that he goes and wants me with him / More than he used to do, / Never he sees my faithful phantom / Though he speaks thereto" (*Thomas Hardy,* edited by Samuel Hynes [Oxford: Oxford University Press, 1994] 86). This vanishing woman speaks, but she speaks in order to tell us that she cannot be heard (80). I am grateful to Susan Wolfson for her help with thinking about the literary genealogy of the vanishing woman.

7   Sigmund Freud, "Female Sexuality," in Sigmund Freud, *Standard Edition of the Complete Psychological Works of Sigmund Freud* (London: Hogarth, 1895–1938), 21: 228.

8   Diana Taylor, for example, writes of the *desaparecidos* of Argentina:
    Any attempt to think about the material facticity of the body poses problems. Nonetheless, I feel the urgency of holding on to the material body even if that body's existence and meaning cannot at the present be fully theorized. In dealing with the Dirty War, and other situations in which collective fantasies and phobias are embodied and fought out on human bodies, it seems to me imperative to guard against seeing the *othered* body as *only* the container of social anxieties, *only* the negative marker of social indifference and stratification, *only* the embodiment of other people's fears and passions to be annihilated and absorbed at will. . . . But how to hold on to the materiality of the individual body even as we accept the social production of subjectivity?

(*Disappearing Acts: Spectacles of Gender and Nationalism in Argentina's "Dirty War"* [Durham: Duke University Press, 1997], 149).

9 Klaus Theweleit, *Male Fantasies* (Minneapolis: University of Minnesota Press, 1987), xi.

10 Jacques Derrida writes, "Now the height of the conjuring trick here consists in causing to disappear while producing 'apparitions,' which is only contradictory in appearance, precisely, since one causes to disappear by provoking hallucinations or by inducing visions" (*Specters of Marx: The State of the Debt, the Work of Mourning, and the New International,* translated by Peggy Kamuf [New York: Routledge, 1994], 127–28).

11 See Eric Rentschler, *The Ministry of Illusion: Nazi Cinema and Its Afterlife* (Cambridge: Harvard University Press, 1996), 272–73, for further information about the Third Reich's film ratings.

12 Siegfried Zielinski, *Veit Harlan* (Frankfurt am Main: R. G. Fischer, 1981), 217.

13 Walter Benjamin, "The Work of Art in the Age of Mechanical Reproduction," in *Illuminations,* edited by Hannah Arendt (New York: Schocken, 1968), 233.

14 Juliet Mitchell, *Mad Men and Medusas: Reclaiming Hysteria* (New York: Basic Books, 2000), 230.

15 Questioning the ethical imperative to hold tightly on to the material body, Judith Butler writes: "Against the claim that post-structuralism reduces all materiality to linguistic stuff, an argument is needed to show that to deconstruct matter is not to negate it or to do away with the usefulness of the term. And against those who would claim that the body's irreducible materiality is a necessary precondition for feminist practice, I suggest that that prized materiality may well be constituted through an exclusion and degradation of the feminine that is profoundly problematic for feminism" (*Bodies That Matter: On the Discursive Limits of "Sex"* [New York: Routledge, 1993], 29–30). See also Peggy Phelan, *Unmarked: The Politics of Performance* (New York: Routledge, 1993), 6; and Ellis Hanson, *Outtakes: Essays on Queer Theory and Film* (Durham: Duke University Press, 1999), 18–19.

16 For a mere sample of the discussions of Bette Davis in contemporary film theory since the late 1980s alone, see Maria La Place, "Producing and Consuming the Woman's Film: Discursive Struggle in *Now, Voyager,*" *Home Is Where the Heart Is: Studies in Melodrama and the Woman's Film,* edited by Christine Gledhill (London: British Film Institute 1987), 138–66; Mary Ann Doane, *The Desire to Desire: The Woman's Film of the 1940s* (Bloomington: Indiana University Press, 1987); Jackie Stacey, "Desperately Seeking Difference," in *The Female Gaze: Women as Viewers of Popular Culture,* edited by Lorraine Gamman and Margaret Marshment (London: Women's Press, 1988), 112–29; Andrew Ross, *No Respect: Intellectuals and Popular Culture* (New York: Routledge, 1989); Rena Grant, "Characterhysterics II: Repeating Oneself," *Lacanian Ink* 8 (1994): 72–83; Judith Mayne, *Cinema and Spectatorship* (New York: Routledge, 1993); Jackie Stacey, *Star Gazing: Hollywood Cinema and Female Spectatorship* (London: Routledge, 1994); Teresa De Lauretis, *The Practice of Love: Lesbian Sexuality and Perverse Desire* (Bloomington: Indiana University Press, 1994); Martin Shingler,

"Masquerade or Drag? Bette Davis and the Ambiguities of Gender," *Screen* 36.3 (autumn 1995): 179–92; Elizabeth Cowie, "Fantasia," *m/f* 9:70–105; Elizabeth Cowie, *Representing the Woman: Cinema and Psychoanalysis* (Minneapolis: University of Minnesota Press, 1997); Peggy Phelan, *Mourning Sex: Performing Public Memories* (London: Routledge, 1997); Stanley Cavell, *Contesting Tears: The Hollywood Melodrama of the Unknown Woman* (Chicago: University of Chicago Press, 1997); Patricia White, *Uninvited: Classical Hollywood Cinema and Lesbian Representability* (Bloomington: Indiana University Press, 1999); and Jane M. Gaines, *Fire and Desire: Mixed-Race Movies in the Silent Era* (Chicago: University of Chicago Press, 2001).

1 Surplus Bodies, Vanishing Women

1 Quoted in Richard Williams, *The Contentious Crown: Public Discussion of the Monarchy in the Reign of Queen Victoria* (Aldershot: Ashgate, 1997), 34.

2 Quoted in Robert Blake, *Disraeli* (New York: St. Martin's, 1967), 433.

3 Adrienne Munich, *Queen Victoria's Secrets* (New York: Columbia University Press, 1996), 82.

4 Ann McClintock, *Imperial Leather: Race, Gender, and Sexuality in the Colonial Contest* (New York: Routledge, 1995), 61–62.

5 See William Hazlitt, *Reply to the Essay on Population by the Rev. T. R. Malthus* (London, 1807); and William Godwin, *Of Population: An Enquiry Concerning the Power of Increase in the Numbers of Mankind, Being an Answer to Mr. Malthus's Essay on That Subject* (1820; reprint, New York: August M. Kelley, 1964).

6 Robert Malthus, *Essay on the Principle of Population,* edited by Donald Winch (1803; reprint, Cambridge: Cambridge University Press, 1992), 66.

7 Julia Kristeva, *Powers of Horror: An Essay on Abjection* (New York: Columbia University Press, 1982), 3.

8 Catherine Gallagher, "The Body versus the Social Body in Thomas Malthus and Henry Mayhew," *Representations* 14 (spring 1986): 86.

9 "What Shall We Do with Our Old Maids" is the title of an article that appeared in *Fraser's* magazine (November 1862, 594–610) in which Frances Power Cobbe addresses the surplus woman question.

10 B. R. Mitchell, with the collaboration of Phyllis Deane, *Abstracts of British Historical Statistics* (Cambridge: Cambridge University Press, 1962), 6.

11 Martha Vicinus, *Independent Women: Work and Community for Single Women, 1850–1920* (Chicago: University of Chicago Press, 1985), 17.

12 For a more detailed discussion of the beginnings of the Langham Place Circle, see Sheila Herstein, "The Langham Place Circle and Feminist Periodicals of the 1860s," *Victorian Periodicals Review* 26:1 (spring 1993): 24–27.

13 Jessie Boucherett, "On the Cause of the Distress Prevalent among Single Women," *Englishwoman's Journal* (1864):13, 270.

14 Jessie Boucherett, "The Work We Have to Do," *Englishwoman's Review,* 1:1 (October 1866): 3.

15 Jessie Boucherett, "How to Provide for Superfluous Women," in *Woman's Work*

and Woman's Culture: A Series of Essays, edited by Josephine Butler (London: Macmillan, 1869), 29.

16   Although Greg's essay is misogynist in the extreme, treating women like cattle to be exported and paired off at will, Boucherett opens with an expression of gratitude to Greg for his belief that all human suffering can be remedied, a belief that Malthus, of course, did not share. She writes, "Although I attribute the distress prevalent among single women to a cause different from that assigned by Mr. Greg, I cannot, as a woman, refrain from expressing gratitude for the just and kindly spirit in which his essay is written" (ibid., 27).

17   "Emigration," *Englishwoman's Review* (1874): 97.

18   W. R. Greg, "Why Are Women Redundant?" *National Review* 14 (April 1862), 434–60. (emphasis added). See Mary Poovey, *Uneven Developments: The Ideological Work of Gender in Mid-Victorian England* (Chicago: University of Chicago Press, 1988), 1–23, for a further discussion of Greg's essay.

19   It is interesting to note the historical coincidence in 1857 of the founding of Langham Place and the Indian Mutiny.

20   As Edward Said points out, the term *mutiny* is the ideological British designation for what happened in 1857. Indian writers refer to the events as the Rebellion. See Said's *Culture and Imperialism* (New York: Knopf, 1993), 146.

21   *Times,* June 27, 1857, 9.

22   Quoted in ibid., June 29, 1857, 9.

23   Ibid., June 30, 1857, 5.

24   Ronald Hyam, *Britain's Imperial Century, 1815–1914: A Study of Empire and Expansion* (London: B. T. Batsford, 1976), 224.

25   Geoffrey Moorhouse writes, "A much bigger blow than any landed by Company policy, however, fell on the hybrid community when British women began to sail East in quantity in the nineteenth century. Earlier, most Company servants had either openly married native women or had maintained mistresses in a discreet extension to their dwellings, the annex known as the bibi-khana. Such ménages were sometimes blithely polygamous on an exhausting scale." Moorhouse goes on to report that by the 1840s, "the bibi-khana were thought disreputable, and mixed marriages were regarded with distaste. Unions between 'pure' Britons and 'pure' Indians thereafter became very uncommon indeed. At the same time, existing Anglo-Indians found themselves in a social no-man's land between the rulers and the ruled, a sort of outcast society by superior and inferior decree" (*India Britannica* [London: William Collins Sons, 1983], 185).

26   *Times,* August 6, 1857, 6.

27   Ibid., August 25, 1857, 6. It seems that only the clergymen in India were authorized to repeat the graphic details of these stories, as if the title of "reverend" bestowed propriety on otherwise unutterable narratives.

28   Quoted in Jenny Sharpe, *Allegories of Empire: The Figure of Woman in the Colonial Text* (Minneapolis: University of Minnesota Press, 1993), 66.

29   "During My Stay in India," *Household Words: A Weekly Journal,* November 28, 1857, 505.

30 Charles Ball, *The History of the Indian Mutiny* (London: London Printing and Publishing Company, 1858), 1:340.

31 *Times*, September 28, 1857, 8.

32 Albert A. Hopkins, *Magic: Stage Illusions, Special Effects, and Trick Photography* (New York: Munn, 1976), 256.

33 The *Oxford English Dictionary* defines *fakir* as "properly an indigent person, but specially applied to a Mahommedan religious mendicant, and then loosely, and inaccurately, to Hindu devotees and naked ascetics." It is interesting to note that in 1885, Surgeon General Edward Balfour distinguishes between different types of "faqeer": "Sahagia, from Musa Sohag, dress like women, wear female ornaments, play upon instruments, and sing and dance. At the Maharram a number of the lower classes assume the character and garb of fakirs of different ridiculous personations, for the amusement of the populace and the collection of contributions" (Edward Balfour, *The Cyclopeadia of India and of Eastern and Southeastern Asia*, 3 vols. [London: Bernard Quaritich, 1885], vol. 1), 1077. Balfour's comments illustrate the now-commonplace observation that the Indian body of the fakir is also a feminized body, a conflation that was quite pronounced in Victorian magic acts.

34 Collins first wrote about the Indian Mutiny in *Household Words* in an article coauthored with Charles Dickens entitled "The Perils of Certain English Prisoners" (Christmas, 1857). His second article on the subject, "A Sermon for Sepoys," appeared on February 27, 1858. For the debate surrounding imperialism and *The Moonstone,* see John Reed, "English Imperialism and the Unacknowledged Crime of the Moonstone," *Clio* 2 (1973): 281–90; Ashish Roy, "The Fabulist Imperialist Semiotic of Wilkie Collins's *The Moonstone,*" *New Literary History* 24 (1993): 657–81; and Ian Duncan, "*The Moonstone,* the Victorian Novel, and Imperialist Panic," *Modern Language Quarterly* 55.3 (September 1994): 297–319.

35 Wilkie Collins, *The Moonstone* (1868; reprint, London: Penguin, 1986), 453.

36 Jasper Maskelyne, *White Magic: The Story of Maskelynes* (London: Stanley Paul, 1936), 42. The Davenports were famous spiritualists in the second half of the century. I will discuss the relationship between spiritualism and conjuring in chapter two.

37 William Hazlitt, *The Collected Works of William Hazlitt,* edited by A. R. Waller and Arnold Glover (London: J. M. Dent, 1903), 6: 78–79. I am grateful to James Engell for drawing this text to my attention.

38 *Magic Circular: A Monthly Review* 9.2 (November 1908): 9.

39 Scrapbook, Harry Price Library of Magical Literature, University of London. Henry Ridgely Evans notes, "There is no record extant that the ingenious Conus [*sic*] ever attempted to execute this remarkable feat; his announcement was simply a mystification in rather bad taste, or, as we moderns would put it, an 'advertising dodge.' " (*History of Conjuring and Magic: From the Earliest Times to the End of the Eighteenth Century* [Kenton, OH: Durbin, 1930], 47.

40 Jann Matlock, "Reading Invisibility," in *Field Work: Sites in Literary and Cultural*

Studies, edited by Marjorie Garber, Paul B. Franklin, and Rebecca L. Walkowitz (New York: Routledge, 1996), 184–95.

41 See *Magic,* (April 1906, nos. 5–6) 52, for a facsimile of the poster for Anderson's trick, and (December 1904. nos. 5–6) 21, for a facsimile of Robin's poster. It is important to note that in Robin's relatively rare example of a male magician making another man disappear the title of the trick suggests that neither the man nor the woman are ever actually absent but are rather simply invisible to the audience. Invisibility creates a different power dynamic on the stage, as I suggest in my discussion of Frances, and we may well ascribe this choice of invisibility over vanishing to the presence of the male assistant.

42 *Escamoter la vrai question,* "to burke the question"; *escamoter,* "to steal, to filch"; *escamoter un emploi à qqn,* "to do someone out of a job"; *escamoter un consentement,* "to obtain someone's consent by a trick." See *Harrap's New Standard French and English Dictionary* (London: Harrap, 1972, vol. 1), E:55. As Jacques Derrida writes of Marx's use of the German form of this word, *Eskamotage,* "The word 'Eskamotage' speaks of subterfuge or theft in the exchange of merchandise, but first of all the sleight of hand by means of which an illusionist makes the most perceptible body disappear" (*Specters of Marx: The State of the Debt, the Work of Mourning, and the New International* [New York: Routledge, 1994], 127–28). Also interesting to note is that the term links vanishing to the medium of photography: *escamoter une plaque,* "to change a plate in the changing box." As I will argue in chapter two, the history of the vanishing lady is inextricably linked to the development of photography and film.

43 Here we might remember *The Moonstone,* in which Blake, who works hardest to expose the one who has made the Moonstone disappear, is himself the thief or escamoteur.

44 Maskelyne first introduced Zoë in 1877 as a companion to the Hindu automaton, Psycho. On her first appearance, the review in the *Morning Post* declared: "Psycho is to be envied. A lovely companion, always smiling, never contradicting him, never troubling him about bills, or talking of the last sweet thing in bonnets" (quoted in Maskelyne, *White Magic,* 55). It is not difficult to see her as another magical response to the excesses of women.

45 Charles Bertram, *Isn't It Wonderful? A History of Magic and Mystery* (London: Swan, Sonnenschein, 1896), 125–27.

46 We might read this interpretation alongside the *Morning Post*'s celebration of the automaton Zoë for her lack of interest in fashion and female consumerism and for her silence on "the last sweet thing in bonnets."

47 Maskelyne, *White Magic,* 44.

48 *Times,* August 26, 1886, 1.

49 Charles Dickens, *The Posthumous Papers of the Pickwick Club,* edited by Mark Wormald (Harmondsworth, Middlesex: Penguin, 1999), 201.

50 William Woodruff, author of *The Rise of the British Rubber Industry in the Nineteenth Century* (1958), wrote in the fourteenth edition of the *Encyclopaedia Britannica* that "The widespread adoption and improvement of vulcanization for mechani-

cal rubber devices (created by the extension of steam and electric power and the needs of ever widening railway networks), resulted in the expansion of the rubber industry both in Europe and North America. The increase of population and the rising standards of living created vast new markets for rubber footwear and clothing."

In 1886, the year of the vanishing lady, Sir Henry Wickham germinated Amazon seeds of the *Hevea brasiliensis* variety of rubber tree, then took them to Ceylon, where he began the Second Plantation, comprising of 211 trees, in order to meet the growing demand for rubber. Oriental rubber was preferred to Amazonian rubber largely because of the difference in labor costs and perceived levels of skill, perceptions that were, at least to some degree, racially determined, as the following passage from Akers makes clear: "The labour for working the rubber plantations in the Orient is drawn from China, India, or local sources, and it is sufficiently abundant to insure large numbers being available at a comparatively low cost for all classes of work in the field or factories. Skilled mechanics are also cheap and plentiful, and the supply of domestic servants is ample. In the Amazon valley the labourers are brought from the States of Ceará, Rio Grande do Norte, Maranhao, and Parahyba, where the bulk of the population is of negro or half-caste blood. Skilled labour is scarce and expensive, no matter whether Brazilians or Europeans are employed, and trained household servants are not obtainable" (C. E. Akers, *The Rubber Industry in Brazil and the Orient* [London: Methuen, 1914], 121–22).

51 For a detailed account of Burmese resistance to British rule, see Ni Ni Myint, *Burma's Struggle against British Imperialism, 1885–1895* (Rangoon, Burma: The University Press, 1983).

52 A. Von Huhn, *The Struggle of the Bulgarians for National Independence under Prince Alexander: A Military and Political History of the War between Bulgaria and Servia in 1885* (London: John Murray, 1886), 55–56.

53 Alexander reappeared with his brother, Prince Francis Joseph, in Podvolociska in Galacia, receiving an extraordinary welcome from the Polish population. See the *Times*, August 28, 1886, 5, for a full report on this event.

54 *Punch; or, the London Charivari*, October 9, 1886, 174–75.

55 This might be a good place to remember Britain's participation in the carving up of Africa after the discovery of gold in the Transvaal in 1886, another example of imperialist escamotage as both disappearance and theft.

2 Insubstantial Media

1 Charles Bertram, *Isn't It Wonderful? A History of Magic and Mystery* (London: Swan, Sonnenschein, 1896), 127.

2 In 1896, Lumière offered to rent the Cinématographe to Maskelyne for one hundred pounds a week, but Maskelyne got a better offer from R. W. Paul, who sold him a similar machine for one hundred pounds. Lumière proceeded to show his films at the Empire Theatre, while Egyptian Hall made exclusive

use of Paul's machine. For further details, see Jasper Maskelyne, *White Magic: The Story of Maskelynes* (London: Stanley Paul, 1936), 92.

3   Erik Barnouw makes a similar observation in *The Magician and the Cinema* (Oxford: Oxford University Press, 1981), describing cinema as "a powerful robot ousting its former master" (9).

4   This theater was the original venue for Buatier de Kolta's L'Escamotage d'une Personne Vivante. It eventually became a movie theater.

5   Anne-Marie Quévrain and Marie-George Charconnet-Méliès, "Méliès et Freud: Un avenir pour les marchands d'illusions?" in *Méliès et la naissance du spectacle cinématographique*, edited by Madelaine Malthête-Méliès (Paris: Klincksieck, 1984), 235.

6   See Paul Hammond, *Marvellous Méliès* (New York: St. Martin's, 1975), 28.

7   Many of these films have been discussed in depth in two important essays: Lucy Fischer, "The Lady Vanishes: Women, Magic, and the Movies," in *Cinematernity: Film, Motherhood, Genre* (Princeton: Princeton University Press, 1996), 37–55; and Linda Williams, "Film Body: An Implantation of Perversions," in *Narrative, Apparatus, Ideology*, edited by Phillip Rosen (New York: Columbia University Press, 1986), 507–34. One might also look at a number of films in the Library of Congress's Paper Print Collection for examples of the ubiquity of vanishing bodies in early film, such as: *Ching Ling Foo Outdone* (1900); *An Artist's Dream* (1900); *The Clown and the Alchemist* (1900); *The Mystic Swing* (1900); *Faust and Marguerite* (1900); *The Magician* (1900); *The Artist's Dilemma* (1901); *Uncle Josh at the Moving Picture Show* (1902); and *A Frontier Flirtation* (1903). All of these films can be viewed on-line at <http://memory.loc.gov/ammem/edhtml/edhome.html>.

8   The importance of this film in the history of cinema is under debate. John Frazer claims that *L'Escamotage d'une Dame Chez Robert-Houdin* represents the first use of the stop-action camera technique, which allows magical substitutions to take place. See John Frazer, *Artificially Arranged Scenes: The Films of Georges Méliès* (Boston: G. K. Hall, 1979). More recently, however, Barry Salt has suggested that the stop-action technique may have first appeared in the United States: "Although there is no question that Georges Méliès' trick films were the source for a wide diffusion of trick effects during the first decade of the cinema, his origination of all (or indeed any) of these tricks is by no means certain. The apparent transformation of objects in the middle of a shot by stopping the camera, and adding or subtracting the objects in question from the scene before starting the camera again, was first carried out in *The Execution of Mary, Queen of Scots* made by the Edison company in 1895, and this film quite probably reached Europe with the Kinetoscope machines before Méliès began making his films in 1896" (*Film Style and Technology: History and Analysis* [London: Starword, 1983], 46).

9   Tom Gunning, "The Cinema of Attractions: Early Film, Its Spectators, and the Avant-Garde," in *Early Film: Space, Frame, Narrative*, edited by Thomas Elsaesser (London: British Film Institute, 1990), 57 (emphasis added).

10 As an example of this type of reemergence of the "cinema of attractions," it's interesting to note that the original chair used by de Kolta for L'Escamotage d'une Dame reappears in Gracie Field's talkie, *Sing as We Go.* Jasper Maskelyne writes: "The same original chair was used recently by Miss Gracie Fields in making her charming talkie, "Sing as we Go," and Gracie vanished as surprisingly in that film as did the original disappearing lady fifty years ago" (*White Magic,* 81).

11 Barry Salt, "Film Form, 1900–1906," in Elsaesser, *Early Cinema,* 40.

12 A number of feminist film critics have done important work on early film, including Lucy Fischer, Anne Friedberg, Jane Gaines, Miriam Hansen, Janet Staiger, and Linda Williams. However, feminist voices in early film studies still remain marginalized. Elsaesser's anthology *Early Cinema,* for example, contains thirty-two essays, but only three of these are written by female scholars. This is not the only way in which early film scholarship becomes complicit in the process of female disappearance. Louise Heck-Rabi writes of Alice Guy Blaché, the first woman film director: "Many of her films were cited as works by others. No one realized and tried to correct published errors more assiduously than Mme. Blaché herself. She anticipated that directing and producing credits for her films would be falsely assigned to her coworkers. She knew that her name, unintentionally or purposefully, would be omitted or demoted in the histories of French and American film" (*Women Filmmakers: A Critical Reception* [Metuchen, NJ: Scarecrow Press, 1984], 2). To make matters worse, Georges Sadoul then wrongly credited her for directing *Les Méfaits d'une Tête de Veau.* Although she was made a knight of the French Legion of Honor at the age of seventy-eight, Alice Guy Blaché died anonymously, without obituary, in New Jersey. I draw this information from Ally Acker's *Reel Women: Pioneers of the Cinema, 1896 to the Present* (New York: Continuum, 1993), 7–12.

13 Constance Balides, "Scenarios of Exposure in the Practice of Everyday Life: Women in the Cinema of Attractions," *Screen* 34.1 (spring 1993): 20.

14 Lucy Fischer, "The Lady Vanishes: Women, Magic, and the Movies," *Film Quarterly* 33.1 (fall 1979): 30.

15 Williams, "Film Body," 527.

16 See the introduction for a discussion of the contributions of these scholars to the development of a theory of vanishing.

17 Jacques Derrida, "Différance," in *Margins of Philosophy,* translated by Alan Bass (Chicago: University of Chicago Press, 1987), 6.

18 Ellis Hanson, ed., *Outtakes: Essays on Queer Theory and Film* (Durham: Duke University Press, 1999), 19.

19 *Aphanisis* was first used in a psychoanalytic context by Ernest Jones, who defined the term as "the fear of seeing desire disappear," which Lacan found to be "absurd." See Jacques Lacan, *The Four Fundamental Concepts of Psychoanalysis,* edited by Jacques-Alain Miller, translated by Alan Sheridan (New York: Norton, 1981), 207.

20 Lacan defines this Greek word as "disappearance" or "fading," but the dictio-

nary—recalling the violence and subjection in which all subjects are formed—defines it also as "thrashed, beaten, obliterated, secreted, concealed, hushed up, removed, and destroyed." See Henry George Liddell and Robert Scott, eds., *A Greek-English Dictionary,* (Oxford: Clarendon, 1925), 1:286. On the necessary subjection of the subject, see the introduction to Judith Butler's *Excitable Speech: A Politics of the Performative* (New York: Routledge, 1997), 1–41.

21 Elisabeth Bronfen, *Over Her Dead Body: Death, Femininity, and the Aesthetic* (New York: Routledge, 1992), 26–27.

22 Maskelyne, *White Magic,* 108–9.

23 Harry Houdini, *A Magician among the Spirits* (New York: Harper and Brothers, 1924), 165. Houdini was more sympathetic to spiritualism than most magicians, yet he consistently offered exposures of fraudulent practices. He writes: "I have no desire to discredit Spiritualism; I have no warfare with Sir Arthur; I have no fight with the Spiritists; but I do believe it is my duty, for the betterment of humanity, to place before the public the results of my long investigation of Spiritualism" (165). It is ironic that the magician, a master of hoodwinking, should emerge as the agent of truth and revelation.

24 Barnouw, *The Magician,* 89.

25 Quoted in Rosalind Krauss, "Tracing Nadar," in *Illuminations: Women Writing on Photography from the 1850s to the Present,* edited by Liz Heron and Val Williams (Durham: Duke University Press, 1996), 38.

26 James Coates, *Photographing the Invisible: Practical Studies in Spirit Photography, Spirit Portraiture, and Other Rare but Allied Phenomenon* (1911, reprint; New York: Arno, 1973), vii.

27 Robert A. Sobieszek, *Ghost in the Shell: Photography and the Human Soul, 1850–2000* (Cambridge: MIT Press, 1999), 15. For a further example of the contemporary fascination with the ghostliness of photography, see the exhibition catalog Andreas Fischer and Veit Loers, *Im Reich der Phantome: Fotographie des Unsichtbaren* (Ostfildern-Ruit: Cantz Verlag, 1997).

28 Eduardo Cadava, *Words of Light: Theses on the Photography of History* (Princeton: Princeton University Press, 1997), 13.

29 Régis Durand, "How To See (Photographically)," in *Fugitive Images: From Photography to Video,* edited by Patrice Petro (Bloomington: Indiana University Press, 1995), 147.

30 Thierry De Duve, "Time Exposure and Snapshot: The Photograph as Paradox," *October* 5 (1978): 121.

31 Quoted in Russell M. Goldfarb and Clare R. Goldfarb, *Spiritualism and Nineteenth-Century Letters* (London: Associated University Presses, 1978), 125. For further discussion of Katie King's beauty, see Tom Gunning, "Phantom Images and Modern Manifestations," in Petro, *Fugitive Images,* 55–56.

32 Gunning's work in particular addresses the importance of spirit photography to early film, but, by his own admission, he only glosses the centrality of gender in the spiritualist movement. Although he claims that he "can only touch on the fascinating cultural relation between women and Spiritualism" ("Phantom

Images," 52), he does point his readers to Ann Braude's *Radical Spirits: Spiritualism and Women's Rights in Nineteenth-Century America* (Boston: Beacon, 1983). Braude does treat this relationship in great depth, but she then pays only minimal attention to the role played by emerging visual technologies. In this chapter, I hope to show that these two aspects of the spiritualist phenomenon—gender and technology—cannot be separated.

33 Arthur Conan Doyle, *The History of Spiritualism* (New York: Arno, 1975), 2:102–3.

34 Theodore Besterman, *Some Modern Mediums* (London: Methuen, 1930), 71.

35 Bisson hosted numerous séances at her home and authored *Les Phenomènes dits de Matérialisation* (Paris: F-Alcan, 1914).

36 Houdini, *Magician among the Spirits*, 179.

37 A. Freiherrn von Schrenck-Notzing, *Materialisationsphaenomene: Ein Beitrag zur Erforschung der Mediumistischen Teleplastie.* Zweite, stark vermehrte Auflage (second, vastly expanded edition). (Munich: Ernst Reinhardt, 1923), 50–51. Unless otherwise noted, all translations are my own.

38 Ibid., 80, quoted in English in Besterman, *Some Modern Mediums*, 84.

39 It is interesting to note that the spirits mirror the observers' obsessive touching of the medium's body. One account from December 1910 and January 1911, for example, reports that a male spirit's forearm brutally grabbed Eva's breast then flung her forcefully back into an armchair. It apparently took her several weeks to recover from the shock of this spiritual assault, although the spirit's actions seem minor compared to the routine examinations she underwent at the hands of her "protectors" on a daily basis. For further discussion of the erotic relationship between Mme. Bisson and Eva C., see Ruth Brandon, *The Spiritualists: The Passion for the Occult in the Nineteenth and Twentieth Centuries* (New York: Knopf, 1983), 151–53. Another interesting discussion of the spiritualistic séance as a site of lesbian haunting appears in Terry Castle's *Noël Coward and Radclyffe Hall: Kindred Spirits* (New York: Columbia University Press, 1996). Castle writes, "The haunting of *Blithe Spirit* by the Hall-Troubridge-Batten configuration suggests at the outset that Coward's play is a rather more 'lesbian' concoction than it is usually taken to be. It allegorizes Hall's uncanny relation with the two women who loved her in life and death. But it also allegorizes Hall's relation with Coward—in the shifting dynamic between Charles and the sublimely comic Madame Arcati. Indeed, through a series of fluid, mercurial, almost ectoplasmic identifications (Arcati is sometimes associated with Coward, at other times with Hall herself), Hall functions as a Lesbian Muse, who prompts Coward to some of his most penetrating and explicitly 'gay' comic flights" (77–78).

40 On other occasions, Schrenck-Notzing does note the examination of the vagina, perineum, and anus, usually by either Mme. Bisson or a midwife. See, for example, Schrenck-Notzing *Materialisationsphaenomene*, 59.

41 Not surprisingly, spiritualist manifestations were regarded by the medical community as a form of hysteria, a disease labeled mediomania in 1874 by R. Frederic Marvin, a professor of psychological medicine and medical juris-

prudence at the New York Free Medical College for women. According to Marvin, this disease, usually preceded by "a genito or venerio-pathological history," generally appeared as the result of a "woman's departure from traditional female roles" (*The Philosophy of Spiritualism and the Pathology and Treatment of Mediomania: Two Lectures read before the New York Liberal Club* [New York: Asa K. Butts, 1874], 35). For further discussion of the relationship between spiritualism, the women's movement, and the medical community, see Baude, *Radical Spirits,* 142–61.

42   Besterman, *Some Modern Mediums,* 102. These cries of "being taken" were often accompanied by rapid breathing, crying, and throwing back of the head, a performance of sexual ecstasy. For Freud and Breuer, too, the hysteric's *absence* mirrored the temporary loss of self experienced in the moment of sexual climax. For further discussion of the hysteric's disappearance, see chapter three.

43   Fred Gettings, *Ghosts in Photographs: The Extraordinary Story of Spirit Photography* (New York: Harmony, 1978), 115.

44   Jean-Luc Nancy, *The Evidence of Film: Abbas Kiarostami,* translated by Christine Irizarry and Verena Andermatt Conley (Brussels: Yves Gevaert, 2001), 46. I am grateful to Eduardo Cadava for bringing this text to my attention.

45   Barnouw, *The Magician,* 89.

46   Geoffrey Batchen, *Burning with Desire: The Conception of Photography* (Cambridge: MIT Press, 1999), 182.

47   Cadava writes, "There has never been a time without the photograph, without the residue and writing light" ("Words of Light: Theses on the Photography of History," *Diacritics* 22.3–4 [fall–winter 1992]: 87).

48   Fred Gettings takes the existence of Schrenck-Notzing's cinematographic record as the ultimate evidence of the "truth" of ectoplasm: "It has proved possible to photograph the materialization and dematerialization of ectoplasm on a movie camera under conditions that utterly preclude fraud" (*Ghosts,* 115).

3   Mother Knows Best

1   Juliet Mitchell, *Mad Men and Medusas: Reclaiming Hysteria* (New York: Basic Books, 2000), 109.

2   Peter Gay, *Freud: A Life for Our Time* (New York: Norton, 1988), 49.

3   Peter Gay, *The Freud Reader* (New York: Norton, 1989), 51.

4   Sigmund Freud, *The Complete Psychological Works* (London: Hogarth, 1966), 11:21.

5   Ernest Jones, *The Life and Work of Sigmund Freud* (Garden City, N.Y.: Anchor, 1963), 14.

6   Jacqueline Rose, " 'Where Does Misery Come From?' Psychoanalysis, Feminism, and the Event," in *Why War? Psychoanalysis, Politics, and the Return to Melanie Klein* (Oxford: Blackwell, 1989), 89–109.

7   At this moment, we have a strong sense that the magician and the doctor are in cahoots. As my discussion in chapter four of Alfred Hitchcock's *The Lady*

Vanishes and Veit Harlan's *Verwehte Spuren* reveals, this is not the only time when such an alliance will be formed for the purpose of making an excessively knowledgeable older woman disappear.

8　Mary Ann Doane, *Femmes Fatales: Feminism, Film Theory, Psychoanalysis* (New York: Routledge, 1991), 47.

9　In thinking about this question of the representation of the Jewish mother, I am struck by the lack of attention given to Jewish women in recent discussions about the representation of Jews in relation to femininity in the field of Jewish studies. Important and challenging as the work of Sander Gilman, Jay Geller, and Daniel Boyarin is, it seems that the relationship between Jewishness and femininity is almost always discussed with exclusive reference to the Jewish male, thus disappearing the Jewish woman. As Ann Pellegrini notes, "in the homology Jew-as-woman, the Jewish female body goes missing. All Jews are womanly; but no women are Jews" (*Performance Anxieties: Staging Psychoanalysis, Staging Race* [New York: Routledge, 1997], 18).

10　For an excellent discussion of the problem for feminists of seeing the mother as our first mirror, see Jane Gallop, "The Monster in the Mirror," and "Reading the Mother Tongue" in *Around 1981: Academic Feminist Literary Theory* (New York: Routledge, 1992) 48–66. See also Monique Plaza, "The Mother/The Same: Hatred of the Mother in Psychoanalysis," *Feminist Issues* 2.1 (spring 1982): 75–100, for a feminist discussion of the role of the mother in psychoanalytic practice.

11　Julia Kristeva, *Black Sun: Depression and Melancholia* (New York: Columbia University Press, 1989), 27–28.

12　Luce Irigaray, "Body against Body: In Relation to the Mother," in *Sexes and Genealogies* (New York: Columbia University Press, 1993), 16.

13　Jean-Joseph Goux, *Oedipus, Philosopher* (Stanford: Stanford University Press, 1993), 17.

14　Ibid., 25. This same sentence reappears two pages later in slightly altered form: "Matricide is the great unthought element of Freudian doctrine" (27).

15　See ibid., 5, 9, and 13, for Goux's descriptions of the myth as deviant. The term *aberrant* appears on page 3.

16　Judith Butler, *The Psychic Life of Power* (Stanford: Stanford University Press, 1997), 135.

17　Freud, *Complete Psychological Works,* 12:129. Friedrich von Schiller's poem reads: "Sie war nicht in dem Tal geboren, / Man wußte nicht, woher sie kam, / Und schnell war ihre Spur verloren, / Sobald das Mädchen Abschied nahm." (She was not born in the valley, / No one knew from whence she came, / And all trace of her was quickly lost, / As soon as the girl took her leave) (*Deutsche Gedichte: Von den Anfängen bis zur Gegenwart,* edited by Benno von Wiese [Düsseldorf: Cornelsen, 1993], 274). The "verlorene Spuren" (lost traces) of the girl in Schiller's poem here prefigure the title of Veit Harlan's 1938 film *Verwehte Spuren* (*Blown Away Traces*), which I analyze in the chapter four.

18　In *Eating Disorders and the Magical Control of the Body: Treatment through Art Therapy*

(New York: Routledge, 1995), Mary Levens argues that the fantasy of anorexia is a fantasy of omnipotence and is deeply associated with the identity of the magician.

19 It is interesting to note that while Freud links the hysteric's absence to the female orgasm Juliet Mitchell points to the inability of her hysterical patients to "vanish" sexually, arguing that these patients are too close to annihilation and death to feel safe enough to experience orgasm (*Mad Men*, 211).

20 Freud, *Complete Psychological Works*, 2:7. Freud employs the same magical discourse of disappearance in the first of the "Five Lectures on Psychoanalysis" (1909), in which he returns to consider the case of Anna O. and how he and Breuer made her absences vanish.

21 Terry Castle, "The Spectralization of the Other in *The Mysteries of Udolpho*," in *The New Eighteenth Century: Theory, Politics, English Literature*, edited by Felicity Nussbaum and Laura Brown (New York: Methuen, 1987), 252.

22 Jeffrey Moussaieff Masson, ed. and trans., *The Complete Letters of Sigmund Freud to Wilhelm Fliess, 1887–1904* (Cambridge: Harvard University Press, 1985), 272.

23 On a biographical note of interest, it seems that the Mrs. Freuds had a habit of disappearing. Amalia Freud, Sigmund's mother, was Jakob Freud's third wife, but until 1968 she was thought to be only the second Mrs. Freud. Until J. Sajner did some research in the Freiberg archives, all record of Jakob's second wife had vanished. Even now, no one knows whether she died, committed suicide, or simply vanished. The death of Jakob's first wife and the disappearance of his second provide a biographical context for Freud's acute anxiety about the disappearance of his caretakers. See Joseph Sajner, "Sigmund Freuds Beziehungen zu seinem Gebortsort Freiberg (Príbor) und zu Mähren," *Clio Medica* 3 (1968): 167–80.

24 Freud's distance from the scene is also reflected in the fact that his "brother" becomes a "half brother" in this later account.

25 As with Freud's patient Little Hans, the image of the mother in the street is doubly threatening. Not only does the street immediately sexualize the woman walking alone in it; it represents the world of public space, which, as Freud writes in his study of Little Hans, is not "quite the right place for 'coaxing' or whatever else this young lover may have wanted" (*Complete Psychological Works*, 10:26).

26 Mary Jacobus, *First Things: The Maternal Imaginary in Literature, Art, and Psychoanalysis* (New York: Routledge, 1995), 7.

27 Jim Swan, "*Mater* and Nannie: Freud's Two Mothers," *American Imago* 31.1 (spring 1974): 5–6.

28 See Daniel Boyarin, "Jewish Masochism: Couvade, Castration, and Rabbis in Pain," *American Imago* 51.1 (1994): 3–36; and "Freud's Baby, Fliess's Maybe: Homophobia, Antisemitism, and the Invention of Oedipus," *GLQ: A Journal of Gay and Lesbian Studies* 2.1–2 (1995): 115–47. Boyarin's excellent articles examine the maternal metaphors in the context of the Jewish tradition of couvade. In particular, Boyarin usefully addresses the ambivalent nature of couvade, which

both attributes the mother with power and appropriates that power from her through the ritual, an ambivalence also present in Freud's letters.

29 Michel Foucault, *Discipline and Punish* (New York: Vintage, 1979), 201.

30 Jacques Derrida, "Coming into One's Own," in *Psychoanalysis and the Question of the Text: Selected Papers from the English Institute, 1976–77,* edited by Geoffrey Hartman (Baltimore: Johns Hopkins United Press, 1978), 114–48.

31 Elisabeth Bronfen, *Over Her Dead Body: Death, Femininity, and the Aesthetic* (New York: Routledge, 1992), 18.

32 See Ehrenreich's foreword to Klaus Theweleit, *Male Fantasies* (Minneapolis: University of Minnesota Press, 1987), xi. See my introduction for a further discussion of Ehrenreich's argument.

33 See Melanie Klein's, 1940 "Mourning and Its Relation to Manic-Depressive States," in *The Selected Melanie Klein,* edited by Juliet Mitchell (New York: Free Press, 1986), 147.

34 Bronfen also identifies Freud's writing of *Beyond the Pleasure Principle* as an act of mourning in itself: "Yet if representation in one sense serves to negate loss, in another it emerges as the work of mourning" (*Over Her Dead Body,* 30).

35 Freud, *Complete Psychological Works,* 18:14–15. This passive, third-person construction also exists in the original German version, which reads "das nach dem übereinstimmenden Urteil der Mutter und des Beobachters keine Interjektion war, sondern 'fort' bedeutete" (Sigmund Freud, "Jenseits des Lustprinzips," in *Das Ich und das Es: Metapsychologische Schriften* [Frankfurt am Main: Fischer, 1992), 200.

4   Violent Vanishings

1 Žižek continues, "[This] is why the disappearance of this woman is a means by which filmic romance takes cognizance of the fact that 'The Woman does not exist' and that there is, therefore, no sexual relationship" (*Looking Awry: An Introduction to Jacques Lacan through Popular Culture* [Cambridge: MIT Press, 1991], 82).

2 Margaret Anne Doody, *The True Story of the Novel* (New Brunswick, NJ: Rutgers University Press, 1996), 311.

3 See David Bordwell and Kristin Thompson, *Film Art: An Introduction* (New York: McGraw-Hill, 1979), 158.

4 Tom Gunning, *D. W. Griffith and the Origins of American Narrative Film: The Early Years at Biograph* (Urbana: University of Illinois Press, 1991), 190.

5 François Truffaut, *Hitchcock* (New York: Simon and Schuster, 1966), 86. There is no consensus among the various sources for this yarn regarding the date on which it took place. Hitchcock tells us it is 1880, Harlan sets the tale in 1867 at the first great World Exhibition, and Slavoj Žižek places the event in 1889 in *Looking Awry* (79).

6 "Bandrika may have a dictator . . . but tonight we're painting it red." Here the ambiguity of the phrase "painting the town red" points to the confusion

between light entertainment and serious politics that the film will proceed to enact.

7 Ethel Lina White's novel, *The Wheel Spins,* forms the basis of the plot of *The Lady Vanishes.* Hitchcock insisted on the insertion of a magician into the story, and, whereas the governess in White's novel is in fact only a governess wrongly suspected of being a spy, Hitchcock's naive governess in tweeds is, of course, a spy.

8 Sam P. Simone, *Hitchcock as Activist: Politics and the War Films* (Ann Arbor: UMI Research Press, 1982), 22.

9 Googie Withers, interview with the author, London, July 1996.

10 *Variety,* August 31, 1938. The review appeared opposite a three-page advertisement featuring a top hat out of which emerge three movie titles, "made possible by the magic touch of showmanship." "Presto! Abracadabra! . . . Universal has the magic!" the poster declares, thereby placing *The Lady Vanishes* within the wider frame of cinema as a magical form of entertainment.

11 *The New Statesman,* October 15, 1938.

12 Raymond Durgnat, *The Strange Case of Alfred Hitchcock; or, the Plain Man's Hitchcock* (Cambridge: MIT Press, 1974), 161–62.

13 Simone, *Hitchcock,* 247–48. As an example of this overstatement, Simone quotes Leif Furhammer and Folke Isaksson, who claim that "in his British picture *The Lady Vanishes,* [Hitchcock] had already warned about the danger of Hitler, and he continued this anti-Nazi line using the same thematic pattern in *Foreign Correspondent* and *Saboteur*" (304, n. 10).

14 Walter Benjamin "The Work of Art in the Age of Mechanical Reproduction," in *Illuminations: Walter Benjamin—Essays and Reflections,* edited by Hannah Arendt (New York: Schocken, 1969), 240–41.

15 Anne Bauchens, "Cutting the Film," in *We Make the Movies,* edited by Nancy Naumberg (New York: Norton, 1937), 212.

16 We have already seen this alliance between the doctor-analyst and the magician at work in Woody Allen's *Oedipus Wrecks* (see chapter three). Indeed, we might read Allen's entire film as an exploration of this relationship.

17 David Forgacs, "Fascism, Violence, and Modernity," in *The Violent Muse: Violence and the Artistic Imagination in Europe, 1910–1939,* edited by Jana Howlett and Rod Mengham (Manchester: Manchester University Press, 1994), 5–21.

18 Adolf Hitler, *Mein Kampf,* translated by Ralph Manheim (1943; reprint, Boston: Houghton Mifflin, 1971), 57.

19 It is interesting to note how Bauchen's use of the male pronoun here vanishes herself along with all the other many female editors of this period.

20 Jean-Louis Baudry, "Ideological Effects of the Basic Cinematic Apparatus" in *Narrative, Apparatus, Ideology: A Film Theory Reader,* edited by Philip Rosen (New York: Columbia University Press, 1986), 287.

21 Andrew Sinclair, ed., *Masterworks of the British Cinema* (London: Faber and Faber, 1990), 36.

22 The *American Heritage Dictionary* defines *legerdemain* as "Sleight of hand. A show

of skill or deceitful cleverness" (1028). I prefer Barbara Maria Stafford's definition — "the visible invisible." See her *Artful Science: Enlightenment, Entertainment, and the Eclipse of Visual Education* (Cambridge: MIT Press, 1994), xxiv.

23 Norbert Grob, "Veit Harlan," in *Cinégraph: Lexicon zum deutschsprachigen Film,* edited by Hans-Michael Bock (Munchin: Text and Kritik, ca. 1984), E1.

24 Veit Harlan, *Im Schatten Meiner Filme: Selbst Biographie,* edited by H. C. Opfermann (Gütersloh: Sigbert Mohm Verlag, 1966), 64.

25 See chapter one for my discussion of India's role in the success of the Vanishing Lady in Victorian Britain.

26 For one of the best discussions of this film, see Eric Rentschler, "The Elective Other: *Jew Süss* (1940)," in *The Ministry of Illusion: Nazi Cinema and Its Afterlife* (Cambridge: Harvard University Press, 1996), 149–70.

27 Siegfried Zielinski, *Veit Harlan: Analysen und Materialien zur Auseinandersetzung mit einem Film-Regisseur des deutschen Faschismus* (Frankfurt am Main: R. G. Fischer, 1981), 217.

28 "Fade-in: a dark screen that gradually brightens as a shot appears. Fade-out: A shot gradually darkens as the screen goes black. Dissolve: A transition between two shots during which the first image gradually disappears while the second image gradually appears; for a moment the two images blend in superimposition" (Bordwell and Thompson *Film Art,* 493).

29 See Marc Ferro, "Dissolves in *Jud Süss,*" in *Cinema and History,* translated by Naomi Greene (Detroit: Wayne State University Press, 1988); and Karsten Witte, "Wie faschistisch ist *Die Feuerzangenbowle?* Bemerkungen zur Filmkomödie im Dritten Reich," *epd Kirche und Film* 29.7 (July 1976): 1–4.

30 See H. G. Wells, *The Island of Dr. Moreau* (1896; reprint, New York: Signet, 1988).

31 In the 1926 edition of the *Encyclopedia Britannica,* specialists declared that "the most striking feature of the early history of the plague . . . is the gradual retrocession of plague from the west . . . and its eventual disappearance from Europe." This "disappearance" of the plague from Europe is accompanied in the report by the appearance of the disease in India: "It used to be held as a maxim that the plague never appeared east of the Indus; nevertheless it was observed during the 19th century in more than one district centre in India." By 1926, the plague had become inextricably linked to India in the popular and scientific imagination. See "Plague," in *Encyclopaedia Britannica,* 13th ed., vol. 21 (London: Encyclopaedia Britannica Co., 1926). It is also interesting to note that by setting the film in the Paris Exhibition of 1867 Harlan locates the story only three years after the British government instituted the Indian Contagious Diseases Act.

32 Eduardo Cadava, "Words of Light: Theses on the Photography of History," *Diacritics* 22.3–4 (1992): 89.

33 Hitler, *Mein Kampf,* 248. For a detailed discussion of the National Socialist use of this metaphor, see Sander Gilman, "The Jewish Disease: Plague in Germany, 1939–89," in *The Jew's Body* (New York: Routledge, 1991), 210–33.

34 Diana Taylor, *Disappearing Acts: Spectacles of Gender and Nationalism in Argentina's "Dirty War"* (Durham: Duke University Press, 1997), x.

5 Shooting Stars, Vanishing Comets

1 Lucy Fischer, *"Sunset Boulevard:* Fading Stars," in *Women and Film,* edited by Janet Todd (New York: Holmes and Meier, 1988), 112.

2 Laura Mulvey, "Visual Pleasure and Narrative Cinema," in *Narrative, Apparatus, Ideology,* edited by Philip Rosen (New York: Columbia University Press, 1986), 205.

3 Claire Johnston, "Women's Cinema as Counter-cinema," reprinted in *Movies and Methods: An Anthology,* edited by Bill Nichols (Berkeley: University of California Press, 1976), 208–17.

4 Michelle Citron, Julia Lesage, B. Ruby Rich, and Anna Maria Taylor, "Women and Film: A Discussion of Feminist Aesthetics," *New German Critique* 13 (winter 1978): 87.

5 See, for example, Steven Cohan, *Masked Men: Masculinity and the Movies in the Fifties* (Bloomington: Indiana University Press, 1997).

6 bell hooks, *Black Looks: Race and Representation* (Boston: South End, 1992), 115–32; Richard Dyer, *White* (London: Routledge, 1997). Some other important works that have challenged the exclusion of ethnicity and race from discussions of gender and film include Trinh T. Minh-ha, *Woman, Native, Other: Writing Postcoloniality and Feminism* (Bloomington: Indiana University Press, 1989); Manthia Diawara, ed., *Black American Cinema* (New York: Routledge, 1993); Valerie Smith, *Not Just Race, Not Just Gender: Black Feminist Readings* (New York: Routledge, 1998); and Jane M. Gaines, *Fire and Desire: Mixed-Race Movies in the Silent Era* (Chicago: University of Chicago Press, 2001).

7 Terry Castle, *The Apparitional Lesbian: Female Homosexuality and Modern Culture* (New York: Columbia University Press, 1993), 3.

8 Patricia White, *Uninvited: Classical Hollywood Cinema and Lesbian Representability* (Bloomington: Indiana University Press, 1993). Other recent works that uncover the potential agency of the absent subject include Avery F. Gordon, *Ghostly Matters: Haunting and the Sociological Imagination* (Minneapolis: University of Minnesota Press, 1997); and Peggy Phelan, *Unmarked: The Politics of Performance* (London: Routledge, 1993). Phelan claims that "By locating a subject in what cannot be reproduced within the ideology of the visible, I am attempting to revalue a belief in subjectivity and identity which is not visually representable. This is not the same thing as calling for greater visibility of the hitherto unseen" (1).

9 Quoted in Walter Benjamin, "The Work of Art in the Age of Mechanical Reproduction," in *Illuminations,* edited by Hannah Arendt (New York: Schocken, 1968), 229.

10 There have been three film versions of *A Star Is Born,* and another, African American version is currently under discussion at Warner Brothers, but even the original film is itself a remake of George Cukor's 1932 *What Price Holly-*

wood? Dorothy Parker and Alan Campbell wrote the screenplay for William Wellman's 1937 version, starring Frederic March as Norman Maine and Janet Gaynor as Esther Blodgett. George Cukor remade the film in 1954 with Judy Garland and James Mason, and it was remade yet again in 1976 by Frank Pierson. The screenplay for the 1976 version was written by Joan Didion and John Gregory Dunne and starred Barbara Streisand and Kris Kristofferson. Oliver Stone is in talks regarding the direction of the rumored African American remake. Will Smith and Alicia Keys are the most likely leads at the time of writing. See <www.upcomingmovies.com/starisborn.html>.

11 For a revealing discussion of the relationship between female sexuality and falling, see Diana Fuss, "Fallen Women: 'The Psychogenesis of a Case of Homosexuality in a Woman,'" in *Identification Papers* (New York: Routledge, 1995), 57–82.

12 In *"Sunset Boulevard:* Fading Stars," Fischer suggests that these films are significant because "the actress is seen by men to constitute a kind of metaphor for women, since there is a perfect 'match' between her perceived qualities and patriarchal attitudes toward the second sex. In her cinematic incarnation she is, then, both the archetypal woman and the exemplary woman in film" (98). Although the idea of the actress as Everywoman is clearly important for feminist film criticism of this genre, the problem remains that by recasting the star as actress, Fischer's analysis misses the resonances of the star metaphor within these films and the way the star invokes the idea of vanishing.

13 Taking the *Oxford English Dictionary*'s broader definition of *star* as any celestial body, we see that Desmond, in choosing to adapt *Salomé* for the screen, explicitly identifies herself with the waxing and waning of the moon.

14 Eduardo Cadava, *Words of Light: Theses on the Photography of History* (Princeton: Princeton University Press, 1997), 29–30.

15 Martin Heidegger, *An Introduction to Metaphysics,* translated by Ralph Manheim (1959; reprint, New Haven: Yale University Press 1987), 99–100.

16 Quoted in Lawrence J. Quirk, *Fasten Your Seatbelts: The Passionate Life of Bette Davis* (New York: Signet, 1990), 420.

17 Quoted in Whitney Stine, *"I'd Love to Kiss You . . ." in Conversations with Bette Davis* (New York: Pocket Books, 1990), 189.

18 See ibid.

19 Judith Butler, *The Psychic Life of Power* (Stanford: Stanford University Press, 1997), 33.

20 *The American Heritage Dictionary*: "comet."

21 When the ice that holds the comet together melts, cometary debris flies into the earth's atmosphere, producing "sporadic meteors," otherwise known as falling or shooting stars. See Carl Sagan, *Pale Blue Dot: A Vision of the Human Future in Space* (New York: Random House, 1994), 296.

22 See chapter three for a discussion of this film.

23 Yvonne Rainer, *The Films of Yvonne Rainer* (Bloomington: Indiana University Press, 1989), 197–98.

24 In the case of *Sunset Boulevard,* the male voice is literally disembodied, for the

body to which the voice belongs lies floating in Norma Desmond's pool. The presence of this voice at all suggests that male screenwriters, even second-rate dead ones, have more staying power than aging female actresses. As Kaja Silverman has argued, "despite its rather rare occurrence in the fiction film, the disembodied voice can be seen as 'exemplary' for male subjectivity, attesting to an achieved invisibility, omniscience, and discursive power" (*The Acoustic Mirror: The Female Voice in Psychoanalysis and Cinema* [Bloomington: Indiana University Press, 1988], 164).

25 Citron et al, "Nomer and Film," 215.

26 Compared to Garbo, in fact compared to any other female Hollywood star, Davis has remarkably few close-ups, a fact that she acknowledges in her autobiography: "I probably had less close-ups as a star than any other actress" (Bette Davis, *The Lonely Life* [New York: Putnam, 1962], 240).

27 Charles Affron, *Star Acting: Gish, Garbo, Davis* (New York: Dutton, 1977), 247.

28 The specter of Hollywood haunts the stage world of *All about Eve* most forcefully through the figure of Bill Sampson, who moves between the two worlds. In an early scene, he tells Margo, "I start shooting a week from Monday. Zanuck is impatient. He wants me, he needs me," to which Margo replies, "Zanuck, Zanuck, Zanuck. What are you two, lovers?"

29 Dyer, *White*, 122.

30 Although Monroe never has the glossy shine of Margo, Addison DeWitt establishes a direct connection between Miss Caswell (Monroe) and Joyce Heath as Juliet when he tells her "I can see your career rising in the east like the sun."

31 "Garbo still belongs to that moment in cinema when capturing the human face still plunges audiences into the deepest ecstasy, when one literally lost oneself in a human image as one would in a philtre" (Roland Barthes, *Mythologies,* selected and translated by Annette Lavers [New York: Hill and Wang, 1972], 56).

32 As Richard Dyer has noted, in technical discussions of the "problem" of lighting black subjects for film or photography one of the recurrent solutions was to lather black skin in a substance that would make it more shiny: butter or oil (Basil Wright, British documentary filmmaker, 1933), lotion (Conrad Hall, 1986), or skin moisturizer (Ernest Dickerson, Spike Lee's cinematographer, 1988). See Dyer, *White*, 97–98. In this scene, then, we might read Davis as a preparing herself for the camera as a nonwhite subject.

33 James Baldwin, *The Devil Finds Work* (New York: Laurel, 1976), 7–8.

34 Gaines, *Fire and Desire*, 32.

35 The reference to Crawford is most apparent when Elliott leaves the studio, saying to the film crew, "Bless you, bless you," one of Crawford's trademark phrases.

36 Quoted in James Spada, *More Than a Woman: An Intimate Biography of Bette Davis* (New York: Bantam, 1993), 393.

37 It's interesting to note that Amazon.com now markets *The Star* using Natalie

Wood's name alone. Davis appears nowhere in the film's description, an external consequence of the older star's disappearance that the film internally enacts.

38 The formulation of this statement echoes the earlier café scene. Just as the waitress remembered Elliott while Bill did not, so Janie Marx's father tells Janie's mother that Elliott is "washed up," implying perhaps that the mother thinks differently. Male and female spectators remember stars in different ways, the film suggests.

39 Michel Chion, *The Voice and Cinema* (New York: Columbia University Press, 1999), 130.

40 For a similar scenario of the possession of bodies by "other" voices, see Kaja Silverman's discussion of Lina Lamont in *Singin' in the Rain* (1952) in *The Acoustic Mirror,* 45–46. Silverman usefully points out the extent to which this fixing of the voice to the body is a gendered phenomenon (see 164–65).

41 Also worth noting at this point is Silverman's critique of Chion's work on the cinematic voice. In particular, in *The Acoustic Mirror* Silverman notes that Chion's argument repeatedly converges with dominant cinema, especially with respect to the question of gender: "Unfortunately, Chion's sorties into the domain of sexual difference seem motivated primarily by the search for poetic props, and so remain for the most part uncritical and devoid of self-consciousness. Indeed, so determinedly does *La Voix au cinéma* circumscribe its discussion of the voice within existing gender demarcations that it assumes much of the symptomatic value of a Hollywood film" (49).

42 The reviewer from *Weekly Variety* noted that Davis had "A Southern accent that gets across," while the *Times* critic stated that "Miss Davis speaks with a most decided Southern drawl" (quoted in Quirk, *Fasten Your Seatbelts,* 82).

43 Davis is dubbed with Crawford's voice again when she calls the liquor store and finds out that Blanche has forbidden the store to fill any more orders for Jane. Director Robert Aldrich wanted Davis to imitate Crawford's voice, but she found this impossible: "In the scene where I was supposed to imitate Joan over the phone, I wasn't able to do it. Joan had to dub in her voice for me. She was very pleased about that" (Shaun Considine, *Bette and Joan: The Divine Feud* [New York: Dell, 1989], 335). Rather than trying to naturalize this moment of dubbing, Davis's contorted and exaggerated facial movements declare adamantly to the spectator, "This is NOT my voice."

44 In *Uninvited,* Patricia White notes the potential usefulness of a similar phenomenon of "retrospectatorship" in *All about Eve,* which for her is built into the structure of the film itself: "The film's flashbacks and returns leave a gap at its heart where its ostensible object of knowledge ought to be, frustrating the drive to closure of the classic text. Addison interrupts his initial narration—"More about Eve later, all about Eve in fact"—without picking up the thread again. This gap is made meaningful through 'retrospectatorship'; our viewing classical Hollywood from a contemporary position, one shaped by classical Hollywood as a cultural and historical experience and by particular stars or

genres or well-loved texts as concrete signifying instances, by the social and cultural, and, for some, personal meanings of lesbianism today" (207).

Afterword

1 As an example of this approach, Kaja Silverman quotes Charles Affron, who writes: "Sound . . . guarantees immediacy and presence in the system of absence that is cinema" (*The Acoustic Mirror: The Female Voice in Psychoanalysis and Cinema* [Bloomington: Indiana University Press, 1988], 43).

Works Cited

Acker, Ally. *Reel Women: Pioneers of the Cinema, 1896 to the Present.* New York: Continuum, 1993.

Adamson, D. B. "The Vanishing Lady: How to Effect the Disappearance." *Amateur Work* 121 (February 24, 1894).

Affron, Charles. *Star Acting: Gish, Garbo, Davis.* New York: Dutton, 1977.

Akers, C. E. *The Rubber Industry in Brazil and the Orient.* London: Methuen, 1914.

Allen, Jeffner, and Iris Young, eds. *The Thinking Muse: Feminism and Modern French Philosophy.* Bloomington: Indiana University Press, 1989.

Amnesty International. *It's about Time: Human Rights Are Women's Rights.* New York: Amnesty International, 1995.

Anzieu, Didier. *Freud's Self-Analysis,* translated by Peter Graham. Madison: International University Press, 1986.

Appignanesi, Lisa, and John Forrester. *Freud's Women.* London: Weidenfeld and Nicolson, 1992.

Armstrong, Isobel. *Victorian Poetry: Poetry, Poetics, and Politics.* London: Routledge, 1993.

Bailey, Peter. *Leisure and Class in Victorian England: Rational Recreation and the Contest for Control.* London: Routledge and Kegan Paul, 1978.

Baker, Roger. *Drag: A History of Female Impersonation in the Performing Arts.* London: Cassell, 1994.

Baldwin, James. *The Devil Finds Work.* New York: Dell, 1976.

Balfour, Edward. *The Cyclopeadia of India and of Eastern and Southeastern Asia.* 3 vols. London: Bernard Quaritich, 1885.

Balides, Constance. "Scenarios of Exposure in the Practice of Everyday Life: Women in the Cinema of Attractions." *Screen* 34.1 (spring 1993): 19–37.

Ball, Charles. *The History of the Indian Mutiny.* 2 vols. London: London Printing and Publishing, 1858.

Balmary, Mary. *Psychoanalyzing Psychoanalysis: Freud and the Hidden Fault of the Father,* translated by Ned Lukacher. Baltimore: Johns Hopkins University Press, 1982.

Barnouw, Erik. *The Magician and the Cinema.* New York: Oxford University Press, 1981.

Barthes, Roland. *Image-Music-Text,* translated by Stephen Heath. London: Fontana, 1977.

——. *Mythologies.* Translated by Annette Lavers. New York: Hill and Wang, 1973.

Batchen, Geoffrey. *Burning with Desire: The Conception of Photography.* Cambridge: MIT Press, 1999.

Baude, Ann. *Radical Spirits: Spiritualism and Women's Rights in Nineteenth-Century America.* Boston: Beacon, 1989.

Baudry, Jean-Louis. "Ideological Effects of the Basic Cinematic Apparatus." In *Narrative, Apparatus, Ideology: A Film Theory Reader,* edited by Philip Rosen, 286–98. New York: Columbia University Press, 1986. Originally published in 1970.

Baum, L. Frank. *The Art of Decorating Dry Goods Windows and Interiors: A Complete Manual of Window Trimming.* Chicago: Show Window Publishing Company, 1900.

——. *The Wonderful Wizard of Oz,* edited by Susan Wolstenholme. Oxford: Oxford University Press, 1997.

Beales, Derek. *From Castlereagh to Gladstone, 1815–1885.* London: Nelson, 1969.

Beckett, I. F. W. *Victoria's Wars.* Aylesbury: Shire, 1974.

Benjamin, Walter. *Illuminations,* edited by Hannah Arendt. New York: Schocken, 1968.

Bersani, Leo. *Homos.* Cambridge: Harvard University Press, 1995.

Bertram, Charles. *Isn't It Wonderful? A History of Magic and Mystery.* London: Schwan Sonnenschein, 1896.

Besterman, Theodore. *Some Modern Mediums.* London: Methuen, 1930.

Bisson, J. *Les phénomènes dits de matérialisation.* Paris: F. Alcon, 1914.

Blake, Robert. *Disraeli.* New York: St. Martin's, 1967.

Booth, Michael. *Victorian Spectacular Theater, 1850–1910.* London: Routledge and Kegan Paul, 1981.

Bordwell, David, and Kristin Thompson. *Film Art: An Introduction.* New York: McGraw-Hill, 1979.

Boucherette, Jessie. "On the Cause of the Distress Prevalent among Single Women." *Englishwoman's Journal* (1864): 13, 270.
———. "The Work We Have to Do." *Englishwoman's Review*, 1:1 (October 1866): 3.
———. "How to Provide for Surplus Women." In *Woman's Work and Woman's Culture: A Series of Essays*, edited by Josephine Butler, 27–48. London: Macmillan, 1869.
Boyarin, Daniel. "Freud's Baby, Fliess's Maybe: Homophobia, Antisemitism, and the Invention of Oedipus." *GLQ: A Journal of Gay and Lesbian Studies* 2.1–2 (1995): 115–47.
———. "Jewish Masochism: Couvade, Castration, and Rabbis in Pain." *American Imago* 51.1 (1994): 3–36.
Brakhage, Stan. *The Brakhage Lectures*. Chicago: Good Lion, 1972.
Brandon, Ruth. *The Spiritualists: The Passion for the Occult in the Nineteenth and Twentieth Centuries*. New York: Knopf, 1983.
Bronfen, Elisabeth. *Over Her Dead Body: Death, Femininity, and the Aesthetic*. New York: Routledge, 1992.
Brooks, Peter. *The Melodramatic Imagination*. New Haven: Yale University Press, 1976.
Brubach, Holly. "Beauty under the Knife." *Atlantic Monthly*, February 2000, 98–102.
Busch, Noel F. "Bette Davis," *Life*, January 23, 1939, 52–58.
Butler, Josephine, ed. *Woman's Work and Woman's Culture: A Series of Essays*. London: Macmillan, 1869.
Butler, Judith. *Bodies That Matter*. New York and London: Routledge, 1993.
———. *Excitable Speech: A Politics of the Performative*. New York: Routledge, 1997.
———. "Imitation and Gender Insubordination." In *inside/out: Lesbian Theories, Gay Theories*, edited by Diana Fuss, 13–31. New York: Routledge 1991.
———. "Against Proper Objects." In *Feminism Meets Queer Theory*, edited by Elizabeth Weed and Naomi Schor, 1–30. Bloomington: Indiana University Press, 1997.
———. *The Psychic Life of Power*. Stanford: Stanford University Press, 1997.
———. "Sexual Ideology and Phenomenological Description: A Feminist Critique of Merleau-Ponty's *Phenomenology of Perception*." In *The Thinking Muse: Feminism and Modern French Philosophy*," edited by Jeffner Allen and Iris Young, 85–100. Bloomington: Indiana University Press, 1989.
Cadava, Eduardo. "Words of Light: Theses on the Photography of History." *Diacritics* 22.3–4 (1992): 84–114.
———. *Words of Light: Theses on the Photography of History*. Princeton: Princeton University Press, 1997.
Camera Obscura: A Journal of Feminist and Film Theory, special issue, "Spectatrix," 20–21 (1989).
Carey, Gary. *More about "All About Eve": A Colloquy with Joseph L. Mankiewicz*. New York: Random House, 1972.
Case, Sue-Ellen. "Toward a Butch-Femme Aesthetic." *Discourse* 11.1 (fall–winter 1988–89): 55–73.
Castle, Terry. *The Apparitional Lesbian: Female Sexuality and Modern Culture*. New York: Columbia University Press, 1993.
———. *Noël Coward and Radclyffe Hall: Kindred Spirits*. New York: Columbia University Press, 1996.

———. "Phantasmagoria: Spectral Technology and the Metaphorics of Modern Reverie." *Critical Inquiry* 15 (autumn 1988): 26–61.

———. "The Spectralization of the Other in *The Mysteries of Udolpho*." In *The New Eighteenth Century: Theory, Politics, English Literature,* edited by Felicity Nussbaum and Laura Brown, 231–309. New York: Methuen, 1987.

Cavell, Stanley. *Contesting Tears: The Hollywood Melodrama of the Unknown Woman.* Chicago: University of Chicago Press, 1996.

———. *The World Viewed: Reflections on the Ontology of Film.* New York: Viking, 1971.

Chion, Michel. *The Voice in Cinema.* New York: Columbia University Press, 1999.

Citron, Michelle, Julia Lesage, Judith Mayne, B. Ruby Rich, and Anna Marie Taylor. "Women and film: a discussion of feminist aesthetics." *New German Critique* 13 (1978): 83–107.

Coates, James. *Photographing the Invisible: Practical Studies in Spirit Photography, Spirit Portraiture, and Other Rare but Allied Phenomena.* 1911. Reprint, New York: Arno, 1973.

Coates, Paul. *The Story of the Lost Reflection: The Alienation of the Image in Western and Polish Cinema.* London: Verso, 1985.

Cobbe, Frances Power. "What Shall We Do with Our Old Maids?" *Frazer's,* November 1862, 594–610.

Cohan, Steven. *Masked Men: Masculinity and the Movies in the Fifties.* Bloomington: Indiana University Press, 1997.

Cohen, Margaret, and Christopher Prendergast, eds. *Spectacles of Realism: Gender, Body, Genre.* Minneapolis: University of Minnesota Press, 1995.

Collins, (William) Wilkie. *The Moonstone.* 1868. Reprint, London: Penguin, 1986.

Conan Doyle, Arthur. *The History of Spiritualism.* Vol. 2. New York: Arno, 1975.

Considine, Shaun. *Bette and Joan: The Divine Feud.* New York: Dell, 1989.

Cowie, Elizabeth. "Fantasia." *m/f* 9 (1984): 70–105.

———. *Representing the Woman: Cinema and Psychoanalysis.* Minneapolis: University of Minnesota Press, 1997.

Crawford, Christina. *Mommie Dearest.* New York: William Morrow, 1978.

Creed, Barbara. *The Monstrous Feminine: Film, Feminism, Psychoanalysis.* New York: Routledge, 1993.

Crimp, Douglas. "Mourning and Militancy." *October* 52 (winter 1989): 3–18.

Culver, Stuart. "What Manikins Want: *The Wonderful Wizard of Oz* and *The Art of Decorating Dry Goods Windows*." *Representations* 21 (winter 1988): 97–116.

Davis, Bette, and Sanford Dody. *The Lonely Life.* New York: Putnam, 1962.

Davis, Bette, and Michael Herskowitz. *This 'N' That.* New York: Putnam, 1988.

Davis, Curt. "Bette Davis: Getting under the Skin." *Encore American and Worldwide News,* November 6, 1978, 30–31.

De Duve, Thierry. "Time Exposure and Snapshot: The Photograph as Paradox." *October* 5 (1978): 111–25.

De Lauretis, Teresa. *Alice Doesn't: Feminism, Semiotics, Cinema.* Bloomington: Indiana University Press, 1984.

———. *The Practice of Love: Lesbian Sexuality and Perverse Desire.* Bloomington: Indiana University Press, 1994.

———. *Technologies of Gender: Essays on Theory, Film, and Fiction*. Bloomington: Indiana University Press, 1987.

De Nicola, Deborah, ed. *Orpheus and Company: Contemporary Poems on Greek Mythology*. Hanover: University Press of New England, 1999.

Derrida, Jacques. "Coming into One's Own." In *Psychoanalysis and the Question of the Text,* edited by Geoffrey Hartmann. Baltimore: Johns Hopkins University Press, 1978: 114–48.

———. *Margins of Philosophy,* translated by Alan Bass. Chicago: University of Chicago Press, 1987.

———. *Specters of Marx: The State of the Debt, the Work of Mourning, and the New International,* translated by Peggy Kamuf. New York: Routledge, 1994.

Diawara, Manthia, ed., *Black American Cinema*. New York: Routledge, 1993.

Dickens, Charles. *The Posthumous Papers of the Pickwick Club,* edited by Mark Wormald. Harmondsworth, Middlesex: Penguin, 1999.

Didion, Joan. *Salvador.* New York: Vintage, 1983.

Doane, Mary Ann. *The Desire to Desire: The Woman's Film of the 1940s*. Bloomington: Indiana University Press, 1987.

———. *Femmes Fatales: Feminism, Film Theory, Psychoanalysis*. New York: Routledge, 1991.

Doane, Mary Ann, Patricia Mellencamp, and Linda Williams, eds. *RE-VISION: Essays in Feminist Film Criticism*. Los Angeles: American Film Institute, 1984.

Doody, Margaret Anne. *The True Story of the Novel*. New Brunswick, NJ: Rutgers University Press, 1996.

Dove, Rita. *Mother Love: Poems*. New York: Norton, 1995.

Duncan, Ian. "*The Moonstone,* the Victorian Novel, and Imperialist Panic." *Modern Language Quarterly* 55.3 (September 1994): 297–319.

Durant, Régis. "How to See (Photographically)." In *Fugitive Images: From Photography to Video,* edited by Patrice Petro, 141–51. Bloomington: Indiana University Press, 1995.

Durgnat, Raymond. *The Strange Case of Alfred Hitchcock; or, the Plain Man's Hitchcock*. Cambridge: MIT Press, 1974.

Dyer, Richard. *Heavenly Bodies: Film Stars and Society*. New York: St. Martin's, 1986.

———. *White*. London: Routledge, 1997.

———. "The Carole Lombard in Macy's Window." In *Fabrications: Costume and the Female Body,*" edited by Jane M. Gaines, 100–121. New York: Routledge, 1990.

Ellison, Ralph. *The Invisible Man*. New York: Vintage, 1972.

Elsaesser, Thomas, ed. *Early Cinema: Space, Frame, Narrative*. London: British Film Institute, 1990.

Evans, Henry Ridgely. *History of Conjuring and Magic: From the Earliest Times to the End of the Eighteenth Century*. Kenton, OH: William W. Durbin, 1930.

Everett, Anna. *Returning the Gaze: A Genealogy of Black Film Criticism, 1909–1949*. Durham: Duke University Press, 2001.

Ferro, Marc. *Cinema and History,* translated by Naomi Greene. Detroit: Wayne State University Press, 1988.

Fischer, Andreas, and Veit Loers. *Im Reich der Phantome: Fotographie des Unsichtbaren*. (exhibition catalogue) Ostfildern-Ruit: Cantz Verlag, 1997.

Fischer, Lucy. *Cinematernity: Film, Motherhood, Genre*. Princeton: Princeton University Press, 1996.

———. "The Lady Vanishes: Women, Magic, and the Movies." *Film Quarterly* 33.1 (fall 1979): 30–40.

———. "*Sunset Boulevard:* Fading Stars." In *Women and Film: Women and Literature,* edited by Janet Todd, 97–113. New Series, vol. 4. New York: Holmes and Meier, 1988.

———. "Two Faced Woman: The Double in Woman's Melodrama of the 1940s." *Cinema Journal* 23.1 (fall 1983): 24–43.

Forgacs, David. "Fascism, Violence, and Modernity." In *The Violent Muse: Violence and the Artistic Imagination, 1910–1939,* edited by Jana Howlett and Rod Mengham. Manchester: Manchester University Press, 1994, 5–21.

Foucault, Michel. *Discipline and Punish: The Birth of the Prison,* translated by Alan Sheridan. New York: Vintage, 1979.

Frazer, John. *Artificially Arranged Scenes: The Films of Georges Méliès.* Boston: G. K. Hall, 1979.

Freud, Sigmund. *The Standard Edition of the Complete Psychological Works of Sigmund Freud,* translated from the German under the general editorship of James Strachey in collaboration with Anna Freud, assisted by Alix Strachey and Alan Tyson, 24 volumes. London: Hogarth, 1953–74.

———. *Das Ich und das Es: Metapsychologische Schriften.* (Frankfurt am Main: Fischer, 1992).

Friedberg, Anne. "Cinema and the Postmodern Condition." In *Viewing Positions: Ways of Seeing Film,* edited by Linda Williams, 59–83. New Brunswick, NJ: Rutgers University Press, 1994.

Fuss, Diana. *Identification Papers.* New York: Routledge, 1995.

Fuss, Diana, ed. *inside/out: Lesbian Theories, Gay Theories.* New York: Routledge, 1991.

Gaines, Jane M. *Fabrications: Costume and the Female Body."* New York: Routledge, 1990.

———. *Fire and Desire: Mixed-Race Movies in the Silent Era.* Chicago: University of Chicago Press, 2001.

———. "The Queen Christina Tie-Ups: Convergence of Show Window and Screen." *Quarterly Review of Film and Video* 11 (1989): 35–60.

Gallagher, Catherine. "The Body versus the Social Body in Malthus and Mahew." *Representations* 14 (spring 1986): 83–104.

Gallop, Jane. *Reading Lacan.* Ithaca: Cornell University Press, 1985.

———. *Around 1981: Academic Feminist Literary Theory.* New York: Routledge, 1992.

Gay, Peter. *Freud: A Life for Our Time.* New York: Norton, 1998.

———. *The Freud Reader.* New York: Norton, 1989.

Gettings, Fred. *Ghosts in Photographs: The Extraordinary Story of Spirit Photography.* New York: Harmony, 1978.

Gifford, Dennis. *The British Film Catalogue, 1895–1985: A Reference Guide.* 1973. Reprint, London: David and Charles, 1986.

Gilman, Sander. *Difference and Pathology: Stereotypes of Sexuality, Race, and Madness.* Ithaca: Cornell University Press, 1985.

———. *The Jew's Body.* New York: Routledge, 1991.

Gledhill, Christine, ed. *Home Is Where the Heart Is: Studies in Melodrama and the Woman's Film*. London: British Film Institute, 1987.

Godwin, William. *Of Population: An Enquiry Concerning the Power of Increase in the Numbers of Mankind, Being an Answer to Mr. Malthus's Essay on That Subject*. 1820. Reprint, New York: August M. Kelley, 1964.

Goldfarb, Russell M., and Clare R. Goldfarb. *Spiritualism and Nineteenth-Century Letters*. London: Associated University Presses, 1978.

Gordon, Avery F. *Ghostly Matters: Haunting and the Sociological Imagination*. Minneapolis: University of Minnesota Press, 1997.

Goux, Jean-Joseph. *Oedipus, Philosopher*, translated by Catherine Porter. Stanford: Stanford University Press, 1993.

Grant, Rena. "Characterhysterics II: Repeating Oneself." *Lacanian Ink* 8 (1994): 72–83.

Green, André. "The Dead Mother." In *On Private Madness*. London: Hogarth, 1986.

Greg, Samuel. "Why Are Women Redundant?" *National Review* 14 (April 1862): 434–60.

Grosz, Elizabeth. *Toward a Corporeal Feminism*. Bloomington: Indiana University Press, 1994.

——. "The Labors of Love. Analyzing Perverse Desire: An Interrogation of Teresa DeLauretis's *The Practice of Love*." In *Feminism Meets Queer Theory*, edited by Elizabeth Weed and Naomi Schor, 292–314. Bloomington: Indiana University Press, 1997.

Gunning, Tom. "The Cinema of Attractions: Early Film, Its Spectator, and the Avant-Garde." In *Early Cinema: Space, Frame, Narrative*, edited by Thomas Elsaesser, 56–62. London: British Film Institute, 1990.

——. *D. W. Griffith and the Origins of American Narrative Film: The Early Years at Biograph*. Urbana: University of Illinois Press, 1991.

——. "Phantom Images and Modern Manifestations: Spirit Photography, Magic Theater, Trick Films, and Photography's Uncanny." In *Fugitive Images: From Photography to Video*, edited by Patrice Petro, 42–71. Bloomington: Indiana University Press, 1995.

Hammond, Paul. *Marvelous Méliès*. London: Gordon Fraser, 1974.

Hansen, Miriam. "Early Cinema, Late Cinema: Transformations of the Public Sphere." In *Viewing Positions: Ways of Seeing Film*, edited by Linda Williams, 134–54. New Brunswick: Rutgers University Press, 1994.

Hanson, Ellis, ed. *Outtakes: Essays on Queer Theory and Film*. Durham: Duke University Press, 1999.

Haraway, Donna. *Simians, Cyborgs, and Women: The Reinvention of Nature*. New York: Routledge, 1991.

Harlan, Veit. *Im Schatten Meiner Filme: Selbst Biographie*, edited by H. C. Opfermann. Gütersloh: Sigbert Mohm Verlag, 1966.

Hart, Linda, and Peggy Phelan, eds. *Acting Out: Feminist Performances*. Ann Arbor: University of Michigan Press, 1993.

Hartmann, Geoffrey, ed. *Psychoanalysis and the Question of the Text*. Baltimore: Johns Hopkins University Press, 1978.

Haskell, Molly. *From Reverence to Rape: The Treatment of Women in the Movies.* 1973. Reprint, New York: Holt, Rinehart and Winston, 1974.

Hazlitt, William. *The Collected Works of William Hazlitt,* edited by A. R. Waller and Arnold Glover. London: J. M. Dent, 1903.

——. *Reply to the Essay on Population by the Rev. T. R. Malthus.* London, 1807.

Heck-Rabi, Louise. *Women Filmmakers: A Critical Reception.* Metuchen, NJ: Scarecrow, 1984.

Heidegger, Martin. *An Introduction to Metaphysics,* translated by Ralph Manheim. 1959. Reprint, New Haven: Yale University Press, 1987.

Herstein, Sheila. "The Langham Place Circle and Feminist Periodicals of the 1860s." *Victorian Periodicals Review* (spring 1993) 26:1 24–27.

Higham, Charles. *Bette: The Life of Bette Davis.* New York: Macmillan, 1981.

Hitler, Adolf. *Mein Kampf,* translated by Ralph Manheim. Boston: Houghton Mifflin, 1943. Reprinted 1971.

hooks, bell. *Black Looks: Race and Representation.* Boston: South End, 1992.

Hopkins, Albert A., ed. *Magic, Stage Illusions, Special Effects, and Trick Photography.* New York: Munn. Scientific American Office, 1898.

Houdini, Harry. *A Magician among the Spirits.* New York: Harper and Brothers, 1924.

Hyam, Ronald. *Britain's Imperial Century, 1815–1914: A Study of Empire and Expansionism.* London: Batsford, 1976.

Hyman, B. D. *My Mother's Keeper.* New York: Morrow, 1985.

Hynes, Samuel. *Thomas Hardy.* Oxford: Oxford University Pres, 1994.

Irigaray, Luce. "Body against Body: In Relation to the Mother." In *Sexes and Genealogies,* translated by Gillian C. Gill. New York: Columbia University Press, 1993: 7–21.

——. *An Ethics of Sexual Difference,* translated by Carolyn Burke and Gillian C. Gill. Ithaca: Cornell University Press, 1993.

——. *Speculum of the Other Woman,* translated by Gillian C. Gill. Ithaca: Cornell University Press, 1985.

Jacobus, Mary. *First Things: The Maternal Imaginary in Literature, Art, and Psychoanalysis.* New York: Routledge, 1995.

Jacobus, Mary, Evelyn Fox Keller, and Sally Shuttleworth, eds. *Body/Politics: Women and the Discourse of Science.* New York: Routledge, 1990.

Jay, Martin. *Downcast Eyes: The Denigration of Vision in Twentieth Century French Thought.* Berkeley: University of California Press, 1993.

Johnson, Barbara. *A World of Difference.* Baltimore: Johns Hopkins University Press, 1987.

Johnston, Claire. "Women's Cinema as Counter-cinema." In *Notes on Women's Cinema.* 1973. Reprinted in *Movies and Methods: An Anthology,* edited by Bill Nicholas, 208–17. Berkeley: University of California Press, 1976.

Jones, Ernest. *The Life and Work of Sigmund Freud.* Vol. 1. New York: Basic Books, 1953.

Kalin, Tom. "Prodigal Stories: AIDS and Family." *Aperture:* "The Body in Question" (special issue) 121 (fall 1990): 22–25.

Kaye, J. W. "The Non-existence of Women." *North British Review* 23 (August 1855): 288–302.

Kent, Susan Kingsley. *Sex and Suffrage in Britain, 1860–1914.* Princeton: Princeton University Press, 1987.

Klein, Melanie. *Love, Guilt, and Reparation and Other Works, 1921–1945.* London: Hogarth, 1975.

Krauss, Rosalind. *The Optical Unconscious.* Cambridge: MIT Press, 1993.

——. "Tracing Nadar." In *Illuminations: Women Writing on Photography from the 1850s to the Present,* edited by Liz Heron and Val Williams. Durham: Duke University Press, 1996.

Kristeva, Julia. *Black Sun: Depression and Melancholia.* New York: Columbia University Press, 1989.

——. "Freud and Love: Treatment and Its Discontents," In *The Kristeva Reader,* edited by Toril Moi. New York: Columbia Press, 1986, 238–271.

——. *Powers of Horror: An Essay on Abjection.* New York: Columbia University Press, 1982.

Lacan, Jacques. *Feminine Sexuality: Jacques Lacan and the École Freudienne,* translated by Jacqueline Rose and Juliet Mitchell. New York: Pantheon, 1982.

——. *The Four Fundamental Concepts of Psychoanalysis,* edited by Jacques-Alain Miller, translated by Alan Sheridan. New York: Norton, 1977.

Lamb, Geoffrey. *Victorian Magic.* London: Routledge and Kegan Paul, 1976.

LaPlace, Maria. "Producing and Consuming the Woman's Film: Discursive Struggle in *Now, Voyager.*" In *Home Is Where the Heart Is: Studies in Melodrama and the Woman's Film,* edited by Christine Gledhill, 138–66. London: British Film Institute, 1987.

Leaming, Barbara. *Bette Davis: A Biography.* New York: Ballantine, 1992.

Levens, Mary. *Eating Disorders and the Magical Control of the Body: Treatment through Art Therapy.* London: Routledge, 1995.

Levin, Martin, ed. *Hollywood and the Great Fan Magazines.* New York: Arbor, 1970.

Magic (London). Various issues, 1900–1920.

Magic Circular: A Monthly Review (London). Various issues, 1906–.

Malthete-Méliès, Madelaine, ed. *Méliès et la naissance du spectacle cinématographique.* Paris: Klincksieck, 1984.

Malthus, Robert. *An Essay on the Principle of Population,* edited by Donald Winch. 1803. Reprint, Cambridge: Cambridge University Press, 1992.

Marvin, R. Frederic. *The Philosophy of Spiritualism and the Pathology and Treatment of Mediomania: Two Lectures Read before the New York Liberal Club.* New York: Asa K. Butts, 1874.

Maskelyne, Jasper. *White Magic: The Story of Maskelynes.* London: Stanley Paul, 1936.

Masson, Jeffrey Moussaieff, trans. and ed. *The Complete Letters of Sigmund Freud to Wilhelm Fliess, 1887–1904.* Cambridge: Harvard University Press, 1985.

Matlock, Jann. "Reading Invisibility." In *Field Work: Sites in Literary and Cultural Studies,* edited by Marjorie Garber, Paul B. Franklin, and Rebecca L. Walkowitz, 184–95. New York: Routledge, 1996.

Mayne, Judith. *Cinema and Spectatorship.* London: Routledge, 1993.

McClintock, Anne. *Imperial Leather: Race, Gender, and Sexuality in the Colonial Contest.* New York: Routledge, 1995.

Merleau-Ponty, Maurice. *The Phenomenology of Perception,* translated by Colin Smith. London: Routledge and Kegan Paul, 1962.

——. *The Visible and the Invisible,* translated by Alphonso Lingis. Evanston: Northwestern University Press, 1968.

Millbourne, Christopher. *The Illustrated History of Magic.* New York: Cromwell, 1973.

Miller, D. A. *The Novel and the Police.* Berkeley: University of California Press, 1988.

Minh-ha, Trinh T. *Woman, Native, Other: Writing Postcoloniality and Feminism.* Bloomington: Indiana University Press, 1989.

Mitchell, B. R., with Phyllis Deane. *Abstract of British Historical Statistics.* Cambridge: Cambridge University Press, 1962.

Mitchell, Juliet. *Man, Men, and Medusas: Reclaiming Hysteria.* New York: Basic Books, 2000.

Mitchell, Juliet, ed. *The Selected Melanie Klein.* New York: Free Press, 1986.

Moore, F. Michael. *DRAG! Male and Female Impersonators on Stage, Screen, and Television: An Illustrated World History.* Jefferson, NC: McFarland, 1994.

Moorhouse, Geoffrey. *India Britannica.* London: William Collins Sons, 1983.

Morey, Anne. "'A Whole Book for a Nickel'? L. Frank Baum as Filmmaker." *Children's Literature Association Quarterly* 20.4 (winter 1995–96): 155–60.

Mulvey, Laura. "British Feminist Film Theory's Female Spectator: Presence and Absence." *Camera Obscura: A Journal of Feminism and Film Theory* 20–21 (May–September 1989): 68–79.

——. "Visual Pleasure and Narrative Cinema." *Screen* 16.3 (autumn 1975): 6–18.

Munich, Adrienne. *Queen Victoria's Secrets.* New York: Columbia University Press, 1998.

Myint, Ni Ni. *Burma's Struggle against British Imperialism, 1885–1895.* Rangoon: Burma: The University Press, 1983.

Nancy, Jean-Luc. *The Evidence of Film: Abbas Kiarostami,* translated by Christine Irizzary and Verena Andermatt Conley. Brussels: Yves Gevaert, 2001.

Naumberg, Nancy, ed. *We Make the Movies.* New York: Norton, 1937.

Newton, Esther. *Mother Camp: Female Impersonators in America.* 1972. Reprint, Chicago: University of Chicago Press, 1979.

Nunokawa, Jeff. "All the Sad Young Men: AIDS and the Work of Mourning." In *inside/out: Lesbian Theories, Gay Theories,* edited by Diana Fuss, 311–23. New York: Routledge, 1991.

Ohmer, Susan. "Female Spectatorship and Women's Magazines: Hollywood, *Good Housekeeping,* and World War II." *The Velvet Light Trap* 25 (spring 1990): 53–68.

Pellegrini, Ann. *Performance Anxieties: Staging Psychoanalysis, Staging Race.* New York: Routledge, 1997.

Petro, Patrice, ed. *Fugitive Images: From Photography to Video.* Bloomington: Indiana University Press, 1995.

Petro, Patrice. "Rematerializing the Vanishing 'Lady': Feminism, Hitchcock, and Interpretation," in *A Hitchcock Reader,* edited by Marshall Deutelbaum and Leland Poague, 122–132. Ames: Iowa State University Press, 1986.

Phelan, Peggy. *Mourning Sex: Performing Public Memories.* London: Routledge, 1997.

———. *Unmarked: The Politics of Performance*. New York: Routledge, 1993.

Phillips, Adam. *On Kissing, Tickling, and Being Bored: Psychoanalytic Essays on the Unexamined Life*. Cambridge: Harvard University Press, 1993.

Plaza, Monique. "The Mother/The Same: Hatred of the Mother in Psychoanalysis." *Feminist Issues* (spring 1982) 2:1 75–99.

Price, Theodore. "The Truth about the Bette Davis 1937 Gangster Movie *Marked Woman*." In *Crime in Motion Pictures,* edited by Douglas Radcliff-Umstead, 24–32. Kent: Kent State University Press, 1986.

Pryse, Marjorie, and Hortense Spillers, eds. *Conjuring: Black Women, Fiction, and the Literary Tradition*. Bloomington: Indiana University Press, 1985.

Punch; or the London Charivari. Various issues.

Quéverain, Anne-Marie, and Marie-George Charconnet-Méliès. "Méliès et Freud: Un avenir pour les marchands d'illusions?" In *Méliès et la naissance du spectacle cinématographique,* edited by Madelaine Malthête-Méliès, 221–239. Paris: Klincksieck, 1984.

Quirk, Lawrence J. *Fasten Your Seatbelts: The Passionate Life of Bette Davis*. New York: Morrow, 1990.

Rainer, Yvonne. *The Films of Yvonne Rainer*. Bloomington: Indiana University Press, 1989.

Rattray, David. *How I Became One of the Invisible*. New York: Semiotext(e), 1992.

Reed, John. "English Imperialism and the Unacknowledged Crime of the Moonstone." *Clio* 2 (1973): 281–90.

Renov, Michael. "Advertising/Photojournalism/Cinema: The Shifting Rhetoric of Forties Female Representation." *Quarterly Review of Film and Video* 2 (1989): 1–21.

Rentschler, Eric. *The Ministry of Illusion: Nazi Cinema and Its Afterlife*. Cambridge: Harvard University Press, 1996.

Ricks, Christopher, ed. *The New Oxford Book of Victorian Verse*. Oxford: Oxford University Press, 1987.

Ringgold, Gene. *The Films of Bette Davis*. New York: Bonanza, 1966.

Rose, Jacqueline. *Sexuality in the Field of Vision*. London: Verso, 1986.

———. *Why War? Psychoanalysis, Politics, and the Return to Melanie Klein*. Oxford: Blackwell, 1993.

Rosen, Philip, ed. *Narrative, Apparatus, Ideology: A Film Theory Reader*. New York: Columbia University Press, 1986.

Ross, Andrew. *No Respect: Intellectuals and Popular Culture*. New York: Routledge, 1989.

Roy, Ashish. "The Fabulist Imperialist Semiotic of Wilkie Collins's *The Moonstone*." *New Literary History* 24 (1993): 657–81.

Russo, Vito. *The Celluloid Closet: Homosexuality in the Movies*. New York: Harper and Row, 1981.

Sagan, Carl. *Pale Blue Dot: A Vision of the Human Future in Space*. New York: Random House, 1994.

Said, Edward. *Culture and Imperialism*. New York: Knopf, 1993.

Sajner, Josef. "Sigmund Freuds Beziehungen zu seinem Geburtsort Freiberg (Príbor) und zu Mähren." *Clio Medica* 3 (1968): 167–80.

Salt, Barry. "Film Form, 1900–1906." In *Early Cinema: Space, Frame, Narrative,* edited by Thomas Elsaesser, 31–34. London: British Film Institute, 1990.

——. *Film Style and Technology: History and Analysis.* London: Starword, 1983.

Schatz, Thomas. "'A Triumph of Bitchery': Warner Bros., Bette Davis, and *Jezebel.*" *Wide Angle: A Film Quarterly of Theory, Criticism, and Practice* 10.1 (1988): 16–29.

Schilder, Paul. *The Image and Appearance of the Human Body: Studies in the Constructive Energies of the Psyche.* New York: International University Press, 1978.

Schrenck-Notzing, A. Freiherrn von. *Materialisationsphaenomene: Ein Beitrag zur Erforschung der Mediumistischen Teleplastie.* Zweite, stark vermehrte Auflage. Munich: Ernst Reinhardt, 1923.

Scrapbooks. Harry Price Library of Magical Literature, University of London.

Screen 25.1 (January–February 1984), special issue on melodrama.

Screen 27.6 (November–December 1986), special issue on melodrama.

Sharpe, Jenny. *Allegories of Empire: The Figure of Woman in the Colonial Text.* Minneapolis: University of Minnesota Press, 1993.

Shingler, Martin. "Masquerade or Drag? Bette Davis and the Ambiguities of Gender." *Screen* 36.3 (autumn 1995): 179–92.

Showalter, Elaine. *Sexual Anarchy: Gender and Culture at the Fin de Siècle.* New York: Penguin, 1990.

Silverman, Kaja. *The Acoustic Mirror: The Female Voice in Psychoanalysis and Cinema.* Bloomington: University of Indiana Press, 1988.

——. *The Threshold of the Visible World.* New York: Routledge, 1996.

Simone, Sam P. *Hitchcock as Activist: Politics and the War Films.* Ann Arbor: UMI Research Press, 1982.

Sinclair, Andrew. *Masterworks of the British Cinema.* London: Faber and Faber, 1990.

Smith, Valerie. *Not Just Race, Not Just Gender: Black Feminist Readings.* New York: Routledge, 1998.

Sobieszek, Robert A. *Ghost in the Shell: Photography and the Human Soul, 1850–2000.* Cambridge: MIT Press, 1999.

Spada, James. *More Than A Woman: An Intimate Biography of Bette Davis.* New York: Bantam, 1993.

Sprengnether, Madelon. *The Spectral Mother: Freud, Feminism, and Psychoanalysis.* Ithaca: Cornell University Press, 1990.

Stacey, Jackie. "Desperately Seeking Difference." In *The Female Gaze: Women as Viewers of Popular Culture,* edited by Lorraine Gamman and Margaret Marshment, 112–29. London: Women's Press, 1988.

——. *Star Gazing: Hollywood Cinema and Female Spectatorship.* London: Routledge, 1994.

Stafford, Barbara Maria. *Artful Science: Enlightenment, Entertainment, and the Eclipse of Visual Education.* Cambridge: MIT Press, 1994.

Steiner, Wendy. *The Scandal of Pleasure: Art in an Age of Fundamentalism.* Chicago: University of Chicago Press, 1995.

Stine, Whitney. *"I'd love to kiss you . . ." Conversations with Bette Davis.* New York: Pocket Books, 1990.

Strachey, Lytton. *Queen Victoria*. San Diego: Harcourt, 1921.

Strand 34 (winter 1902–3): 552–58.

Swan, Jim. "*Mater* and Nannie: Freud's Two Mothers." *American Imago* 31.1 (spring 1974): 1–64.

Swann, Karen. "Harrassing the Muse. In *Romanticism and Feminism,* edited by Anne K. Mellor, 81–92. Bloomington: Indiana University Press, 1988.

Taylor, Diana. *Disappearing Acts: Spectacles of Gender and Nationalism in Argentina's "Dirty War."* Durham: Duke University Press, 1997.

Theweleit, Klaus. *Male Fantasies*. Minneapolis: University of Minnesota Press, 1987.

Thompson, David. *England in the Nineteenth Century*. London: Penguin, 1950.

Thompson, Kristin. "The Concept of Cinematic Excess." In *Narrative, Apparatus, Ideology: A Film Theory Reader,* edited by Philip Rosen, 130–142. New York: Columbia University Press, 1986.

Trollope, Joanna. *Britannia's Daughters: Women of the British Empire.* London: Hutchinson, 1983.

Truffaut, François. *Hitchcock*. New York: Simon and Schuster, 1966.

Tyler, Carole-Anne. "Boys Will Be Girls: The Politics of Gay Drag." In *inside/out: Lesbian Theories, Gay Theories,* edited by Diana Fuss, 32–70. New York: Routledge, 1991.

Van Leer, David. *The Queening of America: Gay Culture in Straight Society*. New York: Routledge, 1995.

Vicinus, Martha. *Independent Women: Work and Community for Single Women, 1850–1920*. Chicago: University of Chicago Press, 1985.

Virilio, Paul. *The Aesthetics of Disappearance,* translated by Philip Beitchman. New York: Semiotext(e), 1991.

Von Huhn, Major A. *The Struggle of the Bulgarians for National Independence under Prince Alexander: A Military and Political History of the War between Bulgaria and Servia in 1885.* London: John Murray, 1886.

Von Wiese, Benno. *Deutsche Gedichte: Von den Anfängen bis zur Gegenwart.* Düsseldorf: Cornelsen, 1993.

Waldorff, Leon. *Keats and the Silent Work of Imagination.* Urbana: University of Illinois Press, 1985.

Walker, Alexander. *Bette Davis: A Celebration.* Boston: Little, Brown, 1986.

Weed, Elizabeth, and Naomi Schor. *Feminism Meets Queer Theory.* Bloomington: Indiana University Press, 1997.

Welles, H. G. *The Island of Dr. Moreau.* 1896. Reprinted, New York: Signet, 1988.

White, Ethel Lina. *The Wheel Spins.* New York: Harper, 1936.

White, Patricia. *Uninvited: Classical Hollywood Cinema and Lesbian Representability.* Bloomington: Indiana University Press, 1999.

Wide Angle 4.2 (1980), special issue on melodrama.

Williams, Linda. "Film Body: An Implantation of Perversions." *Cinétracts* 12 (winter 1981): 19–35.

——. *Hard Core: Power, Pleasure, and the "Frenzy of the Visible."* Berkeley: University of California Press, 1989.

——. *Viewing Positions: Ways of Seeing Film.* New Brunswick, NJ: Rutgers University Press, 1994.

Williams, Richard. *The Contentious Crown: Public Discussion of the Monarchy in the Reign of Queen Victoria.* Aldershot: Ashgate, 1997.

Winnicott, D. W. *Playing and Reality.* New York: Routledge, 1971.

Witte, Karsten. "Wie faschistisch ist *Die Feuerzangenbowle?* Bemerkungen zur Filmkomödie im Dritten Reich." *epd Kirche und Film* 29.7 (July 1976): 1–4.

Wittig, Monique. *The Straight Mind and Other Essays.* Boston: Beacon, 1992.

Zielinski, Siegfried. *Veit Harlan: Analysen und Materialen zur Auseinandersetzung mit einem Film-Regisseur des deutschen Faschismus.* Frankfurt am Main: R. G. Fischer, 1981.

Žižek, Slavoj. *Looking Awry: An Introduction to Jacques Lacan through Popular Culture.* Cambridge: MIT Press, 1992.

Filmography

All about Eve. Joseph Mankiewicz, 1950.
The Artist's Dilemma. Thomas Edison, 1901.
An Artist's Dream. Thomas Edison, 1900.
Ching Ling Foo. Thomas Edison, 1900.
The Clown and the Alchemist. Thomas Edison, 1900.
Dangerous. Alfred E. Green, 1935.
The Disappearance of Aimee. Anthony Harvey, 1976.
Faust and Marguerite. Thomas Edison, 1900.
A Frontier Flirtation. Thomas Edison, 1903.
Hooligan Assists the Magician. Thomas Edison, November 16, 1900.
The Lady Vanishes. Alfred Hitchcock, 1938.
The Magician. Thomas Edison, February 28, 1900.
The Man Who Envied Women. Yvonne Rainer, 1985.
The Mystic Swing. Thomas Edison, March 21, 1900.
Now, Voyager. Irving Rapper, 1942.

Oedipus Wrecks. Woody Allen, 1989.

Parachute Jumper. Alfred E. Green, 1933.

The Poster Girls. AM&B, April 26, 1902.

Psycho. Alfred Hitchcock, 1960.

A Spiritualist Photographer. Georges Méliès, July 6, 1903.

The Star. Stuart Heisler, 1952.

A Star Is Born. William Wellman, 1937.

A Star Is Born. George Cukor, 1954.

A Star Is Born. Frank Pierson, 1976.

Sunset Boulevard. Billy Wilder, 1950.

Uncle Josh at the Moving Picture Show. Thomas Edison, 1902.

Vanishing Lady. Georges Méliès, October–November 1896.

Vanishing Lady. R. W. Paul, 1897.

Vanishing Lady. Thomas Edison, 1898.

Verwehte Spuren. Veit Harlan, 1938.

What Price Hollywood? George Cukor, 1932.

Whatever Happened to Baby Jane? Robert Aldrich, 1962.

Index

Phenomenon: Preliminary Communication," 106–107; in Paris, 96–97; "The Psychopathology of Everyday Life," 113–116; on self-analysis, 98, 111–128; "Studies on Hysteria," 96–97; and vanishing mother, 112–128

Freud, Sophie, 123–127

Friedberg, Anne, 4, 196 n.4

Gaines, Jane M., 174

Gallop, Jane, 102

Gettings, Fred, 83–84, 208 n.48

Ghosts in the Shell, 75

Goux, Jean-Joseph, 101, 102–104

Greg, W. R., 27–31

Gunning, Tom, 63, 77, 86, 131, 206 nn.31, 32

Hanson, Ellis, 69

Hardy, Thomas, 196–197 n.6

Harlan, Veit. See *Verwehte Spuren*

Hazlitt, William, 41–42

Heidegger, Martin, 159–160

Hitchcock, Alfred. See *The Lady Vanishes; Psycho*

Hitler, Adolf, 134–137, 139–143, 148

Hopkins, Albert A., 39, 42, 46

Houdini, Harry, 73, 79, 206 n.23

Hyam, Ronald, 32–33, 38

Hypnosis, 96–97, 107–108

Hysteria: and absence, 98, 105–109; disappearing symptoms of, 96–97; as form of vanishing, 81; male, 93–95; mimetic nature of, 94; and spiritualism, 207–208 n.41; as vanishing discourse, 93–94, 128

Indian magic: basket trick, 42–44; dissected messenger, 44–45; fakirs, 39, 140, 201 n.33; and Hitler, 140; jugglers, 39–42, 58–59; in *The Moonstone,* 40; rope trick, 45; as superior to British conjuring, 39, 41

Indian "Mutiny" (1857): bibighar /

bibi-khana, 32, 200 n.25; British press coverage of, 33–34; Cawnpore massacre, 32–39; and English women, 34–38; or "Rebellion," 31, 200 n.20

Indian Rubber (caoutchouc), 54, 202 n.50

Irigaray, Luce, 101, 122

Jacobus, Mary, 116

Jewish masculinity, 121, 209 n.9, 210 n.28

Johnston, Claire, 154

Keats, John, 196–197 n.6

King, Katie, 76

Kristeva, Julia, 23, 100

Lady Vanishes, The, 9, 12–13, 129–151, 193

Levens, Mary, 210

Magician's assistants, 40, 50–53, 70–71, 164, 192

Malthus, Robert, 22–25

Mannequins, 3–6, 195 n.2

Maskelyne: John Neville (J.N.), 41, 61–62, 72, 203–204 n.2; Jasper (grandson of J.N.), 41, 62

Matlock, Jann, 47

McClintock, Anne, 21

Méliès, Georges, 62–68, 130–131

Mitchell, Juliet, 14, 93–95, 111, 116, 128

Mother: good and bad, 117; as knowledge, 118–128; and matricide, 101–102, 104, 111, 150; monster, 99, 102; tongue, 101–102. *See also* Vanishing mother

Mulvey, Laura, 154–155

Mumler, William, 74

Nadar, 74–75

Nancy, Jean-Luc, 86

National Socialism, 131–151

Karen Beckman is Assistant Professor of English and
Film Studies at the University of Rochester.

Library of Congress Cataloging-in-Publication Data
Beckman, Karen.
Vanishing women: magic, film, and feminism /
Karen Beckman.
Includes bibliographical references and index.
ISBN 0-8223-3125-x (cloth : alk. paper)
ISBN 0-8223-3074-1 (pbk. : alk. paper)
1. Women in motion pictures.   2. Body, Human,
in motion pictures.   I. Title.
PN1995.9.W6 B385   2003   791.43'652042–dc21   2002014074